The Economics of Smoking

The Economics of Smoking

By
Robert D. Tollison
Richard E. Wagner

Center for Study of Public Choice
George Mason University

Kluwer Academic Publishers
Boston/Dordrecht/London

Distributors for North America:
Kluwer Academic Publishers
101 Philip Drive
Assinippi Park
Norwell, Massachusetts 02061 USA

Distributors for all other countries:
Kluwer Academic Publishers Group
Distribution Centre
Post Office Box 322
3300 AH Dordrecht, THE NETHERLANDS

Library of Congress Cataloging-in-Publication Data

Tollison, Robert D.
   The economics of smoking / by Robert D. Tollison, Richard E.
Wagner.
     p. cm.
   Includes bibliographical references and index.
   ISBN 0-7923-9224-8
   1. Smoking—Economic aspects. 2. Tobacco habit—Economic aspects.
3. Tobacco industry—Government policy. 4. Smoking—Economic
aspects—United States. 5. Tobacco habit—Economic aspects—United
States. 6. Tobacco industry—Government policy—United States.
I. Wagner, Richard E. II. Title.
HV5735.T65 1991
338.4'36797—dc20   91-31510
                                               CIP

Printed on acid-free paper.

Printed in the United States of America

Contents

PREFACE

Cigarettes are under political attack at all levels of government in the United States. From Washington, D.C. to state capitals to local governments, proposals abound to increase the cigarette excise tax, to impose smoking bans, to prevent cigarette advertising, to restrict the sale of cigarettes through vending machines, to cut off the export of cigarettes, to earmark the cigarette excise tax for health programs, to divest the stock of cigarette companies, and so on. And all of these are purportedly being advocated in the name of health. Undergirding and abetting the health argument is an economic argument that claims to place a value of up to $100 billion per year on the alleged health costs of smoking to the American economy, which is more than $3 per pack of cigarettes smoked.

As our title suggests, our interest lies in the economics of smoking and not in the health issues surrounding smoking. We are professional economists and not medical scientists. We will focus on what, if any, economic consequences arise for nonsmokers when smokers smoke. For purposes of our discussion, we simply accept the premise that smoking damages health and proceed with our analysis. Since we have not studied the issue ourselves, we have no way of knowing whether such a premise is true. But it really does not matter for getting the economics of smoking right. The important point resides in who pays for whatever costs may be attributable to smoking. If smokers bear all such costs, including any health risks, then surely no issue of public policy or taxation arises, at least within the setting of a free society. But if non-smokers pay part of the costs of smoking, there would be a clear rationale for the intervention of government in taxing and regulating smoking behavior. Resolving this important issue represents the primary focus of this book.

Unlike our previous book on the subject (Tollison and Wagner 1988), our intention in this book is to be comprehensive. We seek to cover all of the economic issues that have been raised with respect to cigarette smoking. In addition to a careful consideration of the argument that smokers impose costs on nonsmokers, we examine the issues surrounding the regulation of environmental tobacco smoke, the advertising of tobacco products, the public health bureaucracy and its associated interest groups, the health-promotion "industry," the earmarking of tobacco taxes, and various other issues related to smoking. Most of these issues, however, derive from the social cost argument. For example, the argument that tobacco advertising should be banned or regulated is based on the proposition that smoking should not be promoted, especially to young people, because it impares health and imposes costs to society. So the root issue remains whether smokers pay their own way in society. For if they do, issues such as the above should become moot, at least when judged against the traditional standards of American democracy, where adults are presumed generally to be free to pursue whatever activities and interests they choose, provided only that they do not interfere with the similar liberties of others in the process.

We will also try to set the issue of smoking in a larger context. If, in fact, smoking is taxed and regulated on strictly majoritarian and unprincipled grounds (smokers equal about one-third and nonsmokers two-thirds of the adult population in the United States), then the arguments that are being used to provide the intellectual basis for such programs are quite dangerous and insidious and can be quite easily applied to virtually every facet of people's everyday lives. Thus, while smoking may be the issue of note today, to allow a faulty economics of smoking to prevail is an open invitation to tomorrow's arguments about the social costs of sugar, sunbathing, saturated fat, recreational injuries, obesity, and on and on and on. Down this road lies not a free society but a totally regulated society with only one acceptable lifestyle as prescribed by the health paternalists. In a world of busybodies it is only a matter of time before something even the busybodies themselves like will come under scrutiny. Getting the economics of smoking right is therefore important.

Although we are economists, we have written this book not just for economists but for everyone who is interested in possible public policy measures concerning smoking. In so doing we have tried to limit our use of technical economic argumentation and concepts, and where we could not avoid such usage, to present it in an understandable fashion.

This manuscript was produced under a grant from The Tobacco Institute. The views expressed are those of the authors and not necessarily those of the Institute or its member companies. We are grateful to Mrs. Carol Robert for her unfailing and unflappable assistance in the preparation and typesetting of the manuscript.

The Economics of Smoking

CHAPTER I

Tobacco Warfare
In America:
An Overview

There can be no doubt that tobacco has become an object of civil warfare in the United States over the past 20 years or so. Smokers and nonsmokers have been waging pitched battles on many fronts throughout the land. Former Surgeon General C. Everett Koop articulated a vision of a "smoke-free America," where if any smoking at all were to take place it would be in the privacy of smokers' homes and only in the company of other smokers. Perhaps inspired by this vision, a Hawaii State Senator introduced, in February 1990, legislation that would have banned the sale of tobacco products throughout Hawaii. While this proposal failed to be enacted, its mere introduction into Hawaii's legislative process surely attests to the ferocity with which the Great American Tobacco War is being waged. Indeed, there are several universities, including West Virginia University and Texas A&M University, that have banned all smoking on campus.

A Battlefield Tour

This image of warfare is conveyed throughout the nation's news media. For instance, an article in the *Wall Street Journal* (24 May 1990) carried the headline: "Tobacco Is Facing New Attacks." That article went on to describe several fronts along which fighting is taking place. One front is epitomized by the organization of the Boston-based Tobacco Divestment Project. Amid much fanfare Harvard University announced that, starting

1

in June 1990, it would sell off its holdings of tobacco stocks, which were valued at over $60 million.[1] The City University of New York has done the same thing, only the value of its holdings are less than $4 million. Proponents of divestment seek to multiply Harvard's action by pressuring pension funds, insurance companies, and other large-scale owners of tobacco stock to sell their holdings.

Economically, it is unlikely that divestment would exert any significant economic impact on the value of tobacco companies. For the value of tobacco stock depends on the returns investors believe they can receive relative to other investments. At first glance, successful pressures for divestment might seem to be a way of depressing the value of tobacco stocks by dumping large amounts of such stock onto the market. However, this will make tobacco stocks more attractive to those investors who are immune to the divestment bug. All that will happen, ultimately, is that people will rearrange their investment portfolios: divestors will own no tobacco stock and will own correspondingly more of other kinds of stock; non-divestors will have increased their ownership of tobacco relative to other stock in an offsetting fashion.[2]

Economically speaking, divestment would seem to be merely symbolic and devoid of economic significance. But even at the level of symbolism, divestment carries the odor of war. Over what else are calls for divestment heard in America? Over South Africa, of course. In this case divestment is advocated as a means of bringing pressure to bear upon whites in South Africa to support the abolition of Apartheid. To be sure, many scholars have argued that divestment from South Africa would primarily harm blacks in South Africa, and that the best way to promote the elimination of Apartheid would be to promote even greater investment in South Africa, because it is the competition for labor and the search for profits that would do the most to undermine Apartheid.[3]

While the subject of this book is smoking in America and not Apartheid in South Africa, divestment links the two subjects and illustrates the warfare mentality surrounding tobacco. While there is considerable controversy over the economic properties of divestment in South Africa, the pressure for divestment is doubtlessly fueled to a substantial extent by a belief in the evil nature of the South African regime. The extension of divestment to tobacco is to place tobacco in the same normative position as Apartheid in South Africa. By this logic decent people should do their best to eradicate both Apartheid and smoking, and divestment reflects and symbolizes this common belief, the cogency of arguments about the ineffectiveness of such policies notwithstanding.

Vending machines are coming to provide another arena for warfare. Cigarettes have long been widely available for purchase through vending machines, just as have soft drinks and candy. Anti-smoking activists are increasingly seeking to restrict the availability of cigarettes through vending machines. Much of the argument in support of these restrictions has been couched in terms of reducing the ability of minors to buy cigarettes. While most states have minimum age requirements for the purchase of cigarettes, it is more difficult to enforce those requirements with vending machine sales than with over-the-counter sales. For this reason it has been advocated that the availability of vending machines be restricted to such places as bars and offices, where minors would rarely be found in the first place.[4]   Alaska, Indiana, and Minnesota enacted such legislation in 1990, while similar legislation was defeated in 21 states. Legislation to ban or to restrict vending machine sales is currently under consideration in about 20 states.

Those smokers who do not frequent bars or work in offices, and who would perhaps constitute a majority among smokers, would be casualties in the vending machine wars. The alleged reason for opening battle along this front is to reduce opportunities for minors to smoke. Whether this claim is reasonable is something we will explore in depth later; we would only note here that it is implausible that vending machine restrictions would have anything approaching the impact implied by the figures cited above. Eighty percent or so of vending machine purchases take place in such places as bars, factories, and military bases, which are not readily accessible to minors. Minors who want to try smoking will find other sources available: older classmates and brothers and sisters being perhaps at the forefront of these other sources. Furthermore, while it has been reported that most adults who smoke began smoking as minors, it is nevertheless true that most minors who try smoking do not continue to smoke as adults. In short, it is unlikely that the vending machine wars will do much by way of restricting cigarette experimentation by minors. But it will clearly further restrict the ability of adult smokers to buy cigarettes.

Starting in the early 1980s, each year around five to ten state legislatures have considered legislation to mandate the development of a "fire-safe" cigarette. Such legislation would require a cigarette to be so constructed that it would not cause an ignition if it were carelessly dropped on bedding and upholstered furniture. There are currently some significant unanswered questions about how even to produce such a cigarette. The federal government's Cigarette Safety Act of 1984 created a Technical Study Group on Cigarette and Little Cigar Fire Safety to examine the technical and commercial feasibility of developing cigarettes that would not ignite such objects as bedding and upholstered furniture. After three years of study, its report issued in October 1987 noted that substantial additional work would be needed to determine if such a product is feasible. Federal legislation was passed in 1990 which authorizes a continued examination of this issue by the Consumer Product Safety Commission.

Sellers often have to work hard to get potential customers to try their products, for it is easy for people to stick with products with which they are satisfied. There are many ways vendors try to overcome such resistance and to get people to try their products. The issuance of coupons is one widely prevalent form. The shipment of free samples through the mail is another. Cigarette companies sometimes try to distribute samples to interested adults. Nebraska has banned the sampling of smokeless tobacco products, while Utah has severely restricted the ability to sample, limiting it to conventions and to retail stores (and then to people who have just purchased a tobacco product). Similar legislation is pending in eight states, having been defeated in two in 1989. And some observers anticipate that around half of the states could be considering such legislation by the early 1990s.

Advertising has long been a part of the tobacco battlefield. Cigarette advertisements have been banned from radio and television since 1971. Warning labels have been required on all advertisements for tobacco products in newspapers and magazines. Potential new sources of restriction are also continually being explored. For instance, tobacco companies sponsor a variety of sporting events, including tennis matches and automobile races. Some anti-tobacco activists have aimed their sights at these kinds of promotional activities, and are seeking to bring down the various tobacco banners displayed at these events.[5]

All of these efforts, and many more like them, seek to drive the presence of tobacco ever further into the distant reaches of American society, and can be seen as part of a program to create, either through legislation or through intimidation, a smoke-free America. Myriad other regulations operate in the same direction, including various efforts to legislate restrictions on smoking in workplaces, restaurants, and other spaces labeled as "public." So too does the imposition of extraordinarily heavy taxes on cigarettes. On a nation-wide basis the retail price of cigarettes averages about $1.50 per pack. Cigarette taxes average about 40 cents per pack, though with considerable variation from state to state: residents of North Carolina pay a combined federal and state tax of 18 cents per pack while residents of Texas pay 57 cents. Absent taxes, cigarettes would sell for about $1.10 per pack, so the tax on cigarettes averages almost 40 percent of the pre-tax value of the product. Not only do existing taxes and regulations reveal a ferocious battle over smoking in America, and a battle that is being similarly waged in many other places throughout the world, but the continuing spate of proposals for even further taxation and regulation shows that the intensity of battle is still escalating.

American Principles, Public Policy, and Tobacco Warfare

The American system of limited government is clearly based on the premise that people as responsible adults should by and large be free to pursue their own interests and pleasures, provided only that they do not infringe upon the similar rights of others in the process. Government exists principally to preserve and protect people's rights; it exists to promote civil peace and order, and most certainly not to foment civil warfare.

Where does government's participation in the ongoing war over tobacco fit within the central principles of American government? Proponents of the tobacco wars portray this participation as representing proper uses of governmental authority within the context of our constitutional framework of limited government. For the battles in this war are portrayed as efforts to preserve the "rights" of nonsmokers in the face of abusive infringements of those "rights" by smokers. Should government serve as an agent for violating the "rights" of smokers for the advantage of nonsmokers, it would violate the American principle of constitutionally limited government. But should it use its authority to prevent smokers from doing things that would otherwise infringe upon the "rights" of nonsmokers, it would use its authority properly within our framework of limited government.

An economic justification for governmental participation in the war on tobacco is expressed by the doctrine of "social cost," which claims that while smokers may pay for the cost of their cigarettes, there are many other ways in which the cost of smoking is borne by nonsmokers. This belief that a substantial share of the total cost of smoking is paid by nonsmokers is derived from the presumption that smoking is harmful to health: in light of estimates about the size of this health toll, an economic value is imputed to that health toll and an effort is made to determine the share of that toll borne by the nonsmoking portion of American society. For instance, in the 1985 report of the Office of Technology Assessment (OTA), *Smoking-Related Deaths and Financial Costs*, smoking was reported to be responsible for between 186,000 and 398,000 deaths in the United States in 1982, and with what OTA regarded as a "best" estimate being 314,000.[6] The same OTA-sponsored study estimated the annual cost in 1985 dollars of these health problems associated with smoking to have ranged from $40 to $100 billion in the United States, and with a "best" estimate of $65 billion, which is $2.17 per pack of cigarettes smoked. Such figures might seem to suggest that while smokers might pay the dollar or so it costs to buy a pack of cigarettes, about twice that amount is being paid by other people, predominately nonsmokers.

Allegations about the harmful health effects of smoking, and the resulting costs to American society, have been at the forefront of justifications for the escalating war on tobacco. In this book we seek to assess these claims about the cost of smoking and to develop their implications, primarily for the nonsmoking majority of Americans. With respect to the $65 billion figure noted above, we ask who in particular pays this bill if we accept this figure for purposes of our analysis. It is commonly said to be a cost to "society," but society cannot pay bills, only individuals can. With respect to smoking we seek to examine whether the cost of smoking rests with smokers or with nonsmokers. If the $65 billion cost attributed to smoking rests with the 50 million or so adult smokers, they are on average sacrificing $1,300 per year, in addition to the price of tobacco products, to satisfy their desire for those products. In a society that remains true to the foundations of the American republic, however, the bearing of any such costs should be the business of smokers and few if any issues of public policy would seem to arise. But if, by contrast, that cost rests on the 100 million or so adult nonsmokers, they are on average sacrificing $650 per year to subsidize smokers. To be sure, the American polity is replete with income and wealth transfers of all kinds, each of which involves one set of people gaining at the expense of others. Nonetheless, assuming the claims about the cost of smoking were correct, within the normative framework of the American republic there would be a plausible basis for seeking to make smokers more fully bear the costs, if any, of their choices to smoke.

Organization of this Book

Our primary purpose in writing this book is to examine the various allegations that have been advanced about the ways in which smoking imposes costs on the members of society generally and not just upon smokers in particular. We do not address the validity of the belief that smoking is a source of harm to health, for to do so would get us far outside our areas of competence. Our interest and competence lie rather in ascertaining the extent to which the costs commonly associated with smoking are paid by nonsmokers instead of by smokers. This book is concerned with the proper articulation of public policy toward smoking in a nation such as the United States founded on principles of responsible individual liberty, according to which people should be largely free to pursue their personal interests, save to the extent they infringe upon the equal rights of other people in the process.

Chapter 2 lays out the standard economic approach to public policy which derives from the branch of economics called "welfare economics," and then seeks to portray how public policy toward smoking might fit within this framework. The primary point of this chapter is to describe circumstances under which various public policy initiatives in the war on tobacco might be seen as means for protecting rights and promoting the general welfare, as against redistributing rights and promoting the welfare of some people at the expense of that of others. At base, the claim here is that smoking is a source of significant cost to the nonsmoking members of society, and that taxation and regulation are means by which those nonsmokers can protect themselves from the burdens that smokers would otherwise impose on them.

While arguments grounded in the principles of welfare economics can be used to justify or rationalize various measures for the taxation or regulation of tobacco, such arguments generally portray, often implicitly rather than explicitly, public policy essentially as being made by disinterested philosopher-kings. But public policy is made and implemented by politicians and bureaucrats, and not by philosopher-kings. Once this is recognized, arguments grounded in welfare economics cannot be accepted so facilely as they might otherwise be. For once a dose of political realism is applied to the examination of public policy, which Chapter 3 provides, it is easy to see that actual public policy choices, including those concerning the taxation and regulation of tobacco, may diverge sharply from those envisioned by the principles of welfare economics. For instance, tax policy toward tobacco might have less to do with traditional normative concepts of efficiency and equity than with the practical politics of finding comparatively easy sources to tax.

In terms of empirical magnitudes, the largest alleged source of social cost from smoking is the lost production claimed to result from smoking. This claim has two main components. The larger of these derives from the claim that on average smokers die earlier than nonsmokers, and that the resulting loss of earnings because of earlier death is a cost to society. Relatedly, it is claimed that smokers miss work more often than non-smokers, and that this loss of earnings is also a cost of smoking. The validity of these claims is critically examined in Chapter 4.

The second-largest alleged source of social cost of smoking is the cost of medical care attributed to the treatment of purportedly smoking-related illnesses. Starting from the presumption that smokers incur higher medical expenses than nonsmokers, the claim is made that these higher expenses indicate that smokers are able to place part of their medical costs on nonsmokers. With the bulk of medical expenses being financed through insurance programs, it is claimed that premiums paid by non-smokers are higher than they would otherwise be, to cover the added costs incurred by smokers. These claims about social cost are examined in Chapter 5.

Not all medical expenses are paid through private insurance programs or personal payments by patients. About one-quarter of medical expenses are financed through Medicare and Medicaid, the former being a governmental program to cover medical expenses for the elderly and the latter being a similar program for the indigent. In this case the argument is advanced that smoking increases the claims made under these programs, which in turn means higher tax payments on everyone to finance those higher claims. Chapter 6 will explore this component of the charge that smokers place costs upon the nonsmoking portion of American society.

The thrust of our argument in Chapters 4-6 will be to explain why smokers do not impose any of those alleged costs on nonsmokers, principally because our economic system itself operates in such a fashion that smokers themselves bear the costs of whatever ill health they might suffer. But even if it were acknowledged that smokers do bear the costs we discuss in these chapters, it could nonetheless be argued that there are other forms of cost that are borne by nonsmokers. For instance, it is commonly claimed that smokers are more costly workers to employ than nonsmokers, in part because they are less productive due to such things as time spent in smoking breaks, and in part because they increase business costs associated with such things as cleaning and ventilation. These claims about cost are examined in Chapter 7.

Relatedly, and more significantly in terms of the intensity of controversy, it is charged that the tobacco wars are justified because smokers impose costs on nonsmokers through the environmental tobacco smoke (ETS) that results from smoking. Even if it is assumed that smokers pay the full costs that might arise from the smoke they inhale, it could be claimed that significant costs are associated with the smoke that nonsmokers are exposed to because they must breathe air which contains ETS. Chapter 8 seeks to untangle the complex arguments surrounding ETS, explaining in the process why even in this case the arguments for taxation and regulation are ill-founded when they are based on grounds of controlling the costs that smokers supposedly impose on the remainder of society.

But these cost components are not the only elements in the claim that smoking imposes costs on American society. It might well be acknowledged that smokers bear the aforementioned costs, for the reasons we explain in Chapter 8, and yet taxation and regulation might be advocated nonetheless. It is claimed with increasing frequency these days that smokers cannot be said truly to have *chosen* to smoke, primarily because advertising and addiction both impel people to smoke despite their better judgments and prevent their quitting once they have realized the error of their ways. Chapter 9 examines this line of argument that seeks to portray the tobacco war as a just war.

The argument through chapter 9 will have explained why there is no justification for a war on tobacco grounded in any principled argument that such a war is necessary either to protect the "rights" of nonsmokers from infringement by smokers or to get smokers to cover their full "costs" of smoking. We could end the book here, but to do so would leave unexamined any of the possible avenues of economic explanation for the tobacco wars which the body of contemporary public choice scholarship, discussed briefly in Chapter 3, suggests may exist. Chapter 10 explains that there is an economic logic to the various legislative efforts to tax and regulate tobacco. This logic largely sees the legislature as a market place where interest groups compete, both to secure special treatment and to avoid bearing the burden required to provide those favors for other groups. Much of the legislative activity concerning tobacco can be explained in this manner.

Chapter 11 looks upon medical and health organizations from this same economic perspective, and explains how their advocacy of anti-tobacco positions is congruent with their economic self interest. In short, there are several reasons why reducing smoking will promote the economic interests of prominent anti-smoking groups. Tobacco is not alone in being faced with claims for taxation and regulation, based on arguments that those claims are justified because of social costs. The same arguments about social cost can be applied to numerous other cases--for instance, to a breakfast of bacon and eggs, hash brown potatoes, and coffee. Chapter 12 concludes the book by exploring how all such arguments reflect a misuse of social cost arguments and by explaining how the resulting policy implications imply an excessive use of governmental authority that it is the proper function of constitutionally limited government to constrain.

NOTES

1. See the informative discussion in "Anti-Smoking Groups Ask Universities to Sever Ties with Tobacco Industry," *Chronicle of Higher Education* (June 20, 1990), p. A1ff.

2. Of course, divestment coupled with political action against the tobacco industry can depress the prices of tobacco stocks and make the returns from "ethical investments" positive.

3. On this theme see Walter Williams (1989, esp. pp. 125-44).

4. Secretary Louis Sullivan of the Department of Health and Human Services recently called for federal legislation to regulate more tightly the sales of cigarettes through vending machines.

5. These efforts extend to the sublime. Recent attention has been focused on claims concerning the positioning of tobacco billboards in baseball and football parks so as to catch major camera angles, thereby associating tobacco and sports for the viewers, some of whom are minors. So, now, the call is to ban the billboards!

6. The 1989 Report of the Surgeon General, *Reducing the Health Consequences of Smoking: 25 Years of Progress*, attributed around 390,000 deaths to smoking in 1985.

Welfare Economics, Public Policy, And Smoking

F or the better part of a century now economists have sought to use the principles of their discipline to shed light on the nature of desirable public policy. For the most part they have accepted the central presumptions of political liberalism, presumptions which were also incorporated into the foundations of American democracy.[1] These presumptions hold that people should largely be free to conduct themselves as they choose, provided only that in the process they do not infringe upon the equal rights of other people to do the same. To be sure, such a broad statement leaves much room for controversy along a vast spectrum of particular issues. The branch of economics now referred to as "welfare economics" represents the efforts of economists to think systematically about public policy in light of such political presumptions.

Much of welfare economics has been animated by a desire to probe the limits of one form or other of "invisible hand" theorem or proposition. The invisible hand refers to the observation that a coordinated network of economic activity generally results within a market economy, even though there is no coordinating authority; people can count on being able to buy their daily bread, even though to be able to do so requires the cooperation of millions of people extending across space and time. Indeed, economics has primarily evolved as an attempt to understand the paradox that people can count more fully upon being able to buy their daily bread when there is no person or office charged with that responsibility than when there is such a person or office. All of the recent comparisons between Eastern and Western Europe are vivid reminders of the debilitating consequences of allowing authorities to plan economic activities. The superior economic position of Western nations clearly rests on the general absence of planning authorities: that economies work better when no one is in charge is one of the central features of economic understanding.

Even though economists acknowledge the superiority of market economies over planned economies, there is considerable controversy among economists over whether in particular instances market outcomes can be improved through public policies. Even though market processes might lead to orderly and coordinated patterns of economic activity, it might be possible to do even better in some instances through correctly designed public policies. Or at least this possibility is the animating force behind welfare economics, which has sought to set forth circumstances or conditions under which governmental authority might lead to a general improvement in economic well-being.[2] In this chapter we describe the ways in which economic arguments grounded in the principles of welfare economics might be brought to bear on issues of public policy toward smoking.

Smoking, The Market Process, and a Free Society

In a free society people relate to one another according to a set of rules that can be described essentially by the principles of property and contract. The principle of property means that rights of ownership over resources exist, and that owners can sell, lease, or otherwise assign those rights as they choose. The principle of contract means that agreement and not force is the basis for choices concerning the use of resources. A "market economy" is nothing but a shorthand expression for the vast and complex network of exchange relationships that emerges when people relate to one another according to the rules or principles of property and contract.

Economic coordination results through the interplay of people pursuing their own interests within the framework of the rules of property and contract. In such a market economy people who own land can use their ownership rights to grow tobacco or to raise chickens as they choose. And they will make those choices in light of their anticipation of the profitability of those alternative activities. Within the system of profit and loss inherent in the institutions of property and contract, people become wealthier as they are more successful in producing what others want. If the strength of consumer desires for cigarettes generally rises relative to that for eggs, the price of cigarettes will initially rise as supplies run short, and the price of eggs will fall in response to the accumulation of inventories. This shift in prices is a signal to producers that consumers have become relatively more interested in smoking relative to eating eggs, and it simultaneously provides producers with an incentive to reduce the production of eggs while increasing the production of tobacco.

A market economy gives producers strong incentives to supply consumer wants efficiently. One of the central features of a market economy is that the price of a product tends to equal its cost of production. Moreover, the cost of producing a product tends in turn to equal the value that consumers place on the other products that were foregone to produce the product in question. To say that the cost of producing a pack of cigarettes is $1.10, then, is equivalent to saying that the value of the other output that could have been produced had the cigarettes not been produced instead is itself worth $1.10 to consumers. Therefore, the price that consumers must pay for one product is equal to the value they place on the alternative output that could have been produced by the resources that were used instead to produce the product in question. It is impossible to rearrange the pattern of production to increase the value of what is produced. Any such rearrangement will substitute output that consumers value less highly for output they value more highly.

This strong tendency of a market economy to deliver to people what they want most, and to do so efficiently, is illustrated hypothetically by Figure 2.1. The line D depicts the willingness of people to buy cigarettes, showing they will buy more as the price falls: at a price of $2.20 per pack they will buy 20 billion packs per year, while they would buy 40 billion packs should the price fall to 55 cents. The line S portrays the willingness of producers to supply cigarettes, with that willingness rising with the price that producers can get: if they can get only 55 cents per pack they will supply only 20 billion packs annually, whereas they will supply 40 billion packs if they can get $2.20 per pack.

Suppose only 20 billion packs were initially being supplied, and that

Figure 2.1 described accurately the desires of consumers on the one hand and the requirements for producers of cigarettes on the other hand. Cigarettes would sell for $2.20, because at any lower price shortages would arise and the competition among consumers for the scarce cigarettes would bid prices up. To some extent farmers might respond by cultivating tobacco more intensively on their land, because additional production that would cost 55 cents per pack would yield up to $2.20 in revenues. More significantly, land formerly used for other purposes would be converted to growing tobacco. In these and in other ways, the production of cigarettes would expand. And as it did two things would happen, both of which are represented on Figure 2.1: (1) cigarettes would become less valuable to consumers, as shown by the declining schedule of demand prices, and (2) cigarettes would become more costly to produce, in part because less suitable land would be called into production, as shown by the rising schedule of supply prices.

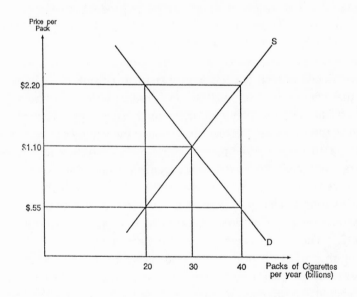

FIGURE 2.1: MARKET FOR CIGARETTES

In the case illustrated by Figure 2.1, when output has risen to 30 billion packs annually, the value of cigarettes to consumers will have fallen to $1.10. So long as output is less than 30 billion packs, the value to consumers will exceed $1.10, as illustrated by D, and this value will exceed the cost producers must incur in producing cigarettes, as illustrated by S. Conversely, should the production of cigarettes exceed 30 billion packs annually, the cost to producers will exceed the willingness of consumers to pay. To produce 40 billion packs, for instance, will cost $2.20 per pack for producers, but consumers will be willing to pay only 55 cents per pack for that many cigarettes. Such an excessive amount of cigarette production will not take place because producers would lose money in trying to do so. So a market economy harnesses efficiently the interests of producers in increasing their net worth to the service of consumer wants.

The bulk of economic scholarship over the past two centuries since Adam Smith wrote his treatise in 1776 on *An Inquiry into the Nature and Causes of the Wealth of Nations*, has been centrally concerned with understanding and explaining the sources of economic progress. Natural resources are largely irrelevant, with freedom of association and enterprise being of paramount importance. For if natural resources were central to the wealth of nations, Japan would be poor and China would be rich. Nor does richness today lead to richness tomorrow. For if it did, Argentina, one of the wealthiest nations in the world in 1930, would be one of the wealthiest still. Instead, she has fallen to a third-world status over two generations. And a generation ago Japan was no wealthier than Peru; since then Peru has been stagnant while Japan has surged ahead.

While there are many arguments among economists over the virtues of particular policy measures, it should also be noted that most of these arguments take place within a general consensus that socialized or otherwise highly centralized economic systems are inferior to relatively decentralized, capitalistic economic systems. And whatever residual support may have remained until recently for centralized, socialized economies has surely been buried by the thoroughgoing rejections of such systems throughout Eastern Europe. Some economists argue that government should do more to preserve forests and wetlands, while others argue that this than can be done more effectively through market processes. Some economists argue that the conservation of petroleum should be promoted through higher taxes on gasoline and through the subsidization of alternative energy sources, while others argue that the best way to deal with future energy needs is to leave it to the individual actions of people trying out numerous different ideas within ordinary market processes.

In these, and in numerous other instances of conflicting policy advice, some suggested approaches would rely more heavily upon market processes while others would put more emphasis on government planning. But these differences, while clearly substantial and important, are small in comparison with the overall magnitudes. One set of policy measures may have the federal government directing 20 percent of the economic activities within the economy, while another set of policy measures may lead to its directing 30 percent of those activities. This difference is significant and substantial, for in the latter case the scope of governmental activity is 50 percent larger than it is in the first case. Nonetheless, in either case economic activities will largely be organized and coordinated through market processes and not through government direction.

Taxation and Regulation in a Market Economy

What, if any, is the proper scope for taxation and regulation within a market economy? To be sure, this is a question that would elicit a variety of specific answers, just as many specific answers might be given to a question concerning the proper extent of government in a market economy. There might be a few libertarians who see no normative scope for government at all, and there probably still remain a few unreconstructed Marxists who wish for the total replacement of markets with planning. While the extent of such controversy should be duly noted, it should also be noted that there is a considerable degree of consensus over the proper scope and type of taxation and regulation. This consensus would hold that taxation and regulation should be general and nondiscriminatory in orientation; taxes and regulations should essentially be universal and not particular in application. This is not to deny that cogent arguments can be articulated in support of particular forms of taxation and regulation, but is only to note that the initial presumption is in favor of universality and generality. After explaining this presumption, we shall examine some of the reasoning that argues for exceptional cases of particular taxation and regulation.

Taxation in a Market Economy

It is generally acknowledged that within a market economy a significant amount of governmental activity will be required. Even a government that conformed to the metaphorical vision of the "nightwatchman" state would have a quite substantial budget these days. For such a state would be in the business of preserving peace and order, both externally and internally. Hence, expenditures of some magnitude on national defense would be required for the preservation of external order, while expenditures for police and justice would be required to preserve internal order. Clearly, there are substantial differences among people in how much spending they believe is required to fulfill such tasks. For instance, some people think defense spending can be cut drastically without harming our security, while others think that significant increases are necessary if we are not to expose ourselves to grave dangers. It is similar with respect to the preservation of internal order: some think that expenditures on police and prisons should be increased, while others think that governmentally guaranteed jobs can substitute for police and prisons.

Despite these differences in personal beliefs, there is a general acknowledgement that such governmental activities provide general benefits for all, as contrasted with providing particular benefits for some. Hence, such activities are generally thought more properly to be financed through general, broad-based forms of taxation than through particular, narrow-based forms. Much of this support for broad-based over narrow-based forms of taxation is grounded in notions of tax neutrality. A truly broad-based tax would avoid the injection of tax-induced biases into the structure of economic activity. To be sure, any practical tax would have some exemptions from the tax base. For instance, even the broadest based consumption or income tax would surely exclude leisure. And other exclusions would be likely as well. Hence, the structure of economic activity will unavoidably be influenced by taxation. Indeed, it is doubtful whether the construct of neutral taxation is anything other than pure fantasy, for even the fabled head tax would surely inspire people to intensify their efforts to avoid the census takers as the amount of tax rose. Even though a truly broad-based, non-distortionary tax may be unattainable, there is surely much scholarly sentiment that a tax system with a relatively broad base would be superior to one with a relatively narrow base, because the range of tax-related sources of discrimination and distortion would be diminished.

Part of the support for broad-based taxation is grounded in considerations of equity. Tax philosophers have articulated two main standards of equity: horizontal equity and vertical equity.[3] Horizontal equity is a requirement that people who have the same income or wealth or expenditure, depending on which of those three categories forms the basis for taxation, should pay the same tax for the support of general governmental expenditures. It is unfair to tax some people more than others for the support of such expenditures, due simply to differences in the sources of their income, the forms of their wealth, or the objects of their expenditure.

In this regard the taxation of cigarettes would seem to create horizontal inequity because people whose expenditures are the same pay different amounts of tax to support general governmental services, depending merely on the particular objects of their expenditure. A sales tax, by contrast, fulfills the requirement of horizontal equity: if you and your neighbor spend the same amount, you pay the same amount of tax. This happens because sales taxes are general or nondiscriminatory levies on all (or most) items of consumption. But excise taxes are discriminatory levies on specific items of consumption. People who spend the same amount pay different amounts of tax to finance general governmental services due simply to differences in the things they buy. People who smoke pay more than people who don't to support governmental services of general public benefit. Hence, smokers are taxed for the benefit of nonsmokers. Any excise tax, including the cigarette tax, is but the converse of a special tax privilege: it is a special tax penalty on a particular form of consumption.

Tobacco taxation also violates most generally accepted formulations of vertical equity, for it imposes a higher rate of tax on people with lower incomes or expenditures than it imposes on people with higher incomes. The share of their incomes that smokers spend on cigarettes generally falls as income rises. For this reason the tobacco tax is a highly regressive levy. For instance, households in the lowest income quintile spent an average of 2.3 percent of their income on tobacco products in a 1981 survey (Bureau of Labor Statistics, 1983, p. 54), while households in the highest income quintile spent an average of 0.42 percent of their income on tobacco products. This point is illustrated by Table 2.1, with reference to three hypothetical smokers. This table conveys the point that smokers spend more on tobacco as their incomes rise, but that the share of income spent on tobacco falls as income rises. When the amount of tobacco tax is expressed as a share of income in the final column, the tax rate falls in half as income rises from $10,000 to $30,000. Furthermore, the use of tobacco products declines as income rises, thereby strengthening the portrait of regressivity.

Table 2.1

Illustration of Regressivity of Tobacco Taxation

Income	Tobacco Purchases	Purchases/ Income	Tobacco Tax *	Tax/Income
$10,000	$200	2.0%	$ 53.33	0.533%
20,000	280	1.4%	74.67	0.373%
30,000	300	1.0%	80.00	0.267%

*Our basic illustration of the cigarette tax is that it raises the price of cigarettes from $1.10 to $1.50 per pack. This means that tobacco taxes constitute 26.7 percent of total expenditures on tobacco.

Vertical and horizontal equity are principles derived from the financing of expenditures of general public benefit. Horizontal equity acts as a protection against the discriminatory imposition of tax burdens upon a subset of people for the benefit of all. The one case where discriminatory taxation might not violate horizontal equity is where the tax revenues are used not to finance expenditures of general benefit but to finance expenditures of particular benefit to the people who are being taxed. In the absence of some sound basis for thinking that tobacco taxation is a means of charging particular beneficiaries for particular services they receive, a possibility that we will explore later, specific excise taxes have little to recommend them. They are a form of tax discrimination, and a highly regressive form, that taxes particular sets of people for the general benefit. The interests of equity and efficiency are better served by using broad, general taxes to finance services of general benefit, and reserving specific excises and fees for the financing of services that benefit specific sets of people who use the services those taxes and fees help to finance.

The roughly $10 billion that various governments in the United States collect from excise taxes on tobacco products are generally paid for by consumers of those products, whose disposable incomes are reduced by the tax. However, the burden that an excise tax imposes on consumers will typically exceed the amount of revenue that governments collect. This additional burden is referred to by economists as *excess burden*. This excess by which the burden of the tax upon consumers exceeds the revenues collected by government results because the tax causes the price of cigarettes (or any other product subject to tax) to exceed its cost: the price of cigarettes will exceed its cost of production by the amount of the tax. To illustrate, suppose cigarettes are taxed at 40 cents per pack and sell at $1.50 per pack, with the cost of producing cigarettes being $1.10 per pack. Consumers value an additional pack of cigarettes at $1.50, while it would cost only $1.10 to produce that additional pack. This cost of production reflects the necessity that to produce more cigarettes will require that fewer other products be produced, reflecting the shift of resources away from other lines of production into the production of cigarettes. Hence, to say that it costs $1.10 to produce an additional pack of cigarettes is to say that the value consumers place on the other output that would have to be sacrificed to produce those cigarettes would be only $1.10. The tax places consumers in the position of being unable to give up something they value at only $1.10 to get something they value at $1.50. The burden of this missed opportunity is an additional burden beyond the payment of tax.

Consumers would be better off by a shift of resources into the production of cigarettes until output had increased sufficiently to lower the price that people would be willing to pay for cigarettes to $1.10. The excise tax makes consumers worse off, beyond the revenues actually collected by the tax, by the extent to which the value they place on additional cigarettes exceeds the cost of producing those cigarettes. It is possible to estimate empirically the extent of this excess burden. A simple approximation of this magnitude is one-half the product of (1) the change in price brought about by the tax and (2) the reduction in consumption caused by the tax.

For instance, suppose that 28 billion packs are sold annually when the tax is 40 cents per pack and the resulting price is $1.50. Further suppose that if the tax were repealed, 32 billion packs would be purchased each year. The tax thus increases price by 40 cents and reduces consumption by 4 billion packs, giving an excess burden, EB, of

$$EB = .5 \times (\$0.40) \times (4 \text{ billion}) = \$800 \text{ million}.$$

In this case the excess burden, which is a measure of the waste associated with the use of the selective excise tax, is more than 7 percent of the $11.2 billion in revenues that governments collect (28 billion packs at 40 cents per pack). For each dollar government collects in tax, consumers of cigarettes lose $1.07--$1 of which is collected by government and $0.07 of which simply evaporates, as it were, because the tax induces a shift of resources away from the production of products that consumers value more highly into the production of products they value less highly. Tobacco taxes are not only regressive and discriminatory levies, but are also wasteful. Tobacco taxation would seem to fare quite poorly by standard norms of equity, justice, and efficiency.

Regulation in a Market Economy

Whatever can be accomplished through taxation can be accomplished alternatively through regulation (Posner 1971). The proper scope for regulation in a market economy would seem to depend largely upon matters concerning the relative efficiencies of legal and regulatory processes. A market economy is one in which people and their activities are regulated by legal processes of property, contract, and tort. It is notable that these rules are universal or nondiscriminatory in their applicability. The same legal principles of contract damages that apply to tobacco transactions apply to economic transactions generally.

In practice, most regulation is specific and not general. The Comptroller of the Currency, as well as the Federal Reserve Bank, issues regulations dealing specifically with banks. It is not that there are general regulations applicable to all branches of commerce, but that there are specific regulations that single out banks for particular treatment. Nonetheless, it is possible to imagine a setting where governments issued general regulations that were applicable universally to commercial transactions. Not to say it would be a good idea, but it would be possible to imagine an agency with the authority to maintain general standards of accuracy in advertising, perhaps somewhat similar to the Federal Trade Commission. This would not involve any specific discrimination against tobacco advertising, but rather would involve standards that were generally applicable to all forms of advertising.

The desirability of any such regulation would be a different matter. For even a market economy without government regulation involves processes through which advertising is regulated. In part, good business practice involves regulation of advertising--self-imposed by businesses as part of their quest for greater earnings. Most commercial transactions involve repeated dealings, and in such a context truthfulness has a high value in fostering a climate conducive to future business. But even absent such considerations of enlightened self-interest, legal sanctions exist to regulate advertising. Puffery may be countenanced, but fraud is not, and the making of claims through advertising will be regulated through legal processes even if there is no government involvement in such regulation.

It is certainly possible to imagine settings where government regulation can serve as an efficient substitute for regulation through legal processes. After all, legal processes are costly: attorneys and judges must be involved, investigations must be conducted, and procedures must be followed. Government regulation of advertising might serve as an efficient replacement for regulation through legal processes. To be sure, there are many reasons for thinking this is unlikely to be the case, reasons having to do with the weakness of incentives within governmental agencies--a topic we shall consider more fully later in this book. But all that is necessary to note here is that the issuance and enforcement of general regulations by government potentially can serve as a substitute to the creation of such regulations through legal processes. But these would be general or universal regulations, just as the legal principles such regulations would replace are general or universal, and would not involve the issuance of regulations that pertained to some industries or types of commercial transactions but not to others.

Welfare Economics and Tobacco Policy

There is much to be said for the application of principles of generality or universality to taxation and regulation. Indeed, such principles would seem to be required if people are to be treated equally under the law. To impose taxes on the sale of cigarettes without imposing identical taxes on other transactions would likewise seem to penalize tobacco transactions relative to other transactions--and so violate the principle of equal treatment under the law.

Yet there can be cases where the principle of equal treatment requires what appears to be unequal treatment if it is to be implemented. These involve cases where the costs or benefits associated with particular transactions are not confined to the parties to the transaction. In the presence of such external costs or benefits, ordinary market transactions may not exhibit the strong tendencies noted above for resources to be utilized in their most valuable uses, as judged by the willingness of consumers to pay for producers' offerings. In such cases, ordinary commercial transactions may fail to incorporate all relevant considerations concerning the values that might be created or extinguished by a transaction. In such cases as these, there are grounds for arguing that *appropriate* governmental policy might improve general economic welfare.[4] In particular, it is commonly argued that smoking is an activity in which smokers place significant external costs on nonsmokers. In the presence of such external costs, the analytical framework of welfare economics can be used to justify both the taxation and the regulation of tobacco products, and in subsequent chapters we will examine carefully these various justificatory arguments.

The war on tobacco features several forms of alleged external cost. Table 2.2 shows that some estimates have portrayed these costs as ranging, in 1985, between $1.27 and $3.17 per pack of cigarettes smoked, with a "best" estimate being $2.17 per pack. It is notable that these figures generally exceed the price that smokers must pay for their cigarettes. Both entries in Table 2.2 reflect the presumption that smoking impairs the health of smokers, and that in turn this impaired health results in lowered economic output and higher medical expenses. The first row shows the estimated impact on production, where the "best" estimate is that smoking-induced reduction in economic production reduces total national output by $43 billion per year, which is $1.45 per pack of cigarettes smoked. The second row illustrates the claim that the treatment of smoking-related illnesses increases the national medical bill by $22 billion annually, which is $0.72 per pack.[5]

Table 2.2

Alleged External Costs of Smoking (1985)

Category	Range Total	Per Pack	"Best" estimate Total	Per Pack
Lost production	$27-$61 billion	$ .90-$2.02	$43 billion	$1.45
Health care	$12-$35 billion	$ .38-$1.17	$22 billion	$ .72
TOTAL	$38-$95 billion	$1.27-$3.17	$65 billion	$2.17

Source: Office of Technology Assessment, *Smoking-Related Deaths and Financial Costs*, p. 4.

Beyond these magnitudes, which might be thought of as representing the economic magnitude of the damages some people portray smokers as inflicting upon themselves, it is further argued that smokers impose significant damages upon third-parties. In this respect, smokers might be seen as personifying A. C. Pigou's (1932) famous smoke-spouting factory, which soils the laundry of nearby residents -- only the smokers spoil the atmosphere and allegedly damage the health of those who must breathe the air the smokers "pollute" with their exhalations. These claims of external damage to third-parties revolve around charges that smokers "pollute" the air around them, with the resulting environmental tobacco smoke being harmful to nonsmokers in the vicinity and a source of increased cost to businesses that employ smokers.

Various policy measures can be justified on the basis of these claims of external cost, though the correctness of the measures depends on the correctness of the claims. For one thing, taxes on cigarettes are capable of justification within the standard framework of welfare economics. Indeed, the theory of "corrective taxation" refers to the use of taxes as instruments for correcting what would otherwise be market failure. According to this theory, if the external cost of smoking were $2 per pack, a tax of this amount would, under certain circumstances to be discussed later, be a means of correcting the market failure that would otherwise be present.

The Pigovian-type arguments for corrective excise taxation view government as seeking to correct market failures that are presumed to result because of some divergence between social cost and private cost at the relevant margins of choice. In the absence of such Pigovian taxes in these cases, it is often argued, competitive market processes will lead to an excessive supply of the good or service in question. For instance, a paper mill may pay for such inputs as water, acid, lumber, and labor, but yet discharge waste water downstream, destroying opportunities for fishing and swimming in the process. The marginal cost of paper to the manufacturer includes the prices of the various inputs it has to hire to produce paper, but the marginal cost to society also includes the reduction in fishing and swimming opportunities that result from the discharge of waste water in the process of producing paper.

This divergence between private and social cost generates a welfare loss, according to this line of argument. As a result, too much paper is produced and too little fishing and swimming take place downstream from the mill. A tax on paper that was equal to the divergence between private and social cost would reduce the amount of paper produced to the correct level, and at the same time would increase the amount of fishing and swimming. Or at least this follows from a simple framework in which the external cost is associated with the production or consumption of service in question and not with the use of particular inputs or particular characteristics of the product. But under these alternative conditions, a corrective tax should be levied not on the product but on the offending input or the particular product attribute. These considerations clearly complicate the knowledge problems involved in trying to create a truly corrective tax.

The Pigovian-type arguments about corrective taxation view government as seeking to correct, through a set of discriminatory, narrow-based taxes, market failures that are presumed to result because of some divergence between social cost and private cost [e.g., Baumol (1972); but see Lee (1985) for a consideration of how exogenous politics might disrupt the standard Pigovian reasoning]. In the absence of such Pigovian taxes, a competitive market process may lead to excessive outputs in cases where private and social cost diverge. To be sure, the literature on corrective taxation explores such distinctions as whether taxes are imposed on outputs, inputs, or product characteristics. While there are many complexities in the theory of corrective taxation, not the least of which is its range of applicability in light of the critiques by Coase (1960) and Turvey (1963), such complexities are peripheral here, for we wish only to note that fiscal principle can also be brought to bear in support of narrow-based, discriminatory forms of taxation.

Tobacco Taxation as Corrective Taxation?

The rationalization for the imposition of a selective excise tax on the consumers of particular products, as against imposing burdens on the general class of consumers, revolves around the possibility that in some cases the market price of a product may not fully reflect its true cost of production. With respect to cigarettes, $1.10 may reflect the cost of such resources as the tobacco, paper, warehousing, shipping, and so on that go into the production of cigarettes. Should someone pay $1.10 for a pack of cigarettes, that payment will compensate the owners of those resources that were used in producing cigarettes.

The central idea of corrective taxation is to impose a tax equal to the external cost that is associated with the consumption of a particular product. If this is not done, there is actually an excess burden from the failure to do so. The argument on this point is symmetrical with the discussion of the excess burden of an excise tax that was presented above. This point may be illustrated with reference to Figure 2.2. As with Figure 2.1, the market forces of supply and demand are represented by S and D respectively, and these forces would produce an outcome of 30 billion packs annually at a price of $1.10 per pack.

Suppose the external costs of cigarette smoking are $49.5 billion annually in the aggregate, which is $1.65 for each of the 30 billion packs smoked. The market supply price, denoted by S, shows the costs that producers must bear, but it excludes these external costs. If those costs could be incorporated into the cost of production, smoking would be more expensive, by $1.65 per pack. This is illustrated in Figure 2.2 by the line S+EC($1.65). When 30 billion packs of cigarettes are smoked, consumers value a pack of cigarettes at $1.10. But the value of other things that must be sacrificed to produce those cigarettes is not $1.10 but is $2.75. Too many cigarettes are being produced, and consumer welfare would be improved by reducing consumption. A tax of $1.65 per pack would accomplish this end. As represented in Figure 2.2, the price would actually rise to $2.20 and only 20 billion packs would be smoked annually. The direct cost of producing cigarettes is shown to have fallen to 55 cents per pack (as less efficient resources would have been shifted to other uses), and the full cost of smoking would be $2.20 per pack, which is equal to the value that consumers would place on cigarettes when only 20 billion are smoked annually.

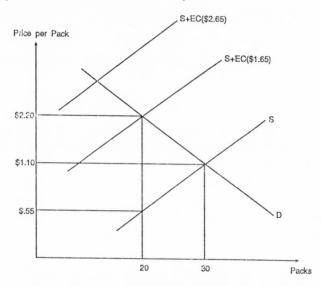

FIGURE 2.2: CORRECTIVE TAX ON CIGARETTES

By reducing the consumption of cigarettes below 30 billion packs, alternative output valued at $2.65 could be acquired by sacrificing something worth only $1.10. The reduction in tobacco consumption will offer such a gain until people come to value their diminished quantity of cigarettes equivalently with the full cost of cigarettes. When consumption has declined to 20 billion packs, keeping in mind that Figure 2.2 is merely illustrative, smokers will pay $44 billion per year ($2.20 x 20 billion packs) for cigarettes. Of this amount, producers will receive $11 billion ($0.55 x 20 billion) as payment for tobacco, paper, and the like, and the government will collect $33 billion ($1.65 x 20 billion) in tax, presumably to serve as compensation for the external costs stemming from smoking. The gain that results from the removal of this excess burden, and which is made possible by the corrective tax, is approximately $8.25 billion, as can be computed by the formula:

$$\text{Welfare Gain} = .5 \times (\$1.65) \times (10 \text{ billion}).$$

Tobacco Taxation: An Overview

Judged by ordinary market standards, federal and state governments discriminate against smokers by taxing them substantially more heavily than they tax anyone else. The federal government taxes cigarettes at 20 cents per pack, and is scheduled to increase this tax to 24 cents in 1993. All states tax cigarettes, at rates ranging from a low of 2 cents per pack in North Carolina to a high of 41 cents in Texas.[6] Moreover, state tax rates have been increasing sharply in recent years. Whereas only three states had cigarette tax rates exceeding 20 cents per pack in 1980, 12 states had such rates by 1984. And by 1990, 28 states had cigarette tax rates in excess of 20 cents per pack.[7]

On average in the United States, the combined federal and state tax on cigarettes is in the vicinity of 40 cents per pack. If a pack of cigarettes sells for $1.50 in such a state, the price net of tax is $1.10. In such a case, the consumption of cigarettes is being taxed at nearly 40 percent, which is about 10 times as high as the tax rate imposed on most products under general sales taxation. There is a rather intense tax discrimination against cigarettes within our prevailing federal and state revenue systems.

Despite these extremely high tax rates, revenue yields are quite low, expressed as a share of total tax collections. Tobacco tax collections, preponderantly from the taxation of cigarettes, though there is some small revenue raised through the taxation of cigars, pipe tobacco, and smokeless tobacco, run around $5 billion annually both at the federal and the state levels of government. While these burdens are substantial to the consumers of those products, they make minuscule contributions to governmental revenue, accounting for somewhat less than 1 percent of total tax collections.

A long tradition of tax analysis explains why tax discrimination is inequitable and inefficient: it is inequitable because it discriminates among people in the tax burdens they are asked to bear, due merely to differences in the things they choose to consume; it is inefficient because it leads people to substitute lower taxed, non-tobacco items which they value less for higher taxed, tobacco items which they value more. But is the taxation of cigarettes and other tobacco products to be seen simply as an expression of political expediency and power? That smokers are a minority in the population surely gives some credence to this possible explanation, for it is an understandable part of human nature to seek to place taxes on other people. Yet it is also possible that such taxes represent efforts to get smokers to cover some of the costs they purportedly impose on nonsmokers, as represented by the economic principle of "corrective taxation." In the next chapter we shall draw more sharply this distinction between principle and expediency as means of understanding the taxation and regulation of tobacco products.

NOTES

1. See, for instance, the careful discussions in Epstein (1985) and Ostrom (1987).

2. There are several approaches to defining what constitutes general improvement. The most popular is the Paretian approach, which holds that improvement results whenever at least one person can be made better off without anyone being made worse off. For surveys of welfare economics, see Baumol (1965), Mishan (1964), Peacock and Rowley (1975), and Van den Doel (1979). See also the collection of essays in Arrow and Scitovsky (1969).

3. For a careful description of vertical and horizontal equity, see Musgrave (1959, Chapters 5 and 8 respectively).

4. Whether this potential for improvement is likely to be translated through existing political processes into actual improvement will be considered below.

5. The 1989 Report of the Surgeon General presents a lower cost estimate of $52 billion. This lower estimate is due to a lower attribution of the cost of lost production, which is placed at $29 billion instead of the $43 billion reported in Table 2.2. The medical costs are nearly the same in both instances.

6. Hawaii taxes cigarettes at 40 percent of wholesale value, which currently runs about 42 cents per pack.

7. For a compendium of information on tobacco taxation, see Tobacco Institute (1990).

CHAPTER 3

The Taxation And Regulation Of Smoking: Principle Vs. Expediency

The application of welfare economics to public policy issues is reminiscent of philosophical discussion, in that public policy questions are approached and presumed to be settled in a disinterested manner through discussion. But with large contemporary governments the stakes in the resolution of policy questions are often exceedingly high, and such disinterestedness may face tough competition from a variety of interest group pressures in the presence of such stakes. Indeed, the contemporary scholarship on public choice processes suggests that public policy outcomes are largely driven by efforts to advance economic interests, and that disinterestedness is largely confined to cases where the stakes are small and no one much cares about the outcomes. Economic policy is accordingly seen as resulting from the interplay of political realists and not from the disinterested discussions of welfare philosophers. This chapter elaborates this distinction, giving particular reference to questions of tobacco taxation and regulation.

Fiscal philosophers are free to articulate whatever tax principles appeal to them, but actual tax choices are made by politicians largely guided by political survival and profit. Actual political outcomes may diverge sharply from those outcomes that seem to be supported by normative reasoning. This can happen because of problems of knowledge. Even a benevolent despot seeking to implement certain normative principles may come up short because of a lack of knowledge of how to do so. For instance,

knowledge of external costs may be weak, thereby reducing the effectiveness of an effort to implement a tax that would truly correct for market
failure. Actual outcomes may also diverge from normatively stipulated
outcomes because of the nature of political incentive. Actual political
processes may not be under the control of some benevolent despot with
a single-minded devotion to enacting a program of corrective taxation.
What may take place instead is an award of tax privileges to politically
powerful groups and a conferral of tax penalties upon politically weak
groups, with both of these being aspects of a generalized market for tax
legislation.

The normative predilections of tax philosophers, as embedded in
models of welfare economics, may have little to do with the outcomes of
actual fiscal processes, driven by political realists. For the incentive to
implement the normative programs of the tax philosophers may be weak
compared with the incentive of the political realists to award tax
privileges to politically powerful groups while imposing tax penalties on
politically weak groups.[1] Merely to develop a justificatory argument does
not imply that such an argument is valid. And should that argument be
invalid, tobacco taxation would have to be explained on other grounds,
and would be seen as accomplishing something other that what the
philosophical justifications claim. This leads, alternatively, into a consideration of positive, explanatory arguments, in which the challenge is to
develop a sensible economic basis for understanding the types of tax
choices that legislatures actually make, and which in some cases may
contrast sharply with the choices the tax philosophers would have them
make.

Realistic Politics and Tobacco Policy

The realistic logic of collective choice starts from the presumption that
people who participate in political processes are essentially the same as
those who participate in market or business processes. Politics is one
form of business activity. The principles of labor supply apply as well to
politics as elsewhere: the higher the rate of pay the greater will be the
amount of labor supplied. People invest in politicians and political parties,
just as they invest in business firms: people contribute more to political
campaigns when government is large than when it is small because large

government exerts a greater impact on economic well-being. In politics, as in business generally, entrepreneurs are continually searching for new products and markets: hearings are held to gauge the demand for possible policy offerings.

Political processes are driven by the same logic of people seeking to increase their well-being through processes of production and exchange as are market processes. To be sure, the rules governing conduct within political processes differ to some extent from those governing conduct within market processes. These differences may induce some differences in the details of conduct in particular cases, but they do not disturb the proposition that politics is as capable of being understood in terms of the principles of economical conduct as is business generally. For instance, the price of a seat on the New York Stock Exchange exceeds the price of a seat on the American Stock Exchange, with the difference reflecting the capital value of the anticipated higher income stream that the NYSE seat would offer. By the same token, people will spend more for a chance to become Governor of California than for a chance to become Governor of Virginia, with that difference also reflecting the higher capital value associated with the ability to legislate in California.[2]

There are several ways in which considerations of political realism grounded in a logic of collective action give different insight into policy processes than would result from a philosophical logic of welfare economics. Consider tax policy. Clearly, there are substantial differences among those scholars who have written about taxation from a normative point of view. Some believe that individual variations in tax burdens should reflect differences in individual valuations for the services provided by government: those who value governmental services more highly should pay more than those who value them less highly. Others believe that variations in individual tax burdens should reflect differences in such measures of economic capacity as income or wealth: people who earn more or are wealthier should pay more for government than those who earn less or are poorer, regardless of the valuations those various people place upon governmental services.

Despite these substantial differences, there is a general agreement among the tax philosophers that tax codes should be fairly stable and should not be subject to substantial change from year to year. While there would be quite a bit of disagreement among the philosophers over how steeply progressive an income tax should be, or even over whether it should be progressive at all, there would be little disagreement with the proposition that whatever tax system is chosen, it should be relatively stable through time, and should be subject to change only at the margins, and not too often at that.

Contrary to the advice of the tax philosophers, tax legislation has become nearly an annual activity over the past two decades. And considerations of political realism give some indication why: a stable tax code offers less business for politicians than a tax code whose provisions are subject to continual change. Tax writing committees will do more business when they allow the tax code to be subject continually to change than if they accord it some form of semi-permanent status.

Furthermore, tax legislation can be sold on both sides of the market. On the one side, a tax code can be changed in a favorable direction. A quite modest change that offers an annual tax reduction of $10 million will be worth some multiple of that amount to the affected industry, with the exact amount depending on such things as discount rates and the expected durability of the legislation. The point here is not to try to sketch out how such a magnitude might be estimated, but rather is only to note that tax favors will be valuable to recipient groups. Everyone can't get tax favors, of course, for then the government would raise no revenue. Those who get the favors would generally be those who bid the most for them, which in turn would generally be those interest groups that faced relatively low costs of organization.

An unfavorable tax change that promises to raise tax liability can also generate business for tax writing committees. People will bid to defeat legislation that threatens to impose losses on them, just as they would bid to support legislation that offers them gains. On both sides of the market, then, the business interests of tax writing legislators leads them to promote a continual churning of the tax code, in sharp contrast to the normative advice of the tax philosophers, advice which notes that stability in the tax code, like legal stability generally, is important in promoting the stability in expectations about the future that is an essential ingredient in advancing the general prosperity.

In 1989, legislation was proposed in Texas that would increase the cigarette tax and would earmark those increased revenues to pay for, among other things, coronary bypass operations. This simple case provides a nice illustration of the contrast between the normative approach to tax policy that stems from welfare economics and a realistic, positive approach. Normatively, such a measure would have to be justified on the grounds that those operations were received by smokers, and by smokers only, and that the tax was an effective way for having those smokers pay for their operations. If the operations were limited to smokers, it could be argued that the earmarked tax program was a form of insurance program, in which all smokers participated, not knowing which particular smokers would need a coronary bypass. But such operations are by no means limited to smokers, and these days there seems to be considerable medical controversy over the possible contributions of smoking, diet, and genetic inheritance to the demand for coronary bypasses. Without doubt, this proposal in Texas, a proposal that is just one instance of many similar proposals throughout the land, cannot in any way be thought to illustrate the agenda of the tax philosophers or welfare economists.

It does, however, illustrate nicely the agenda of the public choice realists. And it does so on both the demand and the supply sides of the market. On the demand side, the subsidy program would increase the demand for bypass operations. Providers of specialized inputs engaged in performing coronary bypasses would thus experience an increase in earnings because of the increased demand. Perhaps the dominant category of specialized input would be the surgeons who perform such operations. But other inputs also in inelastic supply would likewise experience increased earnings. Among these might be specialized nurses, some hospitals, and pharmaceutical companies. In any case, these interest groups would stand to gain by enactment of the proposal, and would be found as participants on the demand side of the market for tax legislation.

The supply side of the market would be populated by those who would be harmed by the legislation. To some extent this would be smokers, who otherwise would be faced with a higher price of cigarettes. But consumers are generally unorganized and relatively ineffective in political processes, save to the extent that their interests coincide with those of other interest groups. One such interest group would be cigarette manufacturers, which have a number of specialized inputs not easily transferable to other uses. Political revenues would thus be reaped on both sides of the market. Those on the demand side pay to get a favorable measure enacted, while those on the supply side pay to get an unfavorable measure defeated. The resulting market outcome will depend on such things as the relative willingness to pay on the two sides of the market and on relative organizational skills. Outcomes where one side or the other win are possible. But so too are compromise outcomes, which in this case would result in some earmarked tax program, but a less extensive one than that advocated by supporters of the measure.

Knowledge and the Improbability of Corrective Taxation

Any effort actually to implement optimal or corrective excise taxes would encounter substantial problems of knowledge, even if it were assumed that the legislature, in choosing to impose excise taxes operated with a single-minded dedication to imposing them in an efficiently corrective manner. At the very core, any such effort must confront the subjectivity of cost and the problem this creates for any effort of a third party or external observer to make inferences about what the participants themselves would do, if only they could.[3] For doing this is central to any effort at corrective taxation.

Refer to the standard Pigovian framework illustrated in Figure 3.1,

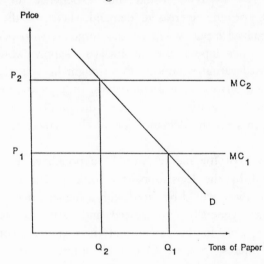

FIGURE 3.1: OWNERSHIP RIGHTS AND CORRECTIVE TAXATION

where MC_1 indicates private marginal cost to the paper mill and MC_2 indicates social marginal cost. The divergence between private and social cost shown there actually represents a counterfactual, hypothetical statement about what the market participants would do under some alternative setting in which people had ownership rights to water. Suppose, in particular, that downstream owners had the right to receive unpolluted water from upstream users. In the presence of such ownership rights, P_2-P_1 might be thought of as the amount that the paper mill would pay downstream users for the right to discharge its waste--with this payment expressed as an average amount per unit of output. But in the absence of such ownership rights, no such trades would actually take place. In this case P_2-P_1 could only represent some hypothetical presumption about what the supply price of that permission might be.[4]

But in any event, the very portrayal of a divergence between private and social cost requires some external observer to make a nonobservable hypothetical statement about what kind of agreements the participants might reach under some counterfactual condition of there being costless agreement. But agreement is costly, and it is those transaction costs that presumably prevent that agreement from being worked out. To be sure, it is certainly a reasonable proposition that so-called transaction costs are as much costs as anything else, so that statements about efficiency must be made in light of realistic statements about transaction costs, and not with hypothetical reference to a world where those costs are zero. But if this is done, there would seem to be no divergence between private and social cost in the first place, for there would exist no unexploited gains from trade among the various participants in the market process.

The existence of a divergence between private and social cost represents the existence of unexploited gains from trade, as Coase (1960) explained. If the river is more valuable as a place to swim and fish than it is as a depository for wastes from the mill, the people who use the river for swimming and fishing will be able to induce the mill to reduce its discharge of wastes. And if relative valuations are in the opposite direction, the mill will be able to induce the swimmers and fishermen to reduce their activities. Which will happen is a matter of which is the more highly valued use of the river. But the efficient use of the river will result in any case, so there will be no divergence between private and social cost. There may be an observed pollution of the river by the paper mill, but this would merely be evidence that the river was more valuable as a receptacle for the mill's wastes than it was as a place for fishing and swimming.

The postulation of a situation described as possessing a divergence between private and social cost is simultaneously the postulation of a situation in which there exist gains from trade to the participants, the exploitation of which would eliminate the divergence between private and social cost. To argue that it is high transaction costs that prevent this exploitation, and to go from there to argue that government can impose the correct outcome, is to posit government as both benevolent and omniscient. Even accepting the presumption of benevolence momentarily, once the presumption of omniscience is acknowledged for what it is, the grounds for suggesting that government can improve matters through corrective taxation would seem to weaken tremendously. In the absence of omniscience, costs will have to be incurred in trying to construct an "as if" network of transactions, and it may well be that the costs of doing so exceed the gain that the participants may think they can achieve. If so, the most efficient outcome is not to put together such a pseudo-transaction, for the gain achieved from doing so will be less than the cost of organizing the transaction.

To be sure, it could be argued that the substitution of some third-party process of governmental choice for a market process of choice by the participants is less costly than the market process, particularly when the number of participants might be large or when some element of bilateral monopoly might exist. There are at least two points that should be raised about this line of argument. One speaks to the presumption that governmental choice might entail lower transaction costs than market processes would entail; the other addresses the comparative accuracy of governmental choice and market processes. Presumably, the central argument in favor of Pigovian taxes in presumed externality situations is that although governmental processes of third-party determination must be less accurate than market processes of first-party determination, this loss in accuracy is more than offset by the saving in transaction costs.

What about the alleged savings in transaction costs that governmental processes are presumed to offer? There is a presumption implicit in much of the literature on corrective taxation that the transaction costs of governmental decision making are virtually zero. This presumption reflects, in turn, the implicit presumption that government is a single mind. To speak of governmental choice is to speak of choice by a single person. While people clearly incur costs in deciding which choices to make personally, those costs are surely compounded when collective choices must be made. In the Pigovian illustrations, transaction costs are presumed to be high usually because the choices of a large number of people must be coordinated, though sometimes it may be just a setting of bilateral monopoly. Governmental choice in this literature is clearly presumed to represent a lower cost substitute for market processes.

But is governmental choice really or plausibly to be viewed as a way of reducing transaction costs? It might be in some cases, to be sure, but it would seem difficult to argue on conceptual grounds that governmental choice must offer significant savings of transaction costs. There is no single person who makes governmental choices on matters of taxation, or about anything else for that matter. A governmental choice of a tax rate on a single product will involve various processes of collective choice, including both legislative processes of developing and enacting legislation and bureaucratic processes of providing information pertinent to the enactment of that legislation and of implementing that legislation. Even should a legislature truly desire to enact an efficiently corrective tax, it would have to go through a costly process of hearings, lobbying, and meetings to put together some tax program. To think of governmental decision making as involving lower transaction costs than market processes by thinking of the former as representing a unified choice by a single mind is fatuous. While there may be particular cases where governmental decision making has lower transaction costs than market processes involving negotiation among the participants, there would seem to be no ground for suggesting that this would universally be the case. Nor does there seem to be ground for suggesting that transaction costs within governmental processes, even if they might be thought to be lower than transaction costs within market processes, are orders of magnitude smaller than transaction costs within market processes.

Even if it were presumed that governmental processes of corrective taxation involved lower transaction costs than market processes of exchange among the participants, the difference would be nothing like the dramatic differences that would be implied by the presumption that governmental processes involve simply the choice of a single person. And against that possible saving in transaction costs must be set the cost of the sacrificed accuracy that must result under governmental processes because of the lack of omniscience. This reduction in accuracy has been expressed and described in various ways in different types of literature. Within the literature on the theory of economic calculation, it represents the argument that a system of market socialism would not be able to duplicate the results of an actual market economy.[5] And this reduction in accuracy would be compounded by the questions of incentive that would arise once it is acknowledged that it is implausible to model legislators as having a single-minded, benevolent dedication to correcting market failures when they impose excise taxes.

Even should it be plausible to model governmental processes as having a single minded dedication to implementing a set of Pigovian corrective taxes, such a government might actually end up imposing no taxes.[6] It is not obvious that governmental processes offer significant savings in transaction costs over market processes. And by substituting the choices of some third party for the choices that the participants would have made themselves necessarily introduces some inaccuracy into processes of resource allocation. A benevolent government might well decide to forego any effort to implement a program of corrective taxation, and concentrate its energies instead on policing and protecting property rights, thereby maintaining a framework within which the participants can exploit opportunities for mutual gain.

Political Incentive and Actual Tobacco Taxation

The abstract theory of corrective taxation is generally simpler than the reality such efforts at taxation address. Even in a world of benevolence, in which tax policy could be described as reflecting a single-minded devotion to the implementation of principles of corrective taxation, a difficult question of knowledge would have to be overcome concerning the formation of a correct, or even a reasonably informed judgment of external cost. A market system generally produces such knowledge as a by-product of its internal operation. For instance, a failure by a firm to cover its cost of production means that the value that consumers place on its output is less than the value they place on the alternative output that was sacrificed to produce the product in question. And the converse conclusion can be reached in the case of a firm that makes a profit. But when a direct market test is absent, as is necessarily the case with external costs, for the very concept implies that some aspects of resource usage are not reflected in market transactions, the problem of securing knowledge is more difficult.

Moreover, a market system provides a strong incentive for people to make knowledgeable choices, because poor choices will result in losses. A growing body of contemporary literature on political economy and public choice has explained why political incentives often operate less strongly to promote economic efficiency than market incentives. In politics, the costs and gains of accurate or inaccurate choice are concentrated less strongly on those who make those choices, because more of those costs and gains are diffused generally throughout the citizenry. The loss from a governmental choice that is more costly than it need be is spread over all taxpayers, rather than being concentrated on those responsible for making that choice.

The principle of corrective taxation is not an explanatory statement about the actual practice of excise taxation. A particular tax may be rationalized on corrective grounds, but the reality of the situation might clash with that rationalization, possibly because the tax does not address accurately the nature of the external costs, or possibly because the alleged external costs are insignificant, or even nonexistent. The real reason for the tax or regulatory measure may be a transfer of wealth. Tobacco taxation may be imposed not as a way of correcting for market failures that result if smokers do not pay the full costs purportedly associated with their smoking, but as a way of transferring tax burdens away from nonsmokers. There is growing recognition, stemming from the literature on public choice processes, that actual tax policies may be adopted for quite different reasons than the justifications commonly advanced in their support. For instance, the imposition of excise taxes on products consumed by a minority can be an effective way of transferring income tax burdens, particularly if the taxed items have relatively inelastic demands.

Recognition that governmental processes are no more grounded on a principle of benevolence than are market processes renders even weaker the normative case for discriminatory taxation. But at the same time, the actual imposition of discriminatory taxation becomes more understandable once it is recognized that governmental processes are as much driven by self interest as are market processes. Within an interest group model of government, the market for legislation is viewed as a process in which the legislature brokers wealth transfers among the citizenry [e.g., McCormick and Tollison (1981)]. Some people are net gainers in this process and others are net losers. There are, to be sure, many particular markets and margins through which the market for legislation can operate. One of these is the market for tax legislation.

Conceptually, it is useful to distinguish two facets of the market for tax legislation, even though both facets are dealt with simultaneously in the legislative process. The first facet recognizes that taxes are necessary for government spending, and that a general increase in desires for such spending amounts *ipso facto* to an increase in desired levels of taxation. The second facet recognizes that people generally prefer to receive preferential tax treatment and to have taxes paid by other people instead of by themselves. These two facets suggest that the market for tax legislation can be conceptualized as a two-stage process, recognizing that both stages occur simultaneously in reality.[7] The first stage is uniform and nondiscriminatory; the second stage is particular and discriminatory. In the first stage, the choice is one of what tax rate to apply to a general, broad-based tax; if that base is income, all income will be taxed at the same rate, and the choice is simply one of which rate. In the second stage, the product of the first stage is revised in consequence of lobbying efforts, where some interest groups seek to get more favorable tax treatment, and where tax reductions for some imply tax increases for others. The tax program that results will contain exemptions from the tax base as well as perhaps having a variety of tax rates.

Consider first the enactment of the initial tax measure--the first draft of the legislation that will ultimately be enacted. While this initial measure will be general, uniform, or nondiscriminatory, there are several particular tax forms that could be used: among the possibilities are head taxes, income taxes, and expenditure taxes. Whichever general tax form is used, the choice of a tax rate can be thought of as resulting from an electoral process, in which an initial tax rate is compared with some higher rate and a vote is taken. Some people will prefer the lower rate, reflecting the belief that the added government spending that the higher tax rate will make possible will be worth less to them than the reduction in disposable income they would have to suffer. Others will support the higher rate, reflecting the belief that the added spending will be more valuable to them than the disposable income they would lose by virtue of the higher rate. One simple way of conceptualizing the outcome of this stage is that the tax rate selected will be the median among the rates preferred by the population, though there are other ways of conceptualizing this process that would give somewhat different results. But in any case, the tax rate will be what it is and not something else because at any other rate political pressures will be predominately on the side of pushing it up or pulling it down.

The second stage in this conceptualization introduces interest groups and the market for tax legislation. Here, the willingness of participants to pay for legislation is reflected in the strength of the political pressure they are able to exert on the fiscal process. It is easy to imagine a world of perfect representation, in which tax rates are put up directly for bid, much like real auctions. In this case people who thought the benefits from additional spending exceeded the cost would submit bids in favor of higher tax rates, while those in the opposite position would submit bids in opposition. And so long as those who favored higher taxes outbid those who wanted lower taxes, it could be said that the benefits from added spending exceeded the costs.

But there are some significant differences between the market for tax legislation and ordinary markets. Tax rates are not subject to any kind of direct auction, and the currency in which transactions take place is only partly pecuniary. There clearly are cases where types of monetary payments, such as campaign contributions, are made to secure policy measures. But much of the currency in the market for tax legislation takes such forms as hiring lobbyists, running newspaper advertisements, and organizing letter-writing campaigns. Political pressure is a far more ambiguous concept than is the market pressure of willingness to pay, though it is surely no less real. Thus, there are likely to be several reasons why actual tax rates might deviate from what would result in a world of perfect representation.

In market processes individual demands are aggregated without any discrimination other than that of willingness to pay. But this is not so in political processes, for some people are able to pursue collective action more effectively than others. Interest group processes require individuals to invest in the promotion of the collective interest of the group's members. As Olson (1965) explains, latent pressure will not automatically be transformed into actual pressure. The interests of some groups of people will be more fully reflected in political processes than the interests of other groups, even though their respective stakes and willingness to pay are identical. Among other things, groups that face lower organization costs will be more predominant in fiscal outcomes than those that face higher costs. Hence, conclusions reached about the equilibrium properties of a model of collective action are not necessarily identical with conclusions reached about the equilibrium properties of a model of welfare economics.

To be sure, an examination of tax policy in terms of a logic of fiscal politics need not be contradictory to such an examination in terms of a logic of welfare economics. Even if we ask not how high the tax rate *should* be, but rather ask how high it *will* be, the answer to the positive question may not be totally unrelated to the answer to the normative question. One aspect of the political benefit surely reflects the perceived external costs that people think they are bearing. If external costs are present, these costs will surely translate into some form of political benefit or demand, as Figure 3.2 illustrates. The line MPC illustrates that opposition to tax increases strengthens as taxes rise; it also shows that there is a sufficiently low rate of tax (and of public spending) where tax increases would encounter no opposition. The line MPB illustrates that the intensity of political support for higher taxation will decline as tax rates increase, because ever larger numbers of people will come to conclude that additional public spending is worth less to them than the loss of disposable income they would suffer. One source of support for higher taxation would surely be the desire to curb the imposition of external costs. This would increase the amount of political pressure exerted in support of higher taxation, as illustrated by MPB* and the associated higher tax rate, t*.

But external costs are not the only source of such political demand. Spending constituencies desire revenues, and these form a source of political demand that would exist even if external costs were zero. Tax increases, of course, go into a general fund, for which various spending constituencies compete. Such a framework was implicit in the construction of Figure 3.2. Both the support for and the opposition to tax increases are conditioned by the public goods nature of tax revenues. However, if the revenues from a particular tax can be earmarked for a particular expenditure program, tax revenues would be transformed into a private good, for a property right would have been created in the tax revenue. Consequently, the political demand for taxation should rise, as illustrated by the shift from MPB to MPB* in Figure 3.2. In this manner rent seeking can also enter the logic of fiscal politics.

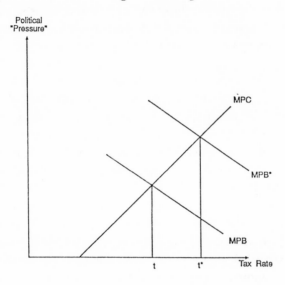

FIGURE 3.2: FISCAL POLITICS AND RENT SEEKING

In any case, the first draft, nondiscriminatory tax code is unlikely to survive the political process by which tax legislation is enacted. Suppose the broad-based tax in question is a consumption tax. For each product category, a representation something like Figure 3.2 could be developed. If these representations were identical across products, the initial, nondiscriminatory tax code would not be modified in the market for tax legislation. But if costs of political organization were lower in some industrial groupings than in others, the political costs of taxation would rise and the resultant tax rates would fall. Questions of external cost aside, the first-draft, broad-based tax is unlikely to survive the political process without modification. Such survival would result only so long as the relationships between marginal political benefit and marginal political cost were the same for all relevant markets and margins. Survival would result, as it were, only if a disaggregation of Figure 3.2 in terms of categories of expenditure (for a tax on the sources side) or types of markets (for a tax on the uses side) led to the same MPC-MPB relationship for each particular category that could be subject to differential tax treatment.

But if the participants in those various markets differ in such things as the costs of organization and the degree of geographical concentration, those interest groups that are particularly effective at political organization will, by raising the marginal political cost of taxation, be able to secure tax reductions. These reductions could occur through lower rates or they could occur through exclusions from the tax base, but in any event a pattern of differential taxation will emerge. More effectively organized groups will secure lower tax burdens than less effectively organized groups, because more effectively organized groups raise the marginal political cost of taxation.[8] With legislation being a product of the ability of various interest groups to bring political pressure to bear on legislators, those groups that face relatively low cost of political organization will be able to secure wealth transfers, which in the case of taxation will be various types of exclusions, exemptions, and deductions. And for those groups that are relatively less effective in this process, the result will be a rise in taxes. Winners in the market for tax legislation will pay lower taxes; losers will pay higher taxes.

Rationale, Reality, and Tobacco Regulation

Besides the continual pressure for increased taxation, tobacco faces intense pressure in several directions for ever more extensive government regulation. Much of this regulatory pressure concerns the ability of smokers to smoke in places other than in their own homes. A wide variety of what might, generically, be called clean indoor air acts have restricted the ability of people to smoke in closed spaces outside their homes. Smoking is now banned on nearly all domestic airline flights. Government buildings typically have rules on where smoking is allowed or prohibited. It is common for governments to regulate smoking policies in a variety of workplaces and restaurants. And new policy measures are continually being invented and advocated.

The justification for clean indoor air acts seems to be a straightforward case of government issuing regulations to control external costs. But as we shall examine in a later chapter, the case for such legislation is not as strong as it might appear on first glance. For one critical difference in the indoor smoking case is that indoor air is subject to private ownership. Hence, the analytical support for clean indoor air legislation may vanish upon closer inspection.

But yet the demand for such legislation continues unabated. If the arguments of the policy philosophers cannot explain the persistent demands for such legislation, can the arguments of the political realists offer any insight? The question here is whether clean indoor air acts can offer any gains to particular people, for if they do they can become a candidate for incorporation into the market for public policy, the nonapplicability of the philosophical arguments of welfare economics notwithstanding. There are numerous ways in which such gains might possibly arise, and we shall examine some of these more fully in later chapters.

Tobacco Policy in Constitutional Perspective

There might be a substantial cleavage between the normative lines of argument that support the taxation and regulation of tobacco, as represented by external cost arguments, and the properties of the actual political processes through which such legislation emerges. Even if such legislation is modeled as the outcome of a benevolent process, the knowledge necessary to legislate in the manner envisioned by the theory of external cost and corrective taxation is unlikely to be present. Furthermore, legislation is really the outcome of a self-interested process of interest group competition. For reasons noted above, tobacco taxation and regulation may have more to do with the forces of interest-group politics than with any imperatives of social or external cost.

This is not to deny that they might not be possible circumstances under which excise taxes might serve socially valuable purposes. But such a possibility would seem to be a matter of the constitutional rules that pertain to processes of tax legislation. Principles of corrective taxation envision government using its power to tax to bring about a complex network of exchanges that would otherwise not have transpired. The extent to which the actual tax enactments of actual governments can be reconciled with this normative vision would seem to depend on the extent to which the constitutional rules that constrain political processes prevent the use of government as a means of imposing disabilities on some people for the benefit of others.

Yet the opportunity for discriminatory taxation points to some severe constitutional questions for democratic political systems. Bruno Leoni (1960) points out that "no taxation without representation" originally meant no taxation without the consent of the taxpayer. A principle of non-discrimination would seem very much to be a related element of a constitutional approach to taxation, as William Hutt (1966) argued in his review essay on *The Calculus of Consent*. While it is reasonable to think of democracy as, among other things, a process of self-taxation, in that we choose to tax ourselves, it is unreasonable to think of it legitimately as a process by which some people choose to tax others. A tax measure that gets a two-thirds majority may be fine when the majority are among the taxpayers. But when the taxes are concentrated among the minority, what may result is a system of a majority choosing to tax not themselves but to tax other people, and a severe conflict with the principles of constitutional government becomes quickly apparent.

A salient illustration of this point arose in California in a referendum that passed in November 1988. This referendum proposed to increase the cigarette tax by 25 cents per pack, and to earmark those revenues primarily to finance medical expenses for people without insurance and to support anti-smoking educational programs. Could this referendum be seen as one particular implementation of the benefit principle, in which people agree to tax themselves to finance services they value? The 58:42 margin by which the referendum passed might seem to indicate a fairly high degree of consensus for the program, which would suggest the tax could reasonably be viewed instead as a quasi-user charge. However, the degree of support for the tax was similar to the proportion of non-smokers to smokers in the population (around 70:30) and this suggests the program could be seen alternatively as a form of income redistribution in which a majority voted to award benefits to itself, financed by tax burdens it chose to impose on a minority.

NOTES

1. For a seminal treatise on issues that arise in seeking to develop an explanatory approach to fiscal processes, see Buchanan (1967). Some relationships between public finance and public choice are surveyed in Buchanan (1975). For a wide-ranging survey of the market for legislation, see Tollison (1988). For interesting efforts to place taxation in the context of a market for legislation, see Doernberg and McChesney (1987) and Hettich and Winer (1988).

2. Ownership of stock exchange seats is secure and transferable, while the possession of governorships is insecure and nontransferable. What this means is that income streams for governorships are discounted over a shorter period of time than those for stock exchange seats. But the economic principles are the same in both cases.

3. On the subjectivity of cost and the obstacles this imposes for third party calculations, see Buchanan (1969).

4. Alternatively, P_2-P_1 might be thought of as representing the supply price to the paper mill owner of building some type of facility to treat the water before discharging it.

5. For expositions of this long-standing topic, see Vaughn (1980) and Lavoie (1985).

6. This theme is developed in a general context in Tollison and Wagner (1991).

7. This conceptualization of tax legislation is developed in Wagner (1990).

8. It is, of course, possible that such a tax base could be earmarked for a particular spending program, which would also increase the marginal political benefit from taxation. The effect on the tax rate is indeterminate in this case, though the amount of political activity will increase on both sides of the transaction.

CHAPTER 4

Smoking And The Economic Cost Of Lost Production

The 1989 report of the Surgeon General, "Reducing the Health Consequences of Smoking: 25 Years of Progress," claimed that "approximately 390,000 Americans died in 1985 as the result of smoking." Such figures as these, along with associated figures on rates of illness among smokers, have in turn been expressed as equivalent economic magnitudes. For instance, the prominently cited survey sponsored by the Office of Technology Assessment, summarized in Table 2.2 above, placed these magnitudes at between $38 billion and $95 billion for 1985. This survey went on to postulate a "best" estimate of $65 billion, which is $2.17 per pack of cigarettes. These cost estimates distinguish between "direct" and "indirect" costs. Direct costs refer to the various medical expenses that are claimed to be associated with smoking, while indirect costs refer to the lost production that is estimated to result because of the purported illnesses and deaths attributed to smoking. With respect to the $65 billion estimate, about one-third, $22 billion, were direct costs, while the remaining two-thirds, $43 billion, were indirect costs.

So in attempting to estimate the claims concerning economic costs of smoking, it is necessary to start with an effort to gauge the reported health consequences of smoking. For it is those alleged consequences that provide a point of departure for estimating the economic magnitudes of the direct and indirect costs. This chapter describes and assesses the methods that have been used to estimate claims concerning indirect costs, while the next chapter does the same thing for the claimed direct costs. First, however, it will be helpful to describe briefly the method by which estimates of the alleged health consequences of smoking are made.

Smoking and Health: The Method of "Attributable Risk"

The central logic behind the construction of estimates for the cost of smoking is simple and straightforward, even if the actual implementation of that logic is fraught with difficulties. The presumption that smoking damages health is the point of departure for any effort to assess the social cost of smoking, for if this presumption is invalid there is no point in talking about any cost of smoking beyond the cost of producing and distributing cigarettes. Although quite a number of diseases have been associated statistically with smoking, the three diseases that have dominated the analysis of the reported health consequences of smoking are lung cancer, cardiovascular disease, and chronic obstructive lung disease (bronchitis and emphysema). Table 4.1 shows estimates, compiled in 1985 by the U. S. Office of Technology Assessment, of smoking-related deaths for 1982 by these three categories.[1] These estimates are

Table 4.1

Smoking-Related Deaths (1982)

Disease	Range	"Best" est.	Life-Yrs. Lost
Cancer	89,000 - 174,000	139,000	
Cardiovascular	48,000 - 170,000	123,000	
Chronic lung	49,000 - 54,000	52,000	
TOTAL	186,000 - 398,000	314,000	5,300,000

Source: Office of Technology Assessment, *Smoking-Related Deaths and Financial Costs*, p. 2.

compiled by constructing a measure of attributable risk for each disease category, which purports to describe the share of the total deaths from a particular disease that can be attributed to smoking. Thus, if there were one million deaths from various cardiovascular diseases during a year and if the attributable risk assigned to smoking were 15 percent, 150,000 of those deaths would be labeled smoking-related.

The first step in any effort to estimate the cost of smoking is to estimate the extent to which smoking is thought to harm health, for the "cost of smoking" represents merely the placement of a valuation upon "the health impairment attributed to smoking." Despite numerous difficulties in attempting to construct such an estimate, the principle behind that construction is a simple one and is commonly described as the method of "attributable risk." First, a sample of people containing both smokers and nonsmokers is selected. Second, the experiences of those people with the diseases under study are recorded. Third, those experiences are compared, and any resulting difference in mortality or morbidity rates between the two sets of people is attributed to smoking. Regardless of the disease to be examined and regardless of whether it is mortality rates or morbidity patterns that are to be examined, the implementation of the attributable risk approach is the same.

The essential idea behind the attributable risk approach is illustrated in simple but accurate fashion by the hypothetical data illustrated in Table 4.1. Suppose the task is to determine how many deaths from lung cancer to attribute to smoking. Table 4.2 illustrates a sample of 2,000 people, 800 (40 percent) of whom are smokers. During the year, 88 deaths were

Table 4.2

Hypothetical Lung Cancer Deaths

	Smokers	Nonsmokers	Total
Sample size	800	1,200	2,000
Number of deaths	64	24	88
Percentage of deaths	8.0%	2.0%	4.4%
Deaths at 2% rate	16		
Smoking-related deaths	48		

attributed to lung cancer, with 24 of the decedents being nonsmokers and the remaining 64 being smokers. It would be wrong to claim that all of the 64 lung cancer deaths among smokers were smoking-related. Because nonsmokers also die from lung cancer, even if it were accepted that cigarette smoking causes lung cancer, some of those smokers would have died from lung cancer even if they had not smoked.

Suppose it were assumed that the only significant difference among the sample of 2,000 people was in whether or not they smoked. During the year 2 percent of the nonsmokers died from lung cancer, while the death rate among smokers was 8 percent. If those 800 smokers had been nonsmokers instead, the expected number of lung cancer deaths among those people would have been 16 (2 percent of 800). Since the actual number of lung cancer deaths among the smokers was 64, it would seem reasonable to attribute 48 of those deaths (64 - 16) to smoking. By this method 54.5 percent of the 88 lung cancer deaths during the year would be attributed to smoking.

Table 4.3 illustrates the construction of the "best" estimate of 139,000 smoking-related deaths from cancers that is presented in Table 4.1. The central principle of the method of attributable risk described above is readily apparent in Table 4.3. During 1982, 433,795 deaths were ascribed

Table 4.3

Smoking-Related Cancer Deaths, 1982

Sex & age group	Total Cancer Deaths	Attributed Risk	Smoking-Related Deaths
Male -- under 65	84,965	50%	42,000
Male -- 65 & over	148,862	41%	61,000
Male -- all ages	233,864	44%	103,000
Female -- under 65	74,484	23%	17,000
Female -- 65 & over	125,420	15%	19,000
Female -- all ages	199,931	18%	36,000
Both sexes -- all ages	433,795		

Source: U.S. Office of Technology Assessment (1985).

to cancers, nearly 234,000 to men and just under 200,000 to women. For men 44 percent of all cancer deaths were attributed to smoking, while for women the attribution rate was 18 percent. Table 4.3 also shows that attribution rates vary with age. So too would those rates vary across types of cancer; the rates portrayed in Table 4.3 are an average across all cancers. Given information about the rate of attributable risk for a particular disease and the number of deaths ascribed to that disease, it is a matter of simple arithmetic to compute the number of so-called smoking-related deaths.[2]

How Accurate Are Measures of Attributable Risk?

It certainly should not be thought that the method of attributable risk yields exact answers that are free from ambiguity and controversy. Indeed, Table 4.1 itself illustrates that the estimation of smoking-related deaths is far from exact. The high end of the range of cancer deaths attributed to smoking is twice that of the low end. OTA's "best" estimate attributes 32 percent of all cancer deaths to smoking. But some scholars have attributed only 20 percent of cancer deaths to smoking, while other scholars have attributed as much as 40 percent to smoking. And even greater variation pertains to the attribution of cardiovascular diseases to smoking. The OTA's "best" estimate of 123,000 deaths reflects an attribution rate of 13 percent (of nearly 968,000 total deaths ascribed to cardiovascular diseases in 1982). But the attribution rates other scholars have developed range from 5 to 18 percent, so the high estimate in this case is nearly four times that of the low estimate.

The method of attributable risk operates by using a sample of people to develop a measure of attributable risk, and then applies that measure to the population at large. The accuracy of this method depends critically on two presumptions: (1) the only relevant difference among the people in the sample is that some smoke and others don't; and (2) the sample is an accurate reflection of the total population to which the estimates are being applied. There are plenty of grounds for recognizing that both presumptions are inaccurate, though how inaccurate and to what effect is something about which no agreement exists. While it turns out that the economic assessment of the costs of smoking, if any, to people other than smokers does not depend on the accuracy of estimates of attributable risk, we do think it is useful to understanding something about the procedures and pitfalls that necessarily characterize any effort to assess the alleged health consequences of smoking.

Table 4.2 describes a hypothetical sample of 2,000 people, 800 of whom are presumed to smoke. Eight percent of the smokers die from lung cancer while 2 percent of the nonsmokers do so. To be able accurately to attribute the additional 6 percent death rate among smokers to smoking requires the presumption that everyone in the sample is alike in all relevant respects, save that some smoke and others do not. But what if a significant number of the smokers are steel or coke oven workers, while few if any of the nonsmokers work in those occupations? These occupations are relatively strongly associated with lung cancer compared with other occupations (Sterling 1975). The presence of such people in the sample would violate the presumption that the sample group that is used to construct the measure of attributable risk is identical in all relevant respects, save that some smoke and others do not.

The resulting measure of attributable risk would be biased in the direction of exaggerating the number of smoking-related deaths. This can be seen in either of two ways. On the one hand, the steel and coke oven workers could be removed from the sample. This would reduce the death rate among the remaining smokers. Alternatively, steel and coke oven workers could be introduced into the sample of nonsmokers. This would raise the death rate from lung cancer among nonsmokers. In either case, the differential death rate from lung cancer between smokers and nonsmokers would be narrowed.

While we have illustrated this point with respect to lung cancer, it has general validity for all disease categories. For instance, in his study on of smoking and heart disease, Carl Seltzer (1980, p. 276) found that "ex-smokers showed statistically significant differences from smokers who continued the habit in a number of cardiovascular symptoms, socio-personal characteristics, and metabolic and miscellaneous traits." This means, Seltzer went on to note, that "ex-smokers are not a representative sample of smokers with regard to their CHD-related characteristics or the extent of the smoking habit." Hence, a statistical finding that ex-smokers have less heart disease than smokers does not by itself make it possible to infer that smokers can reduce their likelihood of heart disease to that of ex-smokers by quitting smoking. This is so because the ex-smokers may have had characteristics that would have led to less heart disease in the first place, even if they had continued to smoke. Smokers and ex-smokers may not be identical in all relevant respects save that only some of them are currently smoking; rather, nonsmokers may differ from smokers in other respects that would also lead to a lower incidence of heart disease--for example, nonsmokers may be relatively heavily concentrated among type B personalities, who apparently are reported to have less heart disease than type A personalities.

The second main difficulty with the method of attributable risk lies in its presumption that the sample from which the measure of attributable risk is developed is representative of the population to which the calculations are bring applied. The sample that is used to construct estimates of attributable risk was a million person study put together by the American Cancer Society over the period 1959-65. Measures of attributable risk are constructed on the basis of this sample, and computations are then made for the entire nation under the presumption that the ACS sample is representative of the nation as a whole.

Yet Sterling (1965) suggests that there are several ways in which the ACS sample is quite non-representative of the nation as a whole. To begin, the ACS sample was limited to households that had one adult who was at least 45 years of age, and this limitation itself produced substantial divergence from the underlying characteristics of the total population. For one thing, the ACS sample had 10 percent more females (and fewer males) than would have been representative of the national population. For both males and females, representation in the 45-55 age range generally ran up to 50 percent higher in the ACS sample than was true for the nation as a whole.

The ACS sample of male smokers was 95 percent native-born and white, while only 79 percent of the American male population had that characteristic in 1960. While 8 percent of the male population in 1960 was black, the ACS sample had only 1 percent. And where nearly 13 percent of the male population was foreign-born and white, the ACS sample contained only 4 percent representation. The ACS sample was about 12 percent more Protestant and nearly 30 percent less Catholic than the nation as a whole. The percentage of men in the ACS sample who lived in metropolitan areas was nearly 20 percent above the national average, while the number who lived in rural areas was more than 30 percent below the national average. In these, as well as in numerous other respects, the characteristics of the ACS sample differed significantly from those of the overall population.

Furthermore, even the attribution of death to a particular cause is subject to error. To say there were 433,795 cancer deaths in 1982 (Table 4.3) sounds like a solid magnitude, even if it might be acknowledged that there are numerous difficulties and ambiguities associated with any effort to attribute a share of those deaths to smoking. But this turns out not to be the case -- even the number of deaths from a particular disease is subject to considerable error and ambiguity.

Table 4.2 postulates 88 deaths from lung cancer in a sample of 2,000 people. But how accurate is this knowledge about the cause of death? For the most part this type of information is taken from death certificates; in the sample illustrated by Table 4.2, 88 of the deaths would have been certified as having been due to lung cancer. Yet there is substantial evidence that such certifications are strikingly inaccurate. Feinstein and Wells (1974) have reported that there is a strong "detection bias" in attributions of death to lung cancer. This bias means that physicians are more likely to certify lung cancer as a cause of death among people whom they know to be heavy smokers than among people they know to be nonsmokers or even light smokers. The accuracy of death certificates can be checked through autopsy. Feinstein and Wells report that in a study where death certificates were checked through autopsy, lung cancer was missed in 38 percent of the cases where it was actually present in nonsmokers, in 20 percent of the cases involving light smokers, and in only 10 percent of the cases involving heavy smokers. Lung cancer is rarely missed among heavy smokers, but is often missed among nonsmokers.

By understating lung cancers in nonsmokers, this detection bias leads to an exaggeration of the attributable risk associated with smoking. This exaggeration can be illustrated with reference to Table 4.2. To minimize the complexity of computation, suppose detection is compete in smokers and only 50 percent complete in nonsmokers; this is a larger difference than Feinstein and Wells reported, but it allows for a simple illustration of the central point. Of the 88 certified lung cancer deaths represented in Table 4.2, 64 were smokers and 24 were nonsmokers. Had autopsies been performed, however, 48 lung cancer deaths would have been detected among the nonsmokers. This gives a true death rate among nonsmokers of 4 percent. If this rate were applied to the 800 smokers, there would have been 32 deaths. Only the excess of lung cancer deaths over this amount would be attributed to smoking. Smoking would have been associated with only 32 of 112 lung cancer deaths, or 28.5 percent of those deaths. In this illustration the removal of detection bias would reduce the attributable risk of smoking nearly in half.

A related source of bias arises because many reported lung cancers really represent metastases from cancers elsewhere. Eysenck (1986, p. 30) reports an autopsy study of 2,826 cases, of which only 747 were primary lung cancers. The other 2,079 were metastases of cancers from other sites. If all metastases were wrongly certified as lung cancer, and if the results of this study were generalizable, 73.5 percent of reported lung cancer deaths would be wrongly certified. And even with moderate assumptions about the extent of erroneous certification, deaths attributed to lung cancer would still decline.

We have pointed out some of the difficulties and ambiguities associated with the construction of measures of attributable risk, not to disparage efforts aimed at acquiring evidence about such matters but rather to give some reasonable understanding of the nature of the foundations upon which particular claims are made about the health consequences of smoking. For claims about economic costs of smoking have been based upon an acceptance of the claims about health consequences, and have sought to place price tags upon those various consequences. The greater the uncertainty and error that characterize such estimates, the greater will be the concomitant variability in estimates of overall economic magnitudes. Yet the possible economic impact of smokers on nonsmokers may be largely the same regardless of this variability, primarily because our economic system works in such a way that smokers bear most of those costs in any event and whatever their magnitude might be.

Economic Measurement of Indirect Costs

Once a description of the claimed health consequences of smoking has been developed, the potential economic significance of those consequences can be assessed. The underlying principles are simple, even if the actual practice is not. The indirect costs associated with the attributed health consequences of smoking have two components. The morbidity component measures the loss in economic output attributed to so-called smoking-related illnesses; the mortality component measures the loss in output attributed to smoking-related deaths. Because different approaches to the estimation of the alleged health consequences of smoking will generate different attributions of smoking-related deaths and diseases, the estimated costs of medical care and lost production will similarly differ, even if there is no disagreement as to the appropriate values to place on illness and lost production. The presence of disagreement about the valuation of such events would increase the range of cost estimates.

These cost estimates are generally quite substantial. Those compiled by the Office of Technology Assessment estimated the health care costs attributed to smoking in 1985 to range from $12 billion to $35 billion, with a "best" estimate of $22 billion. Similarly, the estimated cost of lost production ranged from $27 billion to $61 billion for 1985, with a "best" estimate of $43 billion. The range of cost estimates is obviously quite wide, for the high estimate for total costs of smoking is 2.5 times as large as the low estimate. The width of this range attests to the difficulties of application in moving from the simple conceptual idea to the construction of actual estimates. But in any event, if one accepts the estimates, the magnitudes are quite large, ranging on a per pack basis from $1.27 to $3.17. If cigarettes presently sell for around $1.50 per pack, the full cost of smoking, according to these estimates, would seem to be two or three times that amount.

Several people have tried to estimate the costs they say arise from smoking-related morbidity. Such efforts generally follow a two-step procedure: (1) an estimate is made of the number of days of work missed attributed to smoking-related illnesses and (2) an economic valuation is placed on those days of lost work. For instance, M. H. Peston (1971) estimated that the annual cost of lost production attributable to smoking in Great Britain was 290 million pounds. To construct this figure, he first estimated that 50 million days of work were missed because of illness claimed to be attributed to smoking. After further estimating that the average daily wage rate of those ill workers was 5.8 pounds, he computed the estimated total amount of lost production to be 290 million pounds. For the United States, Luce and Schweitzer (1978) estimated the cost of lost production claimed to be attributed to smoking-related morbidity to be $19.1 billion in 1976. If this latter amount were restated in 1985 dollars, Luce and Schweitzer's estimate for the United States would have been about $36 billion, which is more than $1 per pack of cigarettes. Similarly, Kristein (1977) estimated those costs to be $15.1 billion in

1975, which would extrapolate to about $30 billion in 1985 dollars.

The mortality attributed to smoking is treated in these studies as equivalent to morbidity that lasts until retirement. So the death of a 55 year-old that is attributed to smoking is treated as if that person had suffered a permanently incapacitating illness or injury at that same age. If the work year for such a person was 250 days, and if the daily wage rate was $100, one year's lost work would be valued at $25,000. If this $25,000 annual figure were simply repeated each year until retirement, and if the retirement age were 65, the cost of the lost production that would be attributed to smoking would be $250,000 in this case.

Two types of complications arise in this case. One is the possibility that earnings will be higher or lower in future years. The other is the need to recognize that a dollar to be received next year is worth less now than a dollar to be received now. The reason is that a dollar to be received now can earn interest, and so it is worth more than a dollar to be received one year from now. Alternatively, some amount less than one dollar held now can be converted into a dollar in one year. For instance, at a 10 percent rate of interest and in the absence of compounding, 91 cents now can be converted into $1 in one year. Hence, a dollar to be received in one year is equivalent to only 91 cents now, at an interest rate of 10 percent. While it is not necessary to go into the principles or mechanics of present value discounting here, it should be noted that the estimation of the mortality-related costs of smoking, as contrasted to the morbidity-related costs, does involve such present value discounting.

The aforementioned authors who developed estimates of the morbidity costs of smoking also developed estimates of the mortality costs, with these costs expressed in present value terms. With respect to Great Britain, Peston estimated the present value of the cost of death before the age of 65 to be 147 million pounds per year. He based this calculation on the presumption that there were 23,000 deaths before retirement that could be attributed to smoking each year, and with the average length of time remaining before retirement being four years. The average present value of such a death was estimated to be 6,400 pounds, giving a total cost of mortality of 147 million pounds. For the United States Luce and Schweitzer estimated the lost-production cost of smoking-related mortality to have been $12.3 billion in 1976, which in terms of the deflated value of the dollar a decade later would have been about $23 billion.

Joint Costs and Improper Cost Attribution

Efforts to attribute a cost of lost production to smoking, as well as a cost of medical care, commonly and wrongly attribute to smoking the entire amount of what is really a joint cost. This problem arises because smokers and nonsmokers are not identical in all respects other than smoking. Among other things, smokers have an above-average representation in blue collar occupations, they also consume on average an above-average amount of alcohol, although there are many teetotaling smokers and nonsmoking alcoholics,[3] and they generally exercise less than nonsmokers, although smoking bicyclists, swimmers, and joggers can be found.

In assuming that people are identical except for their smoking, various diseases and their associated costs are improperly attributed to smoking. Consider the hypothetical situation illustrated by Table 4.4. The population is assumed to be evenly divided between smokers and nonsmokers, with nonsmokers having 100 cases of a disease and smokers having 200 cases. This information is shown in column (3) of Table 4.4. If the cost

Table 4.4

Smoking, Exercise, and Health: A Hypothetical Illustration

	Number of Cases		
	Exercisers	Nonexercisers	Total
	(1)	(2)	(3)
Nonsmokers	33	67	100
Smokers	67	133	200
TOTAL	100	200	300

per illness were, say, $1,000, the cost of smoking would be $100,000, according to the common approach, for this would be the product of the 100 excess cases of illness attributed to smoking and the cost per disease.

But now consider the additional information conveyed by columns (1) and (2). The interpretation of this information is that nonsmoking nonexercisers and exercising smokers both have twice the illness rate of nonsmoking exercisers, while smoking nonexercisers have four times the illness rate of nonsmoking exercisers. For both smokers and nonsmokers, there are twice as many cases of illness among nonexercisers than among exercisers. A consideration of this example makes it clear that the $100,000 that is commonly attributed to smoking is wrong, because it attributes to smoking what could alternatively and equally plausibly be attributed to a failure to exercise.

If smokers were replaced by nonsmokers, illnesses would fall from 300 cases to 200 cases, thus appearing to confirm the standard approach to estimating the cost of smoking. In this case, the 67 illnesses among smoking exercisers would be reduced to 33 illnesses among exercising nonsmokers, and the 133 illnesses among smoking nonexercisers would be reduced to 67 illnesses among nonsmoking nonexercisers. However, Table 4.4 can be collapsed by columns as well as by rows. This can be done by replacing the nonexercisers with exercisers. The outcome would be the same as before. The 67 illnesses among nonexercising nonsmokers would become 33 illnesses among nonsmoking exercisers, while the 133 illnesses among smoking nonexercisers would become 67 illnesses among exercising smokers. In this alternative and equally reasonable formulation, the 100 excess cases of illness are attributed not to smoking but to failing to exercise.[4]

While the numbers in this example are hypothetical, the point the example illustrates is no less real: when health, and any associated costs, are a joint product of several variables or activities, it is illegitimate to attribute any health consequences to one particular variable or activity. In the case illustrated by Table 4.4, smoking could be said to cause 100 cases of illness. But it is equally reasonable to say that smoking causes no diseases, with all diseases being attributed instead to the failure to exercise. Furthermore, it would be equally reasonable to distribute the cases equally between smoking and failing to exercise, as it would be to choose any particular distribution of cases between the two sources of illness.

And if the illustration were made more complex and realistic, as by adding information about such other characteristics as drinking, weight, occupation, family stress, and so on, the arbitrariness involved in assessing a "cost of smoking" would multiply. Capriciousness or prejudice can easily replace science in such a setting. Someone who does not like smoking can assign the costs to smoking, someone who does not like sedentary lifestyles can assign the costs to inactivity, someone who does not like alcohol can assign the costs to drinking, and so on. Any proposition can be supported, but equally and by implication, there is no proposition that must be supported--which is to say that there is no unique conclusion that must be drawn from such data.

Who Loses Lost Production: Smokers or Nonsmokers?

The central issue raised by studies dealing with the claimed lost production costs of smoking (as well as of the claimed medical costs) is simply this: Is smoking a source of harm to Americans in general, or is it simply a source of harm to smokers, if, indeed, it is a source of harm to anyone? Even if we accept the proposition that the lost production cost of smoking exceeds the direct cost of cigarettes to smokers by about $50 billion (a proposition fraught with problems), an issue of public policy arises only to the extent that those costs are borne by nonsmokers. For if they are borne by smokers, the situation is the same as it is with any act of consumption: People pay for what they buy. In this case the $50 billion saving that would purportedly result from the cessation of smoking would not accrue to the residents of the nation in general, something that would have given them an average gain of $200 per person per year, but rather would accrue to the 50 million or so smokers, who would each gain about $1,000, though at the sacrifice of the benefits they derive from smoking.

It is essential to distinguish between a cost to an individual and a cost to "society." For example, suppose a paper mill discharges wastes into a river, thereby destroying fishing and other recreational uses downstream. The buyers of the mill's products must pay for such resources used directly in the mill's production as wood, acid, labor, and the like, but not, by assumption, for the damage inflicted on downstream users. The cost to society of the mill's operation is the damage imposed on people who are not party to the transactions between the mill and its customers. To speak of a cost to "society," in other words, is a usage that finds meaning through being opposed to a cost to "customers." A cost to society is a cost that is borne by third parties and not by the parties to a transaction.

It is fallacious to apply principles derived from settings in which diseases are acquired involuntarily because they are inherent in nature to settings in which diseases may be acquired as a by-product of personal choices. In the case of, say, polio or malaria, there is no offsetting beneficial activity for which the disease represents a by-product or possible side effect. But the setting is quite different in such cases as so-called smoking-related diseases or chain saw accidents. In these latter cases, the costs of usage, if any, may be reflected in the demand for the products in the first place, in which case the choice of people to consume the products in question affirms that they value the product more highly than the negative evaluation they place on those costs.

Consider, for example, someone choosing between a chain saw and a hand saw for pruning trees. Chain saws can inflict bodily harm that hand saws cannot begin to emulate. But chain saws also save energy and time. The perceived likelihood or cost of an accident is part of the cost of choosing the chain saw. The more dangerous people perceive chain saws to be, the less will be their willingness to buy chain saws. The choice of someone to buy a chain saw instead of a hand saw means that the buyer values the chain saw more highly than what it costs, which in turn is the value of the things he must give up to get the saw. That cost includes both the direct cost of the chain saw and the indirect cost of such incidents of ownership as the perceived risk of accident.

Why should it be any different for smoking? The cost of smoking includes both the price that people must pay for cigarettes and, in the event that smoking is presumed to damage health, the indirect cost they believe they must bear in terms of diminished health. Someone who chooses to smoke, then, judges that the value that he or she derives from smoking exceeds the sum of the price of cigarettes and cost of any damaged health that is anticipated to result from smoking. Even if smoking were to impair health, there would be no cost to society from smoking. Such cost, if any, would be a personal cost borne by smokers, who in turn by their choices have shown that they value smoking by more than the sum of the price of cigarettes and any diminished health that may result--in precisely the same manner that owners of chain saws reveal that they value power sawing by more than the sum of the price of chain saws and the perceived cost of accidents.

Consider the proposition that smokers are absent from work more often than nonsmokers, a proposition that we shall examine carefully in Chapter 7. It might reasonably be expected that a person who misses more work than another will earn less. If people who take an extra three days off per year earn less than those who do not, this loss of earnings would reflect a cost of smoking, provided the absence was caused by smoking, but this cost would be borne by the smoker. This lost production is reflected in market-determined income payments; those payments already reflect the value of the lost output. Therefore, to count that lost production as a social cost of smoking is to count the same thing a second time.

At first glance it might appear that while this example might be applicable to a piece-rate system of wage determination, it is less than fully applicable to many contemporary industrial settings. For instance, to the extent collective bargaining agreements make uniform provisions for sick leave, a higher rate of absenteeism among smokers than nonsmokers would seem to represent the imposition of a cost on nonsmokers by smokers. As the total amount of absenteeism rises, the average productivity and compensation paid will fall. Other things being the same, firms where employees average 10 absentee days per year will pay more than firms where the average rate of absenteeism is 15 days. Hence, if all workers receive the same compensation regardless of the amount of sick leave they take (up to the allowed limit), those who take less leave are made worse off by those who take more leave. If smokers take 12 days sick leave and nonsmokers take 8 days, and if there are an equal number of smokers and nonsmokers, all workers will receive wages as if they had missed 10 days. Consequently, nonsmokers will receive two days less pay than they actually worked, allowing smokers to receive two days more pay than they actually worked.

However, this situation is not so simple as it might appear. For instance, why were 12 days sick leave allowed in the first place? Why weren't only 8 days allowed? Firms that allow only 8 days leave will be able to pay higher wages than firms that allow 12 days. But if workers place a higher value on the ability to take off four extra days at their discretion than they place upon the higher wages that would otherwise result, they would prefer the employment alternative that offered more sick leave. And people in the opposite position would prefer the other employment option. In either case, sick leave policies are but part of an overall package of compensation, and they will tend to reflect employee preferences.

Furthermore, it is necessary to ask why some people would take only 8 days off when they were allowed 12. It might be that they thought that better attendance would improve their prospects for promotion or for a better assignment. Even though those people who missed only 8 days of work would receive the same income this year as those who missed 12 days of work, they would expect on average to have higher incomes in future years. If so, no questions of social cost arise, because those who are absent more frequently are earning less with respect to expected or lifetime earnings, even if not with respect to present earnings. Alternatively, people with low rates of absenteeism might not like to stay at home because they dislike being around their spouses or children, as well as because they have no interest in fishing or golfing, whereas people with high rates of absenteeism are in the opposite position. In this case, as in the preceding case, the difference in rates of absenteeism does not reflect some transfer between workers but rather reflects differences among workers in their preferences for work, family companionship, and leisure.

What About the Benefits of Smoking?

It is surely peculiar that discussions of smoking have concentrated so intently on the alleged costs of smoking that they have tended almost fully to ignore the benefits of smoking. Yet when we observe people willingly purchasing and using tobacco products, we can infer that the benefits that people derive from smoking is at a minimum equal to the price they pay for cigarettes. Suppose the resource cost (tobacco, paper, and so on) of a pack of cigarettes is $1.10, but the price of cigarettes is $1.50 per pack because taxes are 40 cents per pack. Further suppose that people buy 28 billion packs annually when the price is $1.50. The value of an additional pack of cigarettes is $1.50, but the cost of an additional pack is only $1.10. In this case, as we explained in Chapter 2, the cigarette tax imposes an excess burden or pure waste, in that it prevents people from exchanging something they value at $1.10 to get something they value at $1.50.

In total smokers are paying $42 billion for cigarettes (28 billion packs at $1.50 per pack). Their benefits from smoking are at least this much, as evidenced by their choice to buy the cigarettes rather than buying something else, and will normally exceed this amount. Cigarettes are worth $1.50 per pack to smokers when 28 billion packs are available annually. But if only a lesser amount were available, say 20 billion packs, smokers will value cigarettes more highly, as evidenced by their willingness to pay more for cigarettes, say $2.40 per pack. And if only 10 billion packs were available, they might be willing to pay, say, $4.20 per pack. The total value of cigarettes to smokers is the sum of the $42 billion and the amount by which the value that smokers would place on various amounts less than 28 billion packs exceeds $1.50.

But where do the alleged lost productivity costs, as well as the claimed medical costs, of smoking fit into this type of analysis? Suppose that in addition to the $42 billion that smokers pay for cigarettes, they bear lost productivity (or medical) costs of $42 billion. Should not this amount be subtracted from any measure of benefits, or, equivalently, added to cost? For instance, suppose in the illustration at hand that the total benefits of smoking were $80 billion. This figure would be the sum of (1) the amount people actually pay for cigarettes and (2) the excess of their willingness to pay over what they actually have to pay. Would not the net benefits of smoking be negative in this case? While the gross benefits are, by postulation, $80 billion, the total costs of smoking are by the same postulation $84 billion.

Despite whatever plausibility such an approach might have at first glance, it involves a form of double counting, and so is erroneous. The double counting arises because such possible health consequences as those regarding lost production are already incorporated into the willingness of smokers to buy cigarettes. To the extent one assumes smoking damages health, increases absenteeism, and reduces earnings, the willingness of people to buy cigarettes will be less than it would otherwise be, in exactly the same way that the willingness of people to buy chain saws will be lower the greater the perceived danger of chain-saw accidents. At any given price, people will buy fewer cigarettes the higher their perception of the health cost. To incorporate lost production as an aspect of the cost of smoking, suppose that smokers are absent four days more per year than nonsmokers, and further suppose that this greater absenteeism is due to smoking. If smokers smoke an average of 400 packs per year, it can be said that each pack is responsible for 1/100th of a day of absenteeism. If smokers earn $100 per day, this means that each pack of cigarettes costs them, in expected value terms, $1 in lost earnings.

The cost of smoking in this hypothetical situation has two components. One component is the price smokers pay, which is $1.50 per pack, including tax. The other component is their greater absenteeism and the lost earnings this implies, which is equivalent to $1 per pack. Consumers buy 28 billion packs, and pay a total price of $2.50 per pack. But the value of a pack of cigarettes in this case is also $2.50. The reason for this is that the market demand for cigarettes reflects any perceived risks that people associate with smoking. This can be seen by asking what would happen to the demand for cigarettes if their alleged health consequences were to vanish. At a market price of $1.50, people would no longer buy 28 billion packs. Rather, they would buy a larger amount, say 42 billion packs, in the same manner that they would buy more chain saws at the same price if the risk of accidents were to fall. In short, we can think of a risk-free demand for cigarettes or for chain saws, as well as an actual demand which represents the risk-free demand discounted by any risks that smokers or sawers think they have to bear.

What this analysis shows is that in such a theoretical calculation while the cost of consuming 28 billion packs of cigarettes per year is $70 billion, this amount is also a *minimum* estimate of the benefit of smoking. Only in this case, smokers pay for cigarettes through two different types of transactions. One transaction is the $1.50 they pay for each pack they buy. The other transaction is the $100 they lose for each extra day of work they miss, which in turn may reveal itself through slower rates of advancement rather than through immediate reductions in earnings, but which will be equivalent to $1 per pack in any event. Hence, smokers pay $42 billion to vendors for cigarettes, and they allegedly forfeit $28 billion (28 billion packs at $1 each) through their absenteeism.

NOTES

1. We should note the report of the Office of Technology Assessment is simply a survey of primary research and is not itself primary research. Its importance is largely political, in that it represents a continuation of efforts to push an official governmental position regarding both the alleged effect of smoking on health and the related economic consequences of that presumed effect.

2. The same method can likewise be applied to estimate amounts of other allegedly smoking-related illnesses. For each category of illness a measure of attributable risk would be constructed which, when multiplied by the number of illnesses in a particular category would represent the number of smoking-related illnesses attributed to a particular disease.

3. Shillington (1977) reports that 92 percent of people classified as alcohol abusers are smokers. (It should perhaps be noted, though, that the preponderant number of smokers are not classified as alcohol abusers.)

4. Lest someone object that our illustration of smoking exercisers is far fetched, we would point out that a survey of runners in the Peachtree 10-KM road race in Atlanta on 4 July 1980 estimated that more than 10 percent of them were smokers (Koplan, et al., 1982).

CHAPTER 5

Markets, Insurance, And
The Medical Costs
Of Smokers

Even though people may miss work because of illnesses or deaths that are attributed to smoking, the cost of any resulting lost production that results is borne by the smokers and not by the nonsmoking members of society. But can the same thing be said about the medical expenses that are associated with the treatment of illnesses some claim are smoking-related? Those expenses are also substantial; they were estimated in the report of the Office of Technology Assessment to be roughly half the size of the costs of lost production -- ranging from $12 to $35 billion in 1985, and with a "best" estimate of $22 billion. This "best" estimate is about 70 cents per pack, which is about twice the present tax burden on cigarettes. The more recent study of *Smoking and Health: A National Status Report* by the U.S. Department of Health and Human Services estimated the health-care bill for smoking at $23.7 billion (in 1985 dollars) out of a grand total including lost production of $52.4 billion.

Some of these medical expenses are, of course, financed personally. To the extent they are, they would seem to be a burden for smokers but not for nonsmokers, and would be analytically equivalent to the cost of lost production. However, a substantial part of medical expenses are financed by third parties, either through private insurance programs or through such tax-financed programs as Medicare and Medicaid. Such third-party financing would seem to open the possibility that an increased use of medical resources by smokers involves a shifting of burdens by

73

smokers onto nonsmokers. The extent to which the medical costs allegedly associated with smoking represent social as opposed to personal costs is the primary subject matter of this chapter.

Attribution of "Medical Costs" To Smoking

The medical expenses attributed to the treatment of so-called smoking-related illnesses are estimated in essentially the same way as the cost of lost production (see Chapter 4). A figure is derived for the total medical expenses associated with a particular illness, an estimate is made of the share of those expenses attributable to smoking, and a figure for the so-called medical cost of smoking is consequently derived. While there are differences in details among particular authors, this general format informs all such studies.

For instance, suppose a hospital's annual expenses are $30 million, with which it is able to provide 100,000 patient or bed-days of care during a year. This gives an average expense of $300 per bed or per patient. Once this determination of overall cost has been made, the next step is to attribute a share of that hospital usage to smokers. Suppose someone estimates that the number of bed-days during a year would be 20 percent less if no one smoked. By the standard procedure for attributing cost, $6 million, or 20 percent of expenses, would be attributed as the hospitalization cost due to smoking.

Essentially the same procedure is used to derive an estimate of the excess physician expenses incurred in the treatment of purportedly smoking-related illnesses. Suppose a physician has 5,000 consultations with patients in one year, the expense of which is $100,000. If someone estimates that the demand for physicians' services would be 25 percent less if no one smoked, 25 percent of the cost of physician services would be attributed to smoking. This would be $25,000 in the illustration at hand.

In the various studies of smoking and health, around 85 to 95 percent of the expenses of hospitals and physicians for the treatment of lung cancer are commonly attributed to smoking, although there are instances of substantial variation among authors. And it is common to treat in the vicinity of 15 to 25 percent of the expenses of hospitals and physicians for the treatment of heart disease and chronic bronchitis and emphysema as being related to smoking, though again with there being instances of substantial variation among authors. The exact rates of attribution vary with a number of factors, including the sex and age of the patient. While various complex considerations can arise in making such attributions, once such an attribution has been made it becomes a relatively simple computational matter to derive an estimated cost of smoking.

For example, consider Shillington's estimate of the medical expenses claimed to be associated with smoking in Canada. He started with data on the number of patient days spent in hospitals for four diseases: lung cancer, coronary heart disease, bronchitis, and emphysema. He estimated that the average expense of a patient-day in Canada in 1971 was $61.71. By multiplying this daily expense figure by the number of patient-days in each of the four disease categories, Shillington derived estimates of the total hospitalization expenses that could be attributed to each of these four categories. These figures were $17.9 million for lung cancer, $174.5 million for coronary heart disease, $13.6 million for bronchitis, and $9.3 million for emphysema. To estimate the share of these expenses that could be attributed to smoking, it is necessary to attribute a share of each illness to smoking -- i.e., to estimate the amount by which those illnesses theoretically would decline if no one smoked.

Shillington developed a method for attribution based on different age categories and also developed a range of attribution rates for each disease to reflect different underlying assumptions. To simplify a complex procedure, the average attribution rates ranged from 48 to 63 percent for lung cancer, from 6 to 15 percent for coronary heart disease, from 29 to 53 percent for bronchitis, and from 28 to 69 percent for emphysema. The multiplication of these rates by the estimated total hospital expenses for each of the four disease categories gives an estimated cost of smoking for each of these categories. These estimated amounts ranged from $8.66 to $11.2 million for lung cancer, from $10.1 to $25.9 million for coronary heart disease, from $4.0 to $7.2 million for bronchitis, and from $2.6 to $6.4 million for emphysema. In total, the hospitalization cost of smoking in Canada for 1971 was estimated to range from $25.3 to $50.7 million. And when the same estimation procedure was applied to the expenses of physician's services, the estimated range was $2.8 to $5.4 million.

This procedure is a standard one, and it has been applied in numerous other instances. For instance, for the United States Luce and Schweitzer estimated the claimed medical cost of smoking to be $13.4 billion in 1975, which would be more than twice as costly in 1990 dollars. Similarly, Egger estimated the hospital costs in 1976-77 in Australia to be in the $20.6 to $31.2 million range. He also developed estimates for the costs of physician's services and prescription drugs attributable to smoking, and these estimates were $4.9 to $8.2 million and $5.9 to $11.5 million, respectively. The recent study of *Smoking and Health* by the U.S. Department of Health and Human Services utilized a similar procedure to estimate health-care costs, with the novel twist of using a software program (SAMMEC) developed by the state of Minnesota to derive state-specific estimates for the various claimed costs of smoking, including hospital and physician costs.

There are plausible grounds for thinking that this common procedure overstates the medical costs of smoking. (We should perhaps restate here that we are speaking of *assumed* and not proven *causal* relationships when we speak of the "medical costs of smoking.") A primary reason for this bias is that lung cancer is a relatively inexpensive form of cancer to treat, but the standard approach to estimating medical expenses assumes lung cancer uses the same medical resources as other forms of cancer. The attribution of 30 percent of cancer deaths to smoking does not warrant the attribution of 30 percent of the estimated medical costs of treating all cancers to smoking. The proper attribution rate would be considerably lower. Most lung cancer deaths occur relatively quickly after diagnosis, and do not involve elaborate, long-term methods of treatment. Just how much of a bias results from such "average cost" pricing, we do not know, but we do know that attributing to smoking a share of the medical expenses equal to the rate at which particular diseases are attributed to smoking overstates any claimed medical costs of smoking.

Moreover, the reliability of the process by which physicians attribute certain diseases to smoking is largely an unexamined issue. As stressed in Chapter 4, the data on which studies of the costs of smoking are based are typically derived from death certificates where the physician indicates a cause of death. Eysenck (1986, pp. 23-32) reviewed this issue in some detail, and his general conclusions were that misdiagnosis is prevalent and that there is a strong possibility of bias in attributing certain illnesses to smoking. For example, several studies have been conducted which use autopsies to verify the cause of death. The frequency of disagreements between the autopsy results and the cause of death as indicated on the death certificate has ranged as high as over 50 percent in these studies. Such disparities may result from a "detection bias" in physician behavior, whereby the doctor has a tendency to find "smoking-related diseases" in smokers rather than nonsmokers. (What, for example, *caused* the death of an overweight smoker?) What drives such behavior is not certain, but the main point is simply that the data on which studies of the costs of smoking are based cannot be judged to be very reliable.

Medical Costs, Personal Responsibility, and Insurance

To the extent people pay their own medical expenses, any medical expenses that are due to the treatment of so-called smoking-related illnesses would be paid by smokers and would not be a burden on nonsmokers. The analysis of medical expenses in such a regime of personal responsibility would be essentially the same as the analysis of lost production presented in Chapter 4. Any such medical expenses would be part of the cost of smoking to smokers, and the higher those costs are, the lower will be the net demand for cigarettes. In other words, the market demand for cigarettes would reflect a discount for the medical expenses people associate with smoking. Medical expenses would be personal and not social costs. Therefore, data such as those presented in the report of the Office of Technology Assessment, and which portray "smoking-related" medical costs in the range of $12-$35 billion, would represent costs that are largely borne by smokers and not by nonsmokers.

While people do pay some of their medical expenses directly out of their own pockets, many of those expenses are covered through various insurance programs. Moreover, over the post-war period personal payments have become of ever diminishing importance in the financing of medical care. Third-party payments, which are payments made either by governments or by insurance companies and not by individuals, now comprise about 90 percent of hospital expenses and over 50 percent of the expenses of physicians. Third-party payments create a network of transfers among people, and those transfers open the possibility that smokers might impose costs on nonsmokers. An increase in the medical expenses that smokers incur will increase insurance premiums for the nonsmoking members of an insurance program, and will increase taxes for nonsmoking taxpayers in the case of government-financed medical care. In either case, any increase in medical costs incurred by smokers would be paid in part by nonsmokers. So long as the provision of medical care is at least partially financed through insurance or taxation, those who make relatively high use of medical resources will in turn place added financial burdens upon those who make relatively low use.

In comparing personal responsibility with insurance as forms of paying for medical care, it is important to distinguish between *ex ante* (before the fact) and *ex post* (after the fact) perspectives. When insurance payments are looked at after the fact, people who are sick more often would seem to be subsidized by those who are not. But this is true of all insurance programs, when they are viewed after the fact. People who have automobile accidents seem to be subsidized by those who do not. People whose homes are damaged or destroyed by fire seem to be subsidized by those whose homes are not. People who require medical care seem to be subsidized by people who do not. All insurance has the *ex post* property of appearing to subsidize some people at the expense of others.

But the appropriate perspective toward insurance is *ex ante*. From this *ex ante* perspective, all participants must look upon their participation as beneficial, for otherwise they would not have chosen to participate in the first place. People choose to participate in an insurance program because they judge the benefits of coverage in the event of accident or illness to be worth the price of participation, even though the most likely outcome is that their total premium payments will exceed their total claims.[1] In principle there is little economic difference between a system where people pay for their medical expenses personally and a system where those expenses are covered by insurance.

To say this is not to claim that insurance programs work perfectly in attributing risk to different categories of buyers. Attribution may be imperfect, and to the extent it is some buyers will be subsidized at the expense of others. In some cases government regulation of insurance can be a source of such subsidization through preventing the refinement of risk categories. This is illustrated, for instance, by the use of automobile insurance regulation, which, by restricting the refinement of risk categories, has the effect of requiring low-risk categories of drivers to subsidize high-risk categories (Keeton and Kwerel, 1984). Insurance is also subject to moral hazard, which we shall examine later in this chapter, by which the availability of insurance reduces care on the part of insured parties and so increases accidents and claims. For this reason medical expenses are likely to be higher under insurance finance than under personal finance, even if people fall into the same risk category. Moreover, insurance can also encounter problems of adverse selection. This can arise because people who are particularly likely to have claims will have particularly strong demands for insurance coverage. If such people have better information about those personal characteristics that govern probable claims than do insurance companies, claims for payment, and, therefore, base premiums, will rise.

The error of pointing to the expenditures for private health insurance as a social cost of smoking is apparently an easy one to make. This approach is taken in the above mentioned studies examining the economic cost of smoking, which were conducted primarily by medical scientists. Nevertheless, good economists can and have also fallen into this fallacy. In particular, the Rand Corporation economists who published a study in the *Journal of the American Medical Association* count private employer and employee contributions for health insurance coverage as a social cost of smoking (see Manning *et al.* 1989, p. 1605). This, as we have explained, is an error. Indeed, the conclusion of the Rand study, that under the most plausible assumptions smokers more than pay their own way in terms of their contributions to and use of public health care programs, would be significantly strengthened if private health insurance payments were correctly excluded from the analysis.

Life Insurance and Nonsmoker Discounts

Life insurance companies generally charge less to insure nonsmokers than to insure smokers. A consideration of this premium differential provides insights about the operation of our free enterprise economic system that will prove useful in a number of places below in examining claims that smokers impose costs on nonsmokers. A central feature of good business conduct in our free-enterprise economic system is that people who desire products that are more costly to provide will have to pay more for those products, while people who desire less costly products will pay less. Buyers of Fords will pay less than buyers of Lincolns; buyers of Nissan

Sentras will pay less than buyers of Nissan Maximas. This relationship between relative costs and prices is a simple feature of survival in a competitive enterprise system. Should Nissan offer its Sentras at Maxima prices, Sentras will go unsold as people buy from other producers instead. And should Nissan offer its Maximas at Sentra prices, it will exhaust its stock of Maximas and loose a lot of money in the process.

What holds for automobiles holds for insurance as well. Smokers on average reportedly die earlier than nonsmokers. Consequently, some life insurance companies use smokers as a marker for policy premiums the same way some automobile insurance companies use grades in school to determine premiums for student drivers. Among other things this presumably means that claims will be filed on behalf of smokers earlier on average, than they will be filed on behalf of nonsmokers. The longer life expectancy of nonsmokers represents a period of time during which life insurance companies can earn money on the premiums nonsmokers have paid. If smokers and nonsmokers were charged the same premiums, any particular insurance company could increase its net earnings by offering nonsmokers lower rates to attract their business. But all insurance companies are in this position. If nonsmokers as a group are cheaper to serve than smokers as a group, competition among life insurance companies will lead those companies to offer lower premiums to nonsmokers, with the differential in the amount of the premium being roughly equivalent to the lower cost of serving nonsmokers.

Somewhere on the order of 90 percent of life insurance companies offer discounts to nonsmokers on individual policies.[2] The amount of discount varies with sex and age, but runs generally in the vicinity of 15 to 20 percent, and with some companies offering discounts as high as 40 percent. When expressed in terms of premiums on a $50,000 universal life policy, the annual discount would run about $50 for a 25 year old male or a 35 year old female, and about $180 for a 45 year old male or a 55 year old female.

Insurance companies began offering nonsmoker discounts in the mid-1960s, in response to the development of actuarial data suggesting that smokers had shorter life expectancies than nonsmokers. As the data accumulated the number of insurance companies offering nonsmoker discounts increased steadily, until now only about 10 percent of life insurance companies do not offer nonsmoker discounts on individual policies. To be sure, there is no reason to expect all insurance companies to offer nonsmoker discounts, even if the actuarial evidence is regarded as foolproof. For those companies that did not offer lower premiums to nonsmokers would not receive their patronage, and would service a clientele predominantly if not exclusively consisting of smokers. Still, people who were more costly to serve would pay higher prices than people who could be served at lesser cost.

Health Insurance and Smoker-Nonsmoker Parity

Health insurance companies typically do not offer discounts to non-smokers: only about 15 percent of health insurers offer nonsmoker discounts, and with those discounts running around 10 to 15 percent. One straightforward explanation for this absence of nonsmoker discount is that health insurance companies do not believe they can increase their earnings by offering nonsmokers lower premiums. The basis for this belief, in turn, would be that nonsmokers are not cheaper to insure with respect to annual medical expenses because the annual medical costs of smokers and nonsmokers are similar.

In Chapter 7 we will examine some claims that smokers are more costly to employ than nonsmokers. One aspect of this claim is that smokers miss work more often than nonsmokers, because of greater rates of illness. In Chapter 7 we will explain why the claim that smokers miss more work than nonsmokers is false. To the extent missed work is attributed to sickness, this evidence would suggest, in turn, that there is no morbidity component of missed work and lost production attributable to smoking, despite the lines of argument noted in Chapter 4. Hence, the observation that health insurers do not charge lower premiums to nonsmokers is consistent with evidence, which we will consider in Chapter 7, that smokers as a whole do not generally miss more work than nonsmokers--and both of these are consistent with the proposition that smokers do not incur higher medical costs than nonsmokers.

A different possible explanation for the different prevalence of nonsmoker discounts between life and health insurance resides in the different methods by which life and health insurance are marketed. Individual sales of life insurance are much more common than are individual sales of health insurance; health insurance is predominately sold on a group basis. While 90 percent of life insurance companies offer nonsmoker discounts on individual policies, only 15 percent offer nonsmoker discounts on group policies. It so happens that about 80 percent of health insurance coverage is organized on a group basis, typically employment-related.

There is no reason why group health plans, or group life insurance plans, cannot include discounts for nonsmokers. An employer who makes coverage available free of charge to nonsmokers could require a fee from smokers, and this fee would equal the value of what the nonsmoker discount would be. And should employees make some contribution for their coverage, a greater contribution could be required from smokers. There is certainly nothing in the mechanics of group coverage that precludes nonsmoker discounts; indeed, the presence of such discounts in group life insurance plans, even though it is a small presence, shows that group coverage can accommodate differences in premiums charged to smokers and nonsmokers.

While the actuarial data about the relative medical care costs of smokers and nonsmokers is ambiguous, suppose for purposes of discussion that smokers are more costly to insure on an annual basis than nonsmokers. By way of illustration, suppose a particular group is evenly divided between smokers and nonsmokers, and that group health insurance is offered for $1,000 per year. Suppose the actuarial data suggest's that smokers are $100 more costly per year to insure. Such data might seem to suggest that nonsmokers should receive a $100 discount, with smokers being charged $1,050 and nonsmokers $950. In the absence of such a discount, it would seem as though smokers, who receive coverage at $50 below cost, are being subsidized by nonsmokers, who pay $50 above cost.

But in this case we must probe a little more deeply into the operation of insurance as a business and the provision of group coverage. Among the reasons for group coverage are those dealing with tax savings and administrative savings. With respect to tax savings, the provision of such fringe benefits as health insurance is not treated as taxable income to employees. But if employees were to receive an equivalent increase in income to replace the insurance coverage, they would have to pay tax on that income. For someone in the 28 percent federal tax bracket, $1,000 of insurance coverage would require $1,390 of direct earnings to have the same after tax impact as $1,000 of insurance coverage. And with respect to administrative cost, it is often cheaper to offer insurance on a group basis. If the same insurance coverage offered on an individual basis cost $1,100, nonsmokers would pay $1,000 after the $100 discount. The group policy, in this case, is not so much a means by which nonsmokers subsidize smokers as a means by which insurance coverage is provided for all in a lower cost manner.

In other words, it is possible that the cost differences that might exist between smokers and nonsmokers are so small that allowing for them would incur sufficiently high administrative costs as to make the effort to charge different premiums not worthwhile. It is common, for instance, for medical insurance plans to allow optional coverage for maternity benefits. Maternity expenses are high and the condition is the result of personal choice. But if through some form of technological breakthrough, maternity costs came to be similar to those of having a wart removed, it is doubtful if insurance companies would find it worthwhile to create such a particular risk category and to set a separate fee for coverage.

In any event, the profit-seeking incentives of insurance companies make it in their interests to develop separate risk categories whenever there appears to be an actuarial basis for doing so and whenever the differences in expected costs between the categories exceeds the added cost of administering these additional categories. Hence, if it were to be the case that smokers were placing costs on nonsmokers through group insurance, it would also be the case that the costs of preventing those costs, as through the development of more refined risk categories, would entail even larger costs.

Smoking and Fire Costs

It is typical in efforts to assess the social cost of smoking to include the losses due to fires which are attributed to careless handling of smoking materials. The cost of smoking attributed to fire loss is typically a small portion of the total costs attributed to smoking. The major economic element of fire loss is the damage to property due to fire. The other elements of cost are the hospitalization expenses of those injured in careless smoking-caused fires and the present value of the loss of future income resulting from death in a smoking-caused fire. In their study of

California, Glantz and Schweitzer (1978) estimated fire losses to be only about 2.5 percent of the total costs of smoking. In contrast, medical costs were estimated to comprise over 80 percent of the cost. In his survey article, Wilson (1978) reports a similar figure (2.6 percent) for Canada, based on a 1966 study of Hedrick. While the relative amounts are small, the absolute amounts can be large nonetheless. For instance, Luce and Schweitzer (1978, p. 570) estimate the fire losses due to careless smoking to be $175,900,000 in the United States in 1976.

While it might at first glance seem reasonable to count these fire losses as a social cost of smoking, more careful inspection shows this common practice to be inappropriate. The studies of fire losses due to careless smoking suffer from a failure to distinguish the personal or private cost of smoking from the social cost. With respect to public policy, private cost raises no issues, for the cost is borne wholly by the person who undertakes the activity. Issues arise only when some of the cost is borne by other people, and it is these costs that give rise to what has been called the problem of social cost. If the fire losses attributable to careless smoking can be said to contain elements of social cost, it must be because some of this cost is borne by people other than those who cause the fires.

How do the costs borne by a smoker actually fit into this perspective? The act of buying is *prima facie* evidence that the buyer judges the benefits to exceed the costs. The question of social costs concerns whether or not the losses from fire are one of the components of cost borne by smokers. Generally, it can be said that smokers do bear this component of the cost of smoking. If the house of a careless smoker burns down or is damaged, little, if any, social cost will be involved. If the smoker has no fire insurance, he will clearly bear the loss himself. If he is insured, the effect will be roughly the same. It is possible that his insurance premiums would be higher because of his smoking, thereby reflecting the greater risk of fire. Almost certainly an actual experience with a fire loss would lead to higher premiums subsequently. Smokers can be said generally to bear the costs of property damage related to careless smoking. And it is similar with regard to the costs of hospitalization and death, for reasons explained in those sections of this paper and not reiterated here.

In undertaking an effort to assess the *social* costs of smoking, the losses incurred by a careless smoker due to fires can reasonably be neglected, for they are predominately private rather than social costs. In the absence of contagion from fire, the risk of fire loss is much like the risk of a traffic accident. People drive despite the risk of accident because they judge the benefits from doing so to exceed the cost, which includes that risk.

It might be thought that fire losses must involve a social cost because when a house burns down in a fire caused by smoking, resources must be taken away from other uses to rebuild the house. There certainly are costs involved in rebuilding the house, but these are in no sense social costs. In the case of the fire losses due to careless smoking, the smoker bears the cost of rebuilding his house, in an actual sense if he is uninsured and in a probablistic sense if he is insured. In a private property system of resource allocation, there is no sense in which these costs are exported to others. It is no different than in the case of a family that is hard on its cars. There are costs to replacing the broken cars, but these costs rest with the family.

But, still, the argument might persist that society has one less house. Do not fire losses, then, represent a social cost of smoking? The answer is again no, and for the same basic reasons. Society in no relevant sense bears the cost of the lost house. The individual smoker bears these costs. And it should be emphasized that the smoking example is only one small example of how analysts can go wrong in analyzing the costs of individual activities in the economy. For example, consider the case of drinking water. Drinking water entails such consequences as urination, and people will seek to deal economically with these consequences. Are the costs of toilets therefore a social cost due to drinking water? Again, the answer is no. These costs are borne entirely by individuals, as they adapt to the consequences of drinking water. Some will have indoor toilets, and some outdoor, but in all cases, these costs will be internalized by individual behavior. There are no social costs from drinking water, except perhaps to the extent that one person's toilet drains into another person's water supply. Likewise, private losses from careless smoking-related fires are not social costs.

Moral Hazard and Insurance Costs

We noted briefly in passing early in this chapter that the mere presence of insurance may be a source of higher costs. This possibility is referred to as "moral hazard." The idea behind moral hazard is elementary: the presence of insurance reduces the loss any individual bears, so that individual will have less of an incentive to prevent the occurrence of the condition insured against. If bicycles are insured against theft and damage, owners will have less of an incentive to keep them locked and located in sheltered places. The presence of insurance would thus lead to a higher incidence of bicycle thefts and to more frequently damaged bicycles.

Perhaps the extreme version of moral hazard results when insurance coverage exceeds 100 percent of the value of the item insured. Should a building valued at $300,000 be insured for $800,000, arson may be quite tempting. Short of arson, there would surely be little if any incentive to worry about electrical wiring, and it would not be surprising to find the owner gleeful at the prospect of severe thundershowers and tornadoes in the area. It is for reasons like this that insurance companies never intentionally allow insurance in excess of 100 percent, and generally provide less than 100 percent coverage. When coverage is less than 100 percent, the person being insured has some incentive to prevent the loss insured against.

There are many particular ways coverage at less than 100 percent is achieved. Often this is through the use of deductible requirements, where the person insured pays a particular amount first, with insurance covering only the residual loss. Automobile collision insurance with the first $500 deductible will lead drivers to be more careful in parking lots, because they will bear most of the costs of any body work that may be required through accidents. Co-insurance is often used, in which case the insurance company pays only part of the claim. The individual pays the remainder, acting as a co-insurer. For instance, the insurance coverage may extend only to 70 percent of the value of the claim, with the individual paying the rest. Clearly, the higher the rate of co-insurance, the stronger the incentive the individual has to avoid the loss.

But regardless of practices that have evolved within the insurance business, it is unlikely that moral hazard could ever be fully subdued. To some extent the presence of insurance will increase costs of whatever is being insured against. The presence of medical insurance will increase medical costs, as compared to what those costs would be should all payments be made directly by patients. This property of insurance, though, holds for nonsmokers and smokers alike. Everyone will incur higher medical expenses to some extent when those expenses are covered through insurance. The medical expenses of smokers will be higher in the presence of medical insurance, but so will the expenses of nonsmokers. Any such increase in expense would be attributable to the provision of insurance, and not to smoking. We raise this point here, though it perhaps becomes more relevant with respect to government financing of medical expenses, which we examine in the next chapter.

NOTES

1. It should be noted, as we shall discuss more fully below, that only a few health insurers have established different premiums for smokers and nonsmokers, and they have done so "with little supportive actuarial experience that nonsmokers incur fewer claims," according to the 1989 Surgeon General's Report. Also, just because a smoker files a health insurance claim does not mean the claim is smoking-related. Consider the demographic studies which show that a great many smokers are employed in blue-collar occupations, exposing themselves to higher risks and accident rates. In addition, a large proportion of smokers are low-income people, who more often lack preventive health care, ultimately resulting in larger health-care costs.

2. Insurance is examined in the 1989 Report of the Surgeon General, pp. 539-51.

CHAPTER 6

Medicare, Medicaid, And The Social Cost Of Smoking

Not all medical expenses are paid through insurance. A significant share is provided by government, most of which in turn is provided through Medicare, which primarily finances medical care for social security recipients. Government also provides medical care for the indigent under Medicaid. In both of these cases the medical care is financed by taxpayers, with the beneficiaries being the recipients of the care. It might seem as though governmentally provided medical care offers a means for smokers to impose costs on nonsmokers. A commonly expressed sentiment is that everyone has an interest in smoking because such programs as Medicaid and Medicare cover a significant part of the medical bills for smokers. This sentiment was illustrated by the claim in the 11 May 1982 issue of the *Wall Street Journal* that "Uncle Sam has a budgetary interest in the cigarette toll [on health] because Medicaid and Medicare pick up a significant part of the medical bills for afflicted smokers." If smoking damages health, increased claims under Medicare and Medicaid seem a distinct possibility. Indeed, this possible positive relationship between smoking and resulting claims under Medicare and Medicaid has been used to advocate the earmarking of tobacco tax revenues for the support of Medicare.

Smokers and the Cost of Medicare

The claim that smokers make especially heavy use of Medicare has been used to justify or rationalize a wide variety of proposals to increase tobacco taxes and to earmark the proceeds for particular medical care programs. Some of these we discussed in Chapter 3. This argument for higher tobacco taxation is questionable on both factual and analytical grounds. Factually, if these government-funded health programs were being overused by smokers, one could argue that smokers were creating additional costs for others. To the contrary, however, smokers as a group are very much *underrepresented* in the population groups served by these programs. More than 90 percent of Medicare beneficiaries are over age 65--an age group in which only 16 percent are smokers.[1] Thus, given the contributions of smokers to government health-care financing, there is ample reason to suggest that smokers are subsidizing nonsmokers in these programs, not the other way around.

Even if it is assumed that smoking harms health, there is no valid basis for claiming that smokers place an above-average demand on Medicare. It is incorrect simply to compare two sets of people at the same age, to note that the smokers have higher medical bills than the nonsmokers, and subsequently to conclude that smokers consume an above-average amount of medical resources. One facet of any smoking-induced health impairment would be that smokers as a group would tend to have shorter life spans. Assuming for the following analysis that smokers on average die earlier than nonsmokers, one must consider the potential savings which would result from smokers' hypothesized shortened life spans. For instance, Cowell and Hirst (1980) estimate that smokers have a life expectancy that is 7.3 years less than that of non-smokers. If one assumes such figures are accurate, they suggest that smokers should be taxed *less* for lifetime health insurance--and Medicare is a form of open-ended, lifetime health insurance. It is a program whereby people make tax "contributions" during their working lives, in exchange for a health insurance annuity upon retirement. While some studies report that one working adult in three smokes, only one retiree in six smokes. In this situation, many smokers pay taxes to support medicare during their working years, but are not around to collect benefits during their retirement years. Furthermore, with reportedly shorter life spans, smokers would make less use of extended stays in hospitals and convalescent homes in the later years of life, where the expenses can become particularly heavy, and many of which are covered by Medicare.

The correct question regarding subsidization under Medicare does not involve a comparison between smokers and nonsmokers at the same age, but involves a comparison between smokers and nonsmokers with respect to the present value of their lifetime medical expenses. In this regard, Leu and Schaub (1983) developed a simulation model for Switzerland under the assumption that no one smoked after 1876.[2] In so doing, they sought, among other things, to compare actual medical expenses in Switzerland in 1976 with what they projected those expenses would have been if no one had smoked after 1876. Underlying their work was the presumption that smoking damaged health. Therefore, the cessation of smoking in 1876 would have led to a larger and older population in 1976 than the population that actually existed in Switzerland. However, Leu and Schaub estimated that medical expenses would have been roughly the same as they actually were in 1976. In other words, such studies suggest that attributing health consequences to smoking does not imply that smokers impose costs on nonsmokers, even when health care is provided in part by government.

Schelling (1986, p. 555) views on this matter are as follows:

> Uncertain as these figures are, the figures themselves are less dubious than their significance. It is not at all evident that over their lifetimes smokers incur greater medical-care costs than nonsmokers. Those male 60-year-olds in whom respiratory cancer was diagnosed incurred costs (in 1980 dollars) of $9,000 apiece, on average. Most of them died within 2 years of diagnosis. Most of them had no other major health-care costs in their short lifetimes after diagnosis. Most of them in the absence of lung cancer would have lived a decade or two more and their average aggregate health-care costs as they lived into their seventies and eighties could easily have exceeded the figure associated with lung cancer. Careful estimates have not been done for the United States, but it seems a reasonable guess that the health-care costs that are obviated by premature deaths attributable to smoking are of at least the order of magnitude of the health-care costs attributable to fatal smoking-induced illness. Those who do not die promptly may have not only smoking-related health-care costs that are larger, but the other medical costs associated with living to an older age as well.

The figures to which Schelling refers here are those from the OTA Study of the costs of smoking.

The important point to make here is that if one assumes smokers die earlier than others, one must also recognize they leave substantial unclaimed assets at their death. These include such items as unclaimed social security benefits and possibly other benefits from government programs such as veterans' benefits. As Schelling (1986, p. 557) discusses, albeit hypothetically:

> ...; and if we accept the estimate of, say, 300,000 deaths per year currently due to cigarette smoking, deceased smokers leave unclaimed assets of $20 billion per year. Using this estimate we can conclude that smokers who die may leave enough unclaimed benefits behind them to offset most of the direct medical cost attributable to smoking. And since their own medical costs terminate at death, the aggregate "savings" due to their premature deaths may even exceed the net additional medical costs incurred by all smokers, survivors, and decedents.

Moreover, the taxes that smokers pay during their working lifetimes could also be "counted" in such back-of-the-envelope discussions. These would obviously include excise taxes, income taxes, social security taxes, and all other levies collected from smokers.[3] Surely, such a simplistic, arithmetical approach to the issue of who wins and who loses with respect to transfers related to smokers would show that smokers more than pay their own way in the United States. Rather than the common allegation that smokers are "overusing" publicly provided health-care programs, a more careful accounting of smokers' role in public transfer programs would clearly show that, if anything, smokers should be candidates for a tax refund.[4]

But suppose smokers do, over their lifetime in present value terms, make greater use than nonsmokers of medical resources subsidized by government. There is still an analytical question concerning whether this raises an issue of external cost, or whether it raises only an issue of income transfer. There seems little doubt that the growth of third-party medical payments has contributed to the relative shift of resources into the provision of medical care, as is illustrated by Table 6.1. In 1960 health care took up 5 percent of Gross National Product, up only one percentage point from 1940. And in 1965 health care took up 6 percent of GNP. It was then that Medicare and Medicaid began, and with them the start of significant amounts of tax-financed medical care. Within a decade medical care's share of GNP had increased 50 percent to 9 percent, and in the next decade increased at a similar rate.

Table 6.1

Medical Care Spending as Share of GNP

Year	Medical Care Spending (billions)	Percentage of GNP
1950	$ 12.0	4.2
1960	25.9	5.1
1965	38.9	5.6
1970	69.2	7.0
1975	124.7	8.0
1980	237.8	9.0
1982	347.1	10.5

Source: Ann Kollman Bixby, "Social Welfare Expenditures, 1963-83," *Social Security Bulletin* 49 (February 1986), Table 7.

People will clearly consume more of anything, medical care included, when that consumption is subsidized than when it is not. But in economics the distinction between a transfer and a social cost is a fundamental one: the former refers to a redistribution of total income, while the latter refers to a reduction in total income, although, of course, the two may well occur together. Subsidized medical care is clearly a program that transfers income from people who make below-average claims to people who make above-average claims. With respect to smoking, an external cost would arise from subsidized medical care only to the extent that people might smoke more, and with that increased smoking leading, as some would argue, in turn to greater smoking related illness and higher medical expenses.

The presence of subsidized medical care surely gives at most a faint incentive for most people to become more sickly. Hence, removal of subsidized medical care would have little if any effect on the amount of smoking, and, thereby, on the amount of alleged smoking-related disease. Removing the subsidization of medical care would, of course, reduce the claims people make upon medical resources, but this is a quite different matter. Someone may choose to have a silver dental filling if he has to pay the full cost, but choose to have a gold filling if two-thirds of the cost is reimbursed under a dental insurance plan. The insurance plan does not induce people to have more cavities, but it does induce them to be more lavish in securing treatment for the cavities they do have. Similarly, smokers, as well as everyone else, will make more use of medical care when it is subsidized than when it is not. The subsidization of anything increases the amount of it that people will use. Medicare and Medicaid encourage people to make greater use of medical resources, but this does not mean it encourages them to become more sickly than they would otherwise have been. Smoking would seem to have little if any external cost, even if medical expenses are subsidized. The increased use that smokers make of medical resources is identical to the increased use that others make as well, and this is an inevitable outcome of any program of subsidization.

Transfers and Social Costs: A Clarification

It will be worthwhile to explore more fully why it is the case that even if smokers were to place greater demands upon the public health care system than other people, it does not follow that they are a source of social cost. Suppose a smoker on a crowded train platform accidently burns a hole in the coat of a lady standing next to him. Repairing the damage costs her $100. This is clearly an uncompensated cost. The benefit of smoking accrued to the smoker while the cost of the burned coat was paid by the lady. Alternatively, suppose a young motorcyclist suffers an accident. He dies of head injuries because he was not wearing a safety helmet and his widow collects pension payments. The young man enjoyed the benefits of motorcycling, but through his failure to wear a helmet, he created a situation in which everyone must now contribute through taxation to his widow's pension. Does the payment of the widow's pension also represent a social cost?

The source of the lady's $100 loss was clearly the careless smoker standing beside her. But the source of the loss that taxpayers suffer as their share of the widow's pension is surely not the motorcyclist, any more than the tobacco farmer is the source of the lady's damaged coat. The source of the higher extractions from taxpayers is the legislature: the income transfer was created by the state when the legislature decided to provide pensions for widows. The payment from taxpayers to the widow is a product of state policy.

If we try to go beyond this and specify that some types of transfers constitute "social costs" while others do not, absurdities quickly enter and with no reasonable or logical basis for including some as social costs and excluding others. The widow of a heavy drinker, a fat man, a football player, or a mine worker must also, by the same criteria, create a social cost. Also perhaps vulnerable to the charge of creating a social cost are people who work too hard, who do not get the right vitamins, who do not exercise adequately, and so on. In saying this we do not intend to suggest causal relationships here, but only to acknowledge the types of conceptual issues that can easily arise in this area. Such considerations also bring into question whether the objective of the policy is to relieve the plight of widows or to reward the widows of men who "lived right?" In any event, it is the state and not the injured or deceased person that creates the income transfer, and with it the imposition of any possible loss on other taxpayers. Life is rife with "social costs," which in many cases seem to be created by the very existence of society.

The point of contention about transfers reduces to one of the right of access to state-provided benefits and to the conditions placed upon that access. While there are various grounds on which people have supported or opposed transfer programs, we would only note that the mere presence of a transfer payment or system of payments does not legitimize a claim that the recipients of transfers are creating social costs. There may well be social costs in such situations, but making a judgment to this effect involves more than merely observing the existence of a network of transfers from some people to others.

A social cost in the presence of transfers will exist only to the extent such transfers induce changes in personal conduct. Indeed, such changes in personal conduct are an important reason for seeking to foreclose uncompensated costs. Imagine for a moment that every smoker who burned a hole in someone's coat had to pay for the damage. This would remove the uncompensated cost, but more importantly, it would provide a strong incentive to smokers to be careful with their cigarettes. If smokers were liable for such damages, the annual extent of damage to coats would be reduced. The social gain resides in the reduced damage to coats and not in the payments per se to ladies with burned coats. If the necessity to make such payments did not induce smokers to be more careful, and with that increased care thereby reducing the extent of burned coats, there would be no social gain from such payments. In this case such payments would merely represent a reversal of the direction of transfer: smokers would become poorer and ladies wearing coats richer, but the extent of cigarette-inflicted damage to coats would be unchanged. In this vein, it is surely doubtful whether the repeal of widow's pensions would change the conduct of motorcyclists in a way that would reduce the extent of accidents, while it is quite likely that the imposition of damage penalties upon smokers who burn other people's coats will lead smokers to be more careful with their cigarettes.

A transfer can create a problem of social cost only if people change their conduct in response to the presence of the transfer. If, for instance, the personal cost of absenteeism were somehow to be eliminated, which may actually be quite difficult to do because of the ability of absenteeism to be reflected in future earnings, the rate of absenteeism would rise because of the lessened personal cost of absenteeism. The resulting reduction in output would not be paid for by those who were absent but rather by society generally. By insulating a person's decision to be absent from the consequences or costs of that decision, the transfer would create a problem of social, as distinct from personal, cost. This situation is quite unlike the personal reduction in earning that is suffered as a result of injury or illness.

With respect to engaging in such activities as smoking, whether or not the presence of a transfer system for financing medical expenses creates a social cost is ultimately an empirical matter. A social cost will result to the extent that the injection of subsidies into the provision of medical care encourages people to do things that *increase* illness and death. If subsidized medical care were to lead people to smoke more, and if there thus resulted in an increased incidence of illness and death, the transfer program would create a social cost. However, this cost would result from the increased mortality and morbidity resulting from the subsidy-induced increase in the amount of smoking, and would not reside in the medical payments per se.

There is no question that people will make greater use of medical resources if that usage is subsidized. But the mere fact of subsidization raises no issue of social cost, for it represents only a transfer from those who make relatively little use of such resources to those who make relatively large use. A social cost will result from the existence of a system of subsidized medical care only to the extent that people do things that make them sicker. While this outcome is conceivable, it is also a remote possibility, and the magnitudes involved would surely be small at most. What seems to have happened in discussions of the social cost aspects of such transfer programs as subsidized medical care is that people have addressed the wrong question: Whether subsidized medical care will induce people to make greater use of medical resources. The right question that should be addressed is whether subsidized medical care will induce more smoking, which might arguably lead to greater illness and a need for more medical care. While the wrong question can easily and strongly be answered affirmatively, the right question cannot.

Equity considerations have also been injected into discussions of the subsidization of some peoples' medical expenses by others, often under the claim that the tax-transfer system which subsidizes medical expenses provides an unfair subsidy to smokers. This argument about unfairness is worthy of further consideration. The problem with the argument is that there is no clear way to draw the line between smoking, which is seen as a form of voluntary risk, and such activities as skiing, eating too much, swimming, driving, living in urban areas where the air is polluted, and sundry other activities that may also influence health and longevity. All of these activities are self-inflicted in the same sense as is smoking. To try to draw a distinction between these various possibilities is arbitrary, and, moreover, any effort to draw such a distinction would be to place before the public agenda the regulation of numerous facets of personal life.

Furthermore, it is inappropriate to look at only one incident of income transfer to determine whether a *net* cost or transfer exists. Everyone in a society stands in some loss or gain status with respect to particular transfer programs. There are a large number of income transfers taking place, and each person is a winner in some and a loser in others. The motorcyclist was a "winner" with respect to widow's pensions, for his wife will draw more from the pension program than he paid in taxes. But as a consumer of sugar he was a "loser" to the subsidized sugar grower. As a full-time employee he "lost" on his unemployment insurance. Not being a war veteran, he "lost" on veterans' benefits. And having died at a young age, he would never get to collect his own retirement benefits under Social Security. In order to know whether, overall, income was transferred *to* him or *from* him, one would have to examine his entire life span, measuring all the intentional and unintentional income transfers in which he was involved.

Income transfers are a ubiquitous product of our political system; indeed, it is possible to explain a wide variety of political outcomes and practices under the assumption that wealth transfers are its only product.[5] The end effect of any one person's lifestyle may ultimately leave him a "benefactor" of others or a "debtor" to others, in the sense that either more or less was actually taken from him in taxes than he had received through various transfer programs. It is this, above all else, that makes it impossible to say that any particular income transfer constitutes an unfair and uncompensated cost: any particular program represents only one of many such transactions the individual has within an entire network of tax-transfer relationships that characterize a political order.

Proposals for Earmarked Cigarette Taxes

As discussed in Chapter 2, considerable interest has arisen in recent years in the possibility of earmarking at least part of the cigarette excise tax for the support of Medicare. These proposals for earmarking are justified by claims that smokers impose costs on nonsmokers because smoking damages health and this impairment in turn imposes costs on the remainder of the American citizenry in such ways as higher taxes for Medicare. However, even if we assume for purposes of discussion that smoking harms health, it does not follow that this harmed health imposes costs on nonsmokers, costs that represent the supply of particular medical services to smokers, services that in turn could indirectly be charged to users through the cigarette excise tax.

User charging is generally considered superior on both equity and efficiency grounds to general-fund financing in those cases where user charging is a feasible option. Equity is better served with user charging because the amounts that people pay to support a service varies with how much of the service they use. A person who mails twice as many letters as someone else pays twice as much when postal services are financed by user charges. But if postal services were financed from general revenues, the amounts that different people pay to support postal services would depend not on their use of the mails, but on their share of the total tax burden. Two people with the same taxable income would pay the same amount to support postal services, regardless of how many letters they mail. The light user of postal services would pay a greater amount per letter than the heavy user; general-fund financing would subsidize the heavy user at the expense of the light user.

Efficiency is also better served with user charges, because user charges generate information about the value people place on what is being provided. The main question in the provision of any service is whether that service is worth to users what it cost them in their capacities as customers or taxpayers. The prices people pay indicate how highly they value a service. If the sum of those valuations is insufficient to cover cost, information is generated to the effect that users value that service less highly than what it costs. Alternatively, if the amount people are willing to pay exceeds the cost of providing that service, information is generated to the effect that an expansion of output may be desirable. But with general-fund financing, no such information is created about the value that people place on different public services. With less information available, efficiency is diminished. User pricing, then, is a method of financing government that can enhance both the equity and the efficiency with which public services are provided.

Tax earmarking occupies an intermediate position between user pricing and general-fund financing. It is a method of indirectly pricing services that would be difficult or impossible to price directly. The general technique of tax earmarking is to tax something that is used in conjunction with a service that cannot be priced directly, and to earmark the proceeds of that tax for expenditure upon that service.[6] The primary example of tax earmarking in the United States is the earmarking of gasoline tax revenues for expenditures on highways. The services provided by highways are difficult to price directly (toll roads excepted), yet the use of highways is essentially no different than the use of telephones. A telephone is used to transport a person's voice from one place to another; a highway is used to transport his car from one place to another. The only difference between highways and telephones is the pragmatic one that it is relatively easy to charge people for their phone calls and relatively difficult to charge them for their use of highways.

Even though direct user pricing may not be feasible, an indirect form of user pricing through tax earmarking can under some conditions serve as a reasonably close substitute. If the gas tax is 20 cents per gallon, a car that get 20 miles per gallon is paying, indirectly, a user fee of 1 cent per mile for highways. The central test of tax earmarking is whether it is possible to envision a contractual relationship that would have terms that generally correspond to the terms that are generated by the earmarked tax. The use of a 20 cents per gallon gasoline tax as an indirect way of charging people 1 cent per mile for their use of highways would surely seem, at least as a first approximation, to be in reasonable conformity with the contractual test.

This contractual test is, of course, not free from ambiguity, because it requires the person undertaking the test to envision or conjecture the types of agreements people would have made had direct pricing been possible. Nonetheless, it is possible to distinguish reasonable from unreasonable possibilities. The taxation of gasoline may not operate identically to the direct pricing of highway services, but it surely does operate to create some substantial nexus between the amounts people pay and the services they receive in return. By contrast, the use of a gasoline tax to finance Medicare would be inconceivable as an outcome of some contractual agreement. However, the use of gasoline tax revenues to finance mass transit illustrates the irreducible ambiguity that characterizes this contractual test. This use of revenues would not necessarily fail this contractual test. The provision of mass transit might reduce highway congestion, thereby increasing the quality of highway services received by those who continue to drive and to pay the gasoline tax. Even though the diversion of revenues from highways to mass transit might increase the implicit price per mile to, say, 1.25 cents, the resulting reduction in congestion might result in a higher quality of highway service that is worth the higher price, though this need not be so.

Although it is possible to develop principles of tax earmarking as a substitute for user charging, it does not follow that any particular use of tax earmarking necessarily serves, or serves very effectively, in such a capacity. The practice of earmarking may diverge, to a lesser or a greater extent in particular cases, from the principle of earmarking. With respect to proposals to earmark cigarette taxes in recent years, some truly bizarre examples (when viewed from this contractual perspective) can be found.

At the federal level, a proposal was introduced in 1988 to earmark a 16 cents per pack increase in the cigarette tax for public housing subsidies. In Michigan the same year, a proposal for a six cents per pack was introduced, to be earmarked for AIDS research and treatment, along with a different proposal to earmark 4 cents per pack for jails. In Indiana in 1987 a 5 cents per pack tax increase was approved, with the revenues earmarked for soil conservation and maternity care. The same year Nevada approved a 2 cents per pack increase, to be earmarked for the renovation of university buildings.

The closeness of practice to principle may sometimes be difficult to determine, as the example of earmarking gasoline taxes for mass transit illustrates. A point of departure in any effort to reach such a determination is to ask whether the pattern of charges that results from the earmarked tax seems to correspond in general outline to the pattern that would result from the direct charging of users in a contractual setting. How does the earmarking of tobacco tax revenues for Medicare conform to the principles of tax earmarking? The case for earmarking rests upon two main presumptions. One is that smoking causes an increase in the use of medical resources by people aged 65 and over. The other is that, in light of the first presumption, tax earmarking can reasonably be thought to pass the test of contracting in a context where direct pricing is infeasible.

The prices people pay for insurance coverage do, of course, vary with the various risk categories into which they are placed. An earmarked cigarette tax might seem to be a way of charging a higher insurance premium to people who occupy a higher risk category. However, just because smokers are presumed to belong to a higher risk category does not mean that they make particularly heavy use of Medicare. As we noted above, if smokers do indeed belong to a higher risk category, they may actually make less use of a program like Medicare. If one assumes smoking truly does harm health, the shortened life spans that result may mean that smokers make less use of extended stays in hospitals and convalescent homes in the later years of life, when the burdens on Medicare become especially heavy. This possibility is generally consistent with the work of Leu and Schaub, of Wright, and of Shoven, Sundberg, and Bunker, all noted above.

But suppose, to carry the argument one step further, we find that smokers do indeed, over their lifetimes in present value terms, have greater medical expenses than nonsmokers. Even in this case, a case about which there presently exists no convincing data, it does not follow that the earmarking of the cigarette excise tax to support Medicare is a reasonable way of charging smokers for the medical costs associated with their smoking. This line of argument might have validity if Medicare were truly an insurance program. But if Medicare were truly an insurance program, people would pay directly for their anticipated use of medical resources through their premiums, and the coverage people would receive would depend on the premiums they paid. In this case, however, there would be no need for such an indirect method of pricing as tax earmarking in the first place.

Like all of the Social Security programs, Medicare is not truly an insurance program; its operation does not reflect any effort to apply a commercial principle to government. Medicare is fundamentally a program of subsidized medical care for people over age 65, and as such is more a transfer or welfare program than an insurance program, with the directions of transfer primarily being from younger to older people and from relatively healthy to relatively unhealthy people. This characteristic of Medicare, which is by now widely recognized in the scholarly community even if not among the public at large, invalidates the argument that earmarking the tobacco tax for Medicare is a reasonable substitute for user pricing, for the commercial principle is not applicable to Medicare.

Consider two of the several ways in which Medicare is run as a welfare and not as an insurance program. First, even if current tax payments are looked upon as paying for future medical payments, which is most certainly not the case, people who pay different amounts during their lifetimes would receive correspondingly differing degrees of protection after age 65. People who made larger payments would have bought proportionately more protection. This greater protection might result in longer coverage, a lower coinsurance rate, or in any number of numerous other possibilities. But the essential point is that the protection received would vary directly with the payments made under an insurance program. But with Medicare the protection received is the same regardless of the payments made.

Second, if Medicare were truly an insurance program to take effect upon reaching age 65, people would pay funds during their working years that subsequently would be sufficient, with accumulated interest, to pay their hospitalization expenses during their years of retirement. And, concomitantly, the payments made under Medicare to any particular age cohort would be limited to the payments plus accumulated interest previously made into Medicare by that cohort. But when Medicare was instituted in 1965, people immediately began to receive payment of hospitalization expenses, even though they had paid nothing into the program. Medicare in no way embodies contractual principles. Moreover, direct user pricing is surely feasible for Medicare, so there is no case for arguing that tax earmarking is necessary as an indirect form of user charging. Medicare is fundamentally a welfare program--a program that transfers income from some people to others--and not a genuine, contractually-based program of medical insurance.

One could, of course, advocate the extension of the commercial principle to Medicare, but this would entail a drastically different program than now exists. But so long as the commercial principle is not invoked and so long as Medicare remains essentially a transfer program, there is no principled basis for saying that one particular subset of users should be subject to commercial or actuarial principles while other subsets are not. There does, of course, seem to be a widespread public sentiment that people do pay into genuine insurance programs with the various Social Security programs. This sentiment is surely reinforced by the use of a language that speaks of "contributions" rather than of "taxes." Should the Social Security programs come to be seen as welfare programs of taxing and transferring income, and with distributions of winners and losers that commonly seem arbitrary and capricious when compared against the standards commonly thought applicable to welfare programs, the support for those programs might weaken. By helping to dispel the illusion of insurance and replacing it with the reality of welfare, general-fund financing might undermine public support for those programs.

Principle, Expediency, and Wealth Transfers

The claim that smokers impose above-average burdens upon health-care programs would be an argument for charging smokers differentially heavier prices for participation in those programs--if those programs were operated along commercial principles. But clearly they are not designed to operate along commercial principles. Such programs embody various patterns of cross-subsidization or wealth transfers. As with insurance programs, people who incur greater medical expenses than their tax payments to finance the program are subsidized by people in the reverse position. However, save to the extent that insurance programs are constrained by state regulation to create patterns of cross-subsidization, any such ex post cross-subsidization would be unknowable ex ante. Considerations of transaction costs aside, cross-subsidization at an ex ante level must be a matter of political power, with the legislature choosing to subsidize particular sets of people at the expense of others. There are numerous ways in which this happens, both with respect to the financing of medical care and with respect to the financing of most other governmental programs.

What is the merit of a professed desire to implement user-like pricing in one particular case, as by imposing a particularly heavy tax upon smokers to support Medicare, or even simply to support the general-fund, as the cigarette tax now does? Such an effort could, of course, be but one piece of a general program to operate government more along commercial principles. The total program would contain many pieces, including the replacement of the retirement insurance component of Social Security with a system of individual retirement accounts, the elimination of all agricultural price support and crop restriction programs, and the privatization of education, to mention but a few of many, many possible illustrations. Such an approach would represent a principled effort to expand the scope for the application of contractual principles throughout government.

However, the application of such a contractual approach to only one service, as in the case of smoking, can hardly represent the application of principle to politics. Rather, it surely represents expediency backed by power. In light of the minority position of smokers in American society, to say nothing of the predominantly blue-collar status of smokers, which carries relatively low political influence, the imposition of high and growing tax burdens is not surprising, but rather is an understandable reflection of human nature. But rather than say that smokers should pay higher taxes because they make more use of medical resources than others (which is not a demonstrated proposition in any event), it would be more honest to say that smokers should pay higher taxes because that would lower the taxes that the rest of us have to pay.

NOTES

1. As for Medicaid, 45 percent of those served are children.

2. Related findings are developed for Canada in Stoddart, *et al.* (1986).

3. Indeed, smokers have paid excise taxes on cigarettes and other tobacco products since time immemorial. The Tobacco Institute estimates, for example, that since 1863, smokers have paid over $200 billion in excise taxes. Over a substantial portion of this period, there was no publicly provided medical care and hence no basis for any claim of overuse by smokers.

4. This point is developed very clearly by Virginia Wright (1986), whose estimates suggest that each smoker who quits smoking at age 45 adds a net burden to Medicare of around $5,000 in current dollars. Further reinforcing this conclusion are the studies of Shoven, Sundberg, and Bunker (1987), who estimate that smokers "save" the Social Security system billions of dollars. Also see Atkinson and Townsend (1977) for a similar analysis of Great Britain.

5. See, for example, McCormick and Tollison (1981).

6. Aspects of the theory of tax earmarking are presented in Buchanan (1963) and McMahon and Sprenkle (1970). For a comprehensive analysis of user fees and tax earmarking, see Wagner (forthcoming).

CHAPTER 7

Smoking, Business Costs, And Social Cost

Most of the attention surrounding claims that smoking imposes significant costs on the nonsmoking majority of American society has focused on the claims that (1) smoking reduces economic output due to earlier death and greater illness and (2) smoking *ipso facto* increases medical costs. In Chapter 4 we explained why losses in production that may result from smoking are borne by smokers and not by nonsmokers. In Chapters 5 and 6 we undertook the same examination with respect to claims about excess medical expenses.

A somewhat different line of argument holds that smoking impedes the general efficiency of processes of production, and that this impediment results in a general loss for everyone rather than particular losses being borne by smokers. Alchian and Demsetz (1972) articulated nicely the idea that a business firm was engaged in a process of team production, in which case it is impossible to distinguish the separate contributions of individual members of the firm. So if smoking were to interfere with the productivity of the production team the firm represents, the output or productivity of the firm would fall, and with it the earnings of the members of the team would decline. It could, of course, be argued that the owner or manager of the team or firm would have an incentive to establish policies toward smoking that maximized the value of the firm. However, some might argue that competitive processes do not work "perfectly," and that in the face of imperfect competition smoking would exert a generalized negative effect on firm output and earnings. If so, a decrease in smoking would lead to an increase in output and earnings.

In this chapter we examine some aspects of the possibility that smoking impedes the general efficiency of economic processes of production. First, we elaborate on the possibility that smoking may impede team production processes. One of the principal ways it has often been claimed that smokers do this is through being absent from work more frequently than nonsmokers, and we shall examine this claim carefully. Subsequently, we explore related claims that have often been advanced to the effect that smokers in various ways increase the costs of doing business. Finally, we examine from an international perspective some evidence on smoking and economic progress, finding no significant evidence that smoking impedes progress--and actually perhaps finding evidence that could be interpreted as suggesting that it promotes economic progress.

Smoking and the Efficiency of Team Production

In economic theory a business firm is looked upon as a team, the efficiency of which depends upon how well the efforts of its members are coordinated by management. If smoking were to impede the efficiency of the team, it would seem reasonable to suppose that management would have an incentive to institute policies toward smoking that would eliminate the inefficiency and promote the maximization of the value of the firm. Or at least this is an implication of the theory of competitive markets.

To be sure, not all economists agree that the theory of competitive markets is a useful way of looking at all economic processes. Many of these economists would argue that markets are often only imperfectly competitive. One possible implication of this view is that inefficient practices and production processes may persist, perhaps as represented by Leibenstein's (1966) articulation of X-efficiency--the idea that production processes within firms might not be organized in a fully efficient manner.

While there is some controversy over the degree of applicability of the concept of X-efficiency, it does provide a useful framework to assess whether or not smoking leads to some reduction in production efficiency within the firm. If this happens, the firm's cost of production will rise; for the same stock of resources, the firm will be able to produce less output than it could have produced without the smoking-induced increase in the cost of production. To the extent this negative impact on production exists throughout the economy, the aggregate volume of economic production, as represented in such aggregate concepts as Gross National Product and National Income, will suffer. Thus, under this scenario people will be poorer in the society because of smoking and the X-inefficiency it represents.

It is possible to visualize how smoking might impede team production processes. When the members of the team are perfectly coordinated, the firm's production process will be at its greatest level of efficiency. But it is possible to imagine situations where smoking might interfere with that coordination. As one commonly advanced example, it is often argued that smokers have higher rates of absenteeism than nonsmokers. To be sure, merely to advance this line of argument about absenteeism does not automatically render it valid, as we will explain below.

Nonetheless, since we are interested in the construction of arguments grounded in X-inefficiency, it will be useful for purposes of discussion to assume that smoking is a source of absenteeism. A perfectly coordinated production process in a particular firm might involve 300 people engaged in various activities. Now inject absenteeism into that production process. If someone does not show up at work, some element of discoordination might seem to have been injected into the production process. Moreover, the extent of that discoordination might seem to increase directly with the number of people who miss work. One reflection of this discoordination might be that invoices are not prepared and mailed in timely fashion, so payments are in turn received later than they might alternatively have been received, and so the firm loses interest earnings on what alternatively would have been a higher bank balance. A second illustration or reflection might be absenteeism in a section of a warehouse, which leads to orders being completed and filled in slower fashion. With slower shipment, payments are received less quickly and the firm loses the interest earnings it could have received had the shipment been made and payment received earlier.

But absenteeism is not the only way in which smoking might impede a firm's productivity. People who smoke on the job might perform their tasks more slowly than otherwise, which in turn might delay other people in the completion of their tasks. A smoking secretary who thereby slows down the processing of mailing labels may cause congestion in the mailing room where the packages are accumulating while waiting to have the labels affixed. With this congestion, the pace of work in the mailing room might also slow down, perhaps leading the firm to ask people to work overtime or possibly to hire temporary labor, either of which will increase the firm's cost of production.

Alternatively, but equivalently with respect to the possible influence of smoking on the firm's efficiency, smokers may slow down the pace of nonsmokers, thereby injecting discoordination in this fashion. A smoking mechanic in a garage may work as speedily and accurately as a nonsmoking mechanic, but the smoker's smoke might annoy some people who work in the parts department. When these people act with reluctance in dealing with the smoking mechanic, requests for parts are filled more slowly, which in turn slows down the rate at which the garage completes its repairs. With a lower volume of repairs being completed for a given size of operation, the firm's cost of production is obviously higher than it could have been.

To be sure, all of these illustrations of X-inefficiency attributed to smoking raise questions as to whether the managers of the firm would truly allow inefficient production processes to operate. With respect to absenteeism, in many situations by virtue of the law of large numbers it is possible to count on a particular amount of absenteeism. For example, to staff a warehouse with 95 workers would require a labor force of 100 if the rate of absenteeism were 5 percent. In such a setting absenteeism would have no economic impact, and would only have an effect to the extent it were unanticipated. And to the extent that smokers might work more slowly, it might also seem that this should cause little problem of coordination so long as managers were able reasonably to anticipate people's paces of work and the tasks for coordination that this implied. In other words, there is a strong line of reasoning within economic theory that suggests that managers will have an incentive to operate the workplace in its most efficient manner, and will develop policies toward smoking as part of this process. But as we noted above, not all economists accept this fully competitive framework for analysis, and we have accepted for purposes of argument this presumption of X-inefficiency in order to set forth a situation in which smoking could be said to have a negative impact on a firm's productivity--and, by aggregation, on a nation's productivity.

Smoking and Workplace Efficiency

The argument that smoking entails a cost in terms of lost production is sometimes represented by the charge that smoking reduces workplace efficiency. Lost production and workplace efficiency are largely images of one another: the lost production that results from the damaged health of smokers must mean that the workplaces throughout the nation produce less than they would otherwise have produced. And beyond this lost production, it is sometimes claimed that smokers also increase such costs as maintenance and the replacement of furniture. While the significance of these other costs has been shown to be dubious, the matter of absenteeism is worth further consideration.[1] Table 7.1 summarizes aggregate, nationwide data on work loss by smokers and nonsmokers for 1970 and 1976.

Table 7.1

Smoking and Annual Days of Lost Work

	Everyone	Never Smoked	Former Smokers	Current Smokers (amt. smoked/day)			
				all	1-14	15-24	25 & over
1970							
Male	5.0	3.7	5.1	5.8	6.0	5.2	6.4
Female	5.9	5.1	5.3	7.4	7.1	7.9	7.2
1976							
Male	5.0	4.3	5.7	5.2	2.6	5.9	5.7
Female	5.8	5.1	6.3	6.6	6.2	5.7	9.3

Source: For 1970, U.S. Bureau of the Census, *Statistical Abstract of the United States: 1975* (Washington, D.C.: U.S. Government Printing Office, 1975), p. 90. For 1976, *Ibid.: 1980*, p. 130.

A comparison of the columns labeled "never smoked" and "all smokers" conveys the impression of smokers being absent from work more often than nonsmokers. For 1970, nonsmoking men missed 2.1 fewer days of work than smoking men; nonsmoking women missed 2.3 fewer days than smoking women. Stated differently, the rate of absenteeism was nearly 60 percent higher among smoking men than among nonsmoking men. And among women, smokers were absent 45 percent more often than nonsmokers. For 1976, nonsmoking men missed 0.9 fewer days than smoking men, while nonsmoking women missed 1.5 fewer days than smoking women. In this case, smoking men were absent over 20 percent more often than nonsmoking men, while smoking women were absent nearly 30 percent more often than nonsmoking women.

While these pieces of data seem to suggest that smokers are less healthy than nonsmokers and so miss more work, there are also some pieces of data in Table 7.1 that do not, particularly the 1976 data from the National Health Survey. While current smokers on average appear to miss more work than people who never smoked, men who currently smoke on average miss less work than men who formerly smoked. Moreover, men who currently smoke less than 15 cigarettes daily miss nearly two days less work per year than men who never smoked. And women who currently smoke up to 24 cigarettes per day miss less work than women who formerly smoked. So the data on smoking and workplace absenteeism do not tell an unambiguous tale of smoking leading to increased sickness and absenteeism; different tales can be told, depending on how the data are aggregated and categorized.

More than this, it is questionable whether these data are on balance revealing or concealing. There are grounds for suggesting that data like those in Table 7.1 may mislead more than they inform. Many of those data give the impression that smokers miss more work than their nonsmoking coworkers. But this may be a false impression created by aggregation. Smokers are relatively more heavily represented in blue collar occupations than in white collar occupations. This is illustrated by Table 7.2. Among males, a majority of cooks, painters, and mechanics, among others, smoke, whereas less than one-third of engineers, lawyers, and accountants smoke. And among females, nearly half of waitresses, shipping clerks, and assemblers smoke, while less than a quarter of medical technicians, school teachers, and librarians smoke.

Table 7.2

Percentage Smokers by Occupation

Men		Women	
Occupation	% Smokers	Occupation	% Smokers
Garage laborers	58.5	Waitresses	49.6
Cooks	57.5	Shipping & receiving clerks	48.5
Maintenance painters	56.3	Assemblers	43.6
Pressmen & plateprinters	55.7	Bookkeepers	38.6
Auto mechanics	54.6	Nurses	38.4
Assemblers	52.7	Laundry & drycleaning operatives	38.3
Shipping & receiving clerks	50.0	Secretaries	37.3
Draftsmen	34.2	Accountants & auditors	30.8
Accountants & auditors	33.3	Stenographers	28.4
Lawyers	30.3	Technicians, medical & dental	23.6
Aeronautical engineers	26.2	Elementary school teachers	19.4
Electrical engineers	20.3	Librarians	16.4

Source: T. Sterling and J. Weinkam, "Smoking Characteristics by Type of Employment," *Journal of Occupational Medicine* 18 (No. 11, 1976): 743-54.

Blue collar jobs generally entail a stronger separation between work and consumption than white collar jobs. To the extent white-collar workers generally enjoy much more job-related and on-the-job consumption than blue-collar workers, basic economic principles would predict lower rates of absenteeism among white-collar workers than among blue-collar workers. Such a prediction implies in turn more absenteeism among smokers than among nonsmokers, and for reasons having nothing to do with smoking. Daniel Taylor (1979), for instance, shows both that rates of absenteeism are lower in white-collar occupations than in blue-collar occupations, and that within blue-collar occupations rates of absenteeism are lower among skilled than among unskilled workers. Furthermore, Holcomb and Meigs (1972) have shown that while cigarette smokers have a higher rate of absenteeism than nonsmokers (5.9 percent vs. 4.4 percent), pipe and cigar smokers have the lowest rate of absenteeism of all--3.2 percent. Those who seek to infer causation from statistical correlation would, if they were judicious and consistent, have to become advocates of pipes and cigars. But what this observation really shows, of course, is the ever-present danger of treating heterogeneous people as if they were homogeneous. Pipe and cigar smokers are different from cigarette smokers and nonsmokers. With respect to the point at issue here, pipe and cigar smokers are predominantly found in white-collar occupations and professions, where job-related consumption is high, so their lower rate of absenteeism is economically understandable.

Perhaps the most thorough study to date of the alleged impact of smoking on absenteeism was conducted by Ault, Ekelund, Jackson, Saba, and Saurman (1988). They started from the raw observations noted above, that smokers miss significantly more work than nonsmokers. But they also noted that there are many other ways that smokers differ from nonsmokers, and which would lead to greater absenteeism. Consider a very simple illustration to set forth the central point in simplified fashion. Suppose smokers miss work an average of 10 days per year while nonsmokers miss an average of five days, and suppose that blue collar workers miss 10 days of work per year while white collar workers miss five days. These elementary data illustrate accurately the observed relationships that smokers miss more work than nonsmokers and that blue collar workers miss more work than white collar workers.

In conjunction with these realistic relationships, add the admittedly unrealistic assumptions that (1) no smokers are white collar workers and (2) no nonsmokers are blue collar workers. While these assumptions are inaccurate as to detail, they are accurate in terms of the general portrait that smokers are found more heavily in blue collar occupations than in white collar occupations. In terms of the hypothetical formulation, it could be concluded that smokers miss five more days of work per year than nonsmokers. But it could also be concluded that blue collar workers miss five more days of work per year than white collar workers. The open question is whether the extra five days of missed work should be attributed to smoking or to working in blue collar occupations.

It is very easy to attribute missed work to smoking when it should be attributed to the nature of blue collar occupations instead. Table 7.3 presents a hypothetical illustration of this point. This table is constructed on the presumption that blue collar workers miss 10 days per year and white collar workers miss five days; as this table is constructed, smokers and nonsmokers miss the same amount of work, given their occupations. Table 7.3 is constructed under the presumptions (1) that there are 200 workers, divided evenly between smokers and nonsmokers and (2) that the work force is evenly divided between blue collar and white collar workers, *but that 70 percent of the smokers are blue collar workers while 70 percent of the nonsmokers are white collar workers.* Simply by virtue of smokers being relatively heavily concentrated in blue collar occupations, smokers will be attributed with having higher absenteeism rates than nonsmokers. The last row of Table 7.3 shows that smokers would be attributed with missing two more days of work per year than nonsmokers, even though, by the very principles by which Table 7.3 was constructed, there is no impact of smoking per se upon absenteeism.

Table 7.3

Smoking, Occupation, and Absenteeism

	Smokers	Nonsmokers
Number	100	100
Blue Collar Workers	70	30
White Collar Workers	30	70
Days of Work Missed	850*	650**
Absenteeism rate (percent)	8.5	6.5

*The sum of 70 blue collar workers missing 10 days and 30 white collar workers missing five days.

**The sum of 30 blue collar workers missing 10 days and 70 white collar workers missing five days.

To account for such factors as occupation on absenteeism is a complex statistical task. The work by Ault, *et al.* noted earlier did just this. It started from data like that described above, which shows smokers to miss significantly more work than nonsmokers. But Ault, *et al.* also separated out statistically the impact of such things as occupation and alcohol consumption (people who drink more tend on average to miss more work, while people who drink are also more likely to smoke than people who do not). When they made the appropriate allowances for these other impacts on absenteeism, they reported that smoking itself had no significant impact on absenteeism.

It is worth noting briefly that these conclusions by Ault, *et al.* are generally consistent with the presumption, discussed in Chapter 5, that the annual medical expenses of smokers are not significantly higher than those of nonsmokers. If smokers and nonsmokers miss the same amount of work per year due to illness, and if the costs of those illnesses are the same, there would be no basis for claiming that smokers are more costly to treat than nonsmokers. For smokers to incur higher medical expenses, it would be necessary either that smokers have a greater number of illnesses or they have illnesses that have a greater cost per treatment, even if they do not have a greater number of illnesses. The study by Ault, *et al.* provides a strong basis for believing that rates of illness between smokers and nonsmokers are roughly the same. As for costs per episode of illness for smokers and nonsmokers, we know of no reliable data on this point, and would counsel in favor of presuming equal costs of treatment per illness until shown reason for presuming differently.

It is typically suggested that the greater absenteeism of smokers, when multiplied by their wage rate, will give a measure of the cost of sickness claimed to be attributed to smoking, in conformity to the lost earnings approach to the evaluation of illness and death. However, a day spent on sick leave is rarely completely wasted. Even such an activity as lying in bed and watching television is valuable to the sick person, and in principle the value of such activities should be subtracted from the lost earnings in arriving at a cost of the lost production due to illness. Furthermore, a consistent application of the line of analysis that assigns a cost to lost work would have to conclude that weekends, holidays, and vacations also impose a cost of lost production upon society, for production is as much diminished by these types of days away from the workplace as it is by sick leave. Furthermore, sick leave may represent time spent fishing, and the value the worker places on a day of fishing may well exceed his lost output, particularly in blue-collar occupations, and in such cases would actually represent a social benefit rather than a social cost.

Absenteeism by no means implies illness or injury. Rates of absenteeism imply little, if anything, about states of personal health. For instance, the rate of absenteeism in western European nations is generally about three times as high as it is in the United States. And absenteeism in Japan seems to be about half that in the United States. It is implausible that Americans are twice as sickly as Japanese, or that western Europeans are three times as sickly as Americans. It is far more plausible that all are about equally sickly, only they differ in the costs they suffer if they are absent and the rewards they capture if they are not. The lower the cost of absenteeism to workers and the lower the returns to work, the higher will be the rate of absenteeism, and for reasons having nothing to do with personal health. Both the generally higher tax rates in western European nations and the far more extensive programs of social welfare that are found there make it economically understandable why rates of absenteeism are higher.

Workplace Costs: A Further Consideration

Besides absenteeism, allegations are sometimes advanced that the presence of smokers in the work force adds to business costs in other ways. For instance, Kristein (1983) estimates that the added costs to business is in the range of $336 to $601 per smoker per year. And Weis (1981) estimates the added cost to be around ten times higher, in the vicinity of $4,000. Some of the more significant of these cost categories relate to higher insurance costs noted in earlier chapters. But there are also at least three other categories not discussed earlier: (1) a claim that smokers are responsible for increased property damage and increased costs for fire, liability, and accident insurance, (2) a claim that smokers increase costs for ventilation and air conditioning, and (3) a claim that smokers increase costs through the time they spend smoking on the job. We shall consider each of these three elements in turn.

Property damage. It is claimed that smokers damage property in such forms as burned carpets and higher costs for cleaning draperies. To be sure, these forms of damage are easy to see and to attribute to smoking. But it is totally illegitimate to add up such smoking-attributable costs as cigarette burns and call this an excess cost of having smoking workers. For nonsmoking workers might incur costs of a similar nature. Many nonsmokers drink coffee or soft drinks, and which on occasion they spill, sometimes even onto, or into, such expensive office equipment as computers and copying machines. Carelessness by a nonsmoking employee may have led to a shorting out of the electrical system, causing the loss of much computer work in the process.

Employers, of course, have incentives to mitigate accidental damage to property, whether by smokers or nonsmokers. But the kinds of accounting statistics commonly reported in these matters give no convincing basis for concluding that smokers are a source of excess property damage. And in any event, the issues created are ones of individual business policy and not of public policy, for it is the owners of the businesses who bear whatever costs may be incurred.

Ventilation and air conditioning costs. The claim that smokers increase costs of ventilation and air conditioning is the same kind of claim as the preceding one that smokers are sources of property damage. Indeed, in many cases there may be no added ventilation cost that can be reasonably attributed to smoking. To be sure, the inadequacy of ventilation in modern buildings is coming increasingly to be recognized. But in a great many cases, and perhaps in most, there is no assignable cost of ventilation for particular items.

This point is one more illustration of the essential arbitrariness of allocating joint costs. To illustrate, suppose the only two things to be removed from the air are cigarette smoke and on the one hand and dust and pathogenic microorganisms on the other. It is doubtful if a less expensive ventilation system would be installed if there were no cigarette smoke to remove. And once it is recognized that indoor air contains numerous other things as well, the relative significance of cigarette smoke diminishes even further, which in turn makes even less plausible the claim that smoking is a significant source of ventilation costs.

And besides, these costs too are borne by the individual owners of business enterprises. It is at least imaginable that some owners could decide to prohibit smoking within their business, and at the same time choose to install weak ventilation equipment. These costs savings would accrue to the business owners if they were correct in their judgment that without smoking much less ventilation would be necessary. But if they were wrong, the growing unpleasantness and unhealthfulness of the work place would increase their costs of operation, despite the saving of ventilation costs. In either case, business owners bear the costs or gains, and have good incentives to seek efficient outcomes.

Missed work due to smoking breaks. The treatment of time spent on smoking breaks is analytically equivalent to accounting for time lost because of illness. Suppose smokers take four smoking breaks per day, of 15 minutes each. If the standard working day were eight hours, smokers would be viewed as effectively working only seven hours. This would make smokers 12 percent more costly to employ than nonsmokers-- assuming that this was the only difference between smokers and non-smokers.

This assumption, however, is surely without foundation. For it would have us believe that smokers and nonsmokers work equally diligently for seven hours per day, and that nonsmokers continue in the same manner for the eighth hour while smokers sit back and smoke for that eighth hour. Yet experience in any business establishment will show all kinds of ways that nonsmokers can also take what might be called on-the-job leisure: drinking coffee, making shopping lists on a computer, talking about sports with a colleague, and daydreaming while appearing to be thinking, are a few of many possible illustrations.

Perhaps the main difference between smoking and these other illustrations is that smoking is visible and explicit. This is probably particularly so in workplaces that allow smoking only in designated areas and times. Yet even time spent smoking might well be time spent productively. In white collar occupations, this might be time spent composing a letter to be dictated upon return to the desk. In blue collar occupations, a bit of rest time periodically may lead to higher levels of overall performance than would be possible if breaks were not allowed.

Furthermore, it is the task of individual business owners to determine how best to operate their businesses. In this instance, as in the preceding instances, there is no valid economic justification for workplace smoking rules, except those rules which have been voluntarily adopted by firms and workers in the absence of government policy. Firms have clear incentives to produce their output at least cost. In this respect, even if smokers are more costly employees (a point for which we believe no convincing evidence exists), they will be employed because they add more to a firm's revenues than to its costs. To focus on the alleged costs of hiring a particular type of worker is besides the point. The point is to hire the best workers, among which will often be found smokers. Whether through open competition for workers or through collective bargaining, the proper approach to workplace smoking is to allow companies and employees to decide the appropriate smoking policy on a company-by-company basis.

Smoking and Economic Productivity: A Conceptual Framework

As we noted earlier in this chapter, not all economists believe that the economy and the economic process can be aptly characterized by the model of full or perfect competition. Many think that markets are only imperfectly competitive. If this is so, it is possible for X-inefficiency to characterize the economic process. Among other things, it is possible for business firms to produce in a more costly and less efficient manner. And to the extent efficiency suffers in general, such measures of aggregate output as national income should suffer as well. Here we report on some world-wide observations concerning the correlation between changes in the prevalence of smoking and changes in the groth of national output. If smoking retards economic efficiency, nations where smoking is growing most rapidly should exhibit slower rates of economic growth. To be sure, such correlations cannot be used to say anything about causal processes, but they do nonetheless serve to focus attention on relationships and motivate inquiry into those relationships.

In particular, negative correlations between smoking and national output would certainly be consistent with arguments that smoking is a source of economic damage, such as might be represented by a model of X-inefficiency. Similarly, a zero correlation would be consistent with the thesis that smoking is not a source of economic damage, say as represented by the theory of competitive markets. And a positive correlation would similarly suggest that smoking may be beneficial to production processes, a finding that in turn might suggest an inquiry into how this might be possible--and it might also represent a statistical fluke that has no significance.

By way of brief overview, the data presented below do not suggest the existence of a negative relationship between smoking and national output. To the contrary, the data suggest relatively strong evidence of a positive relationship: nations where smoking is growing more rapidly are nations where national output is also growing more rapidly. For the world as a whole, or at least the 95 nations for which observations are available, the Pearsonian correlation coefficient between smoking growth and national output growth over the 1973-83 period is 0.397. With a t-value of 4.18, this coefficient is significantly different from zero at well beyond the 0.01 level of significance. In other words, there is less than one chance in 100 that the true correlation coefficient could be zero. Nations where smoking is increasing most rapidly are nations whose economies are growing most rapidly; this observation comes across strongly in the data.

And what holds for the entire world seems generally to hold up for the various regional subsamples, as Table 7.4 also illustrates. For instance when the data are aggregated in terms of regional averages, the correlation between smoking growth and national output growth is 0.810. Regions of the world where smoking is increasing most rapidly are those regions taht are experiencing the most rapid rates of economic growth. Even though there are only seven observations at this regional level of aggregation, the t-value of 3.12 suggests the correlation is significantly different from zero at about the 0.03 level of significance, meaning that there are only about three chances in 100 that the true correlation could be zero.

Table 7.4

Correlation Coefficients (and t-values)
between Smoking Growth and GNP Growth, 1973-83

Data Set	Observations	Correlation	t
World	95	.397	4.18
Regions (seven)	7	.810	3.12
W. Europe & N. America	19	.312	1.36
C. America & Caribbean	14	.524	2.13
S. America	11	.724	3.15
N. Africa	16	.526	2.31
S. Africa	10	-.151	-0.43
Middle East & S. Asia	14	.235	0.84
Eastern & Southeastern Asia	11	-.375	-1.21

Sources: Cigarette consumption from the *Hardbook of Industrial Statistics*, 1986. GNP from the *World Book Atlas*, 1986.

The remainder of Table 7.4 presents correlation coefficients within the individual regions. Of those seven cases, there are only two cases of negative correlation coefficients--for Southern Africa and for Eastern and Southeastern Asia. With regard to Southern Africa, the t-value of -0.43 is significant at just below the 0.7 level, meaning that nearly 70 percent of the time the true correlation could be zero. The negative correlation coefficient for Eastern and Southeastern Asia has a t-value of -1.21, which is significant at just below the 0.3 level, meaning that there is a nearly 30 percent chance that the true coefficient could be zero.

In terms of the regional data, Eastern and Southeastern Asia is the only region where there appears to be a negative relationship between smoking growth and national output growth, though the significance of the relationship is considerably weaker than any of the positive regional relationships save for that of the Middle East and South Asia. Furthermore, this relationship is due to the influence of Macao, which was the only nation in the region where smoking declined and which had a rate of national output growth more than double that of any other nation in the region. If Macao were eliminated from the sample, the correlation coefficient becomes slightly positive, 0.2, and with a t-value of 0.6 that is not significantly different from zero.

As for the regions with positive correlations, only in the case of the Middle East and South Asia region would it be reasonable to conclude that the coefficient is not significantly different from zero. With a t-value of 0.84, the significance level of the correlation coefficient is just over 0.4, indicating that there is a more than 40 percent chance that the true correlation coefficient is zero. But for the other four regions, the t-values on the correlation coefficients suggest that it is unlikely that the true correlation is zero. For Western Europe and North America, the significance level is about 0.2, suggesting a one-in-five chance that the true correlation could be zero. For the other three regions--Central America and the Caribbean, South America, and Northern Africa--the significance levels are below 0.05, meaning very small odds indeed that the true correlation is zero.

Smoking and Productivity: Discussion of the Data

The data on smoking growth and national output growth give a strong portrait of a positive association. This comes across most clearly in the world-wide aggregation, both the 95 nation analysis and the seven region analysis. This portrait appears to hold a little less firmly in the analysis of individual regions, though at the same time we are necessarily dealing with but a handful of observations in these cases, and the reliability of statistical procedures weakens. To be sure, there exists no satisfactory model of economic growth into which smoking could be embedded as one possible explanatory factor. Perhaps some day such a model will exist. But for now we are limited to correlations, so caution over interpretation is certainly warranted, as we ourselves have noted earlier in other respects.[2]

If a positive correlation between smoking and lung cancer is used at least as some tentative presumption of some underlying causal process, even though such a process has not yet been articulated, it might seem as though something similar might hold for the positive correlation between smoking growth and economic growth. It could, of course, be argued that the positive correlation between smoking growth and national output growth is simply a reflection of the income elasticity of demand for cigarettes being positive. As people get richer they buy more cigarettes. A positive correlation coefficient would be a reflection of this relationship between income and consumption.

But such a line of argument has no room for particular nations to have negative relationships between smoking growth and national output growth. Within the income elasticity interpretation, smoking increases because income increases, which in turn implies that smoking decreases because income decreases. Yet the data show all kinds of cases where income increases while smoking decreases. It seems clear that the data cannot be used simply to tell a story grounded in a positive income elasticity. It is, of course, possible that smoking makes no contribution to economic progress. This would be a proposition that in a correctly specified economic model, rates of economic growth would be independent of rates of smoking growth. In this case smoking would be neither a drag nor a boost to economic progress, but would simply be a reflection of how people choose to spend their money as consumers.

But there are the positive correlations between smoking and economic progress noted above. Accordingly, there would seem to be room for conjecture and speculation on whether such a positive correlation might withstand scrutiny and have some plausible basis. And there do seem to be some plausible lines of thought that would suggest a positive relationship between smoking and economic progress, though we advance these tentatively as possibilities and not definitively as actualities. One possible line of explanation has to do with the costs of regulation; the other has to do with proclivities for risk-taking within a population.

With respect to the costs of regulation, there is a growing economic literature on the ways in which regulation can impede economic progress. For instance, Wayne Gray (1987) estimates that OSHA and EPA regulations were responsible for reducing the rate of productivity growth in manufacturing by 0.44 percentage points--a decline that accounts for nearly 30 percent of the productivity slowdown over the 1970s. Regulations regarding smoking may work in the same way. With respect to the principle of team production, such regulations may impede the efficiency of team production processes, both by requiring firms to undertake inefficient activities and by preventing them from undertaking efficient activities. It seems plausible that there is some positive correlation between the growth of anti-smoking regulation and the decline in cigarette consumption. If the growth in anti-smoking regulation works similarly to such other forms of regulation as OSHA and EPA, an increase in regulation would decrease both smoking and economic progress. Alternatively, a reduction in anti-smoking regulation would both lead to increased smoking and greater economic progress. Smoking and economic progress would be positively correlated, because of the negative impact of regulation, including anti-smoking regulation, on economic progress.

With respect to proclivities for risk-taking within a population, there are well known lines of thought that associate an adventuresome, entrepreneurial spirit with economic progress. By contrast, a lack of adventuresomeness and a strong desire to avoid risk are associated with economic stagnation. It is surely plausible to attribute much of the growing volume of public discussion about risk and safety, in which attention is increasingly riveted on the risks that are thought to follow from some course of action rather than being focussed on the benefits, to a stagnation of the entrepreneurial spirit. A society that comes increasingly to place safety and security first, particularly in the sense of a lexicographical ordering, and which seems to be characterized by a growing volume of regulatory activity, is perhaps likely to be less entrepreneurial and innovative, and, hence, less progressive, than those that do not.

Consider in particular the case of smoking, and simply assume that smoking may be hazardous to some people's health. Judging from the tone of public discussion, it would surely seem that smoking has become an increasingly dangerous activity. And in response to the growing menace, the regulatory army has strengthened its forces and intensified its vigilance. But yet this portrait of reality seems questionable. Even if it is assumed that smoking may be a source of health damage, wouldn't it be concluded that smoking is less of a danger now than it once was? A smaller percentage of people now smoke, and medical diagnosis and treatment have improved for some diseases. Whatever the risks from smoking might be, they would presumably be less now than they were a generation ago. But judging from the tenor of public discussion and advocacy, the opposite would have to be concluded. This might be because the general perception of risk has heightened. If what we are observing is a situation in which people have generally become more concerned in avoiding risks than before, and with a decline in smoking being to some extent a reflection of that change, we should perhaps expect to find the positive correlation between smoking and economic progress that we noted above. In this case a population in which people are more entrepreneurial and less concerned with risk will be both economically more progressive and will smoke more (because people focus less strongly on the risks of smoking relative to the pleasures).

NOTES

1. For strong support for the thesis that smoking has not been shown to impair workplace efficiency, see, for instance, Solmon (1983) and Vogel (1985).

2. Relatedly, with regard to issues concerning the relationship between findings of correlation and statements of causation, Tucker and Friedman (1989) find a strong positive correlation between the extent of obesity in men and the amount of television they watch.

CHAPTER 8

ETS And Governmental Protection Of Consumers And Workers

If the opposition to smoking were based exclusively on the alleged adverse health effects to the smoker himself, it would be easy to counter this opposition by simply noting that paternalism is inconsistent with the principles of individual liberty upon which our free, democratic society is based. Simply stated, if individuals choose to smoke despite possessing knowledge of the possibility of adverse health effects, that is their right, and they would harm no one but themselves in doing so. The choices of individuals concerning the relative riskiness of their personal behavior is their business, and theirs alone, so long as those choices do not infringe on the rights of others. Few of even the most ardent opponents of tobacco should disagree with this proposition.[1] As we have seen in Chapters 4-7, costs of lost productivity and medical care related to smoking would be borne by the smokers themselves.

In recent years a new line of argument has emerged in support of restrictions on smoking. This line of argument suggests that smokers damage the health of nonsmokers who happen to come into contact with tobacco smoke against their will. The claim here is that smokers generate a form of indoor pollution termed environmental tobacco smoke (ETS), and consequently expose nonsmokers in their vicinity to many of the same smoking-related diseases and consequences.

On its surface this argument seems the opposite of the paternalistic claim that the government should restrict smoking in order to "protect" the smoker from himself. There is no direct expression of interest that government act as a busybody or a nanny to protect smokers from themselves. Rather, it is affirmed that government should act as a defender of the rights and liberties of individuals--a governmental role traditionally advocated by even the most ardent proponents of limited governments and free markets. But with respect to smoking this requires government to protect nonsmokers from cigarette smoke. Restrictions on smoking are thus analogous not to laws preventing free speech or other peaceable behavior, but to laws against assault and theft.

It is not our basic purpose here to describe or criticize the claim that there is a link between exposure to ETS and various adverse effects on the health of nonsmokers. Our interest here is with the economics of the behavior of individuals with respect to ETS rather than with any possible direct medical consequences, about which there is a controversy.[2] At the outset, it is important to note that the argument about ETS is *not* an argument about whether or not some nonsmokers dislike tobacco. Obviously, some nonsmokers find tobacco smoke annoying. But by the same token, some non-sports fans find sports fans annoying, some non-vegetarians find vegetarians annoying, and so on. Freedom of choice implies freedom to do things which others may dislike. The proper focus of the argument over ETS is simple: Who would bear the costs? Economically speaking, it is not germane whether or not ETS causes health problems. What is relevant to the economic argument is whether or not smokers impose costs (either health related or not) on others involuntarily.[3]

In this chapter we shall first examine the economics of restrictions on smoking that are ostensibly designed to prevent the generation of external costs by smokers. We will then consider the problem of environmental tobacco smoke from the perspective of the Coase Theorem, considering the extent to which it theoretically represents the imposition by smokers of uncompensated costs on nonsmokers. Given that the Coase Theorem implies that the external costs of smoking are zero, we will next offer an economic explanation for the passage of such laws based on the transfers generated from smokers to nonsmokers. Finally, we will assess the relationship between smoking regulation and the concept of "public health."

The Economics of Clean Indoor Air Acts

Regulations designed to restrict the public consumption of tobacco, which apparently are grounded on the assumption that ETS exposure causes disease in nonsmokers, have been legion in recent years. These forms of legislation are usually referred to as Clean Indoor Air Acts, after the 1979 Connecticut bill by that name. Proposition P in San Francisco, which received tremendous media attention, although technically known as the Smoking Pollution Control Ordinance, is another example. These different Acts range greatly in severity--Connecticut's 1979 law was very limited in the range of places covered, while San Francisco's law has resulted in the prohibition of smoking in many places of work--but all have in common the same basic idea: smokers must be restricted by force of law from exhaling their tobacco smoke on unwilling non-smokers.[4]

The extent of such legislation to regulate smoking in public places has been massive over recent years. At the Federal level nearly 100 bills related to smoking or tobacco use were introduced during the 98th, 99th and 100th sessions of Congress (as of December 1987). Of these 100 bills, 17 were addressed to limitations on smoking in public places. These bills dealt with a variety of issues, such as the prohibition of smoking on domestic airline flights and the regulation of smoking in buildings operated by the Federal government. General federal legislation related to smoking introduced in the 101st Congress rose to a grand total of 200 bills.

Legislative activity with respect to smoking has also been massive and ongoing at the state and local level. Table 8.1 summarizes this activity through 1988. From 1979 to 1987, the number of smoking restriction bills introduced in the states increased by 68 percent. The rate of approval for these bills increased from 7 to 15 percent over the same period. Moreover, according to the data presented in the *Smoking and Health Report* of the Department of Health and Human Services, only 7 states have no laws regulating public smoking--Virginia, North Carolina, Tennessee, Alabama, Illinois, Missouri, and Wyoming. Of these, Virginia recently passed a public smoking ordinance. Table 8.2 gives a few

Table 8.1

Total Number of Smoking Restriction Bills

	State		Local		Total	
	Intr.	Appr.	Intr.	Appr.	Intr.	Appr.
1979	114	8	58	23	172	31
1980	98	1	60	32	149	33
1981	100	10	65	35	165	45
1982	86	4	79	42	165	46
1983	86	5	120	62	206	67
1984	109	4	180	65	289	69
1985	142	26	232	114	374	140
1986	140	17	255	139	395	156
1987	191	28	301	169	492	197
1988	189	18	253	123	411	130

Source: The Tobacco Institute

examples of these state laws and their provisions. At the local level, the HHS Report surveyed the 20 cities with the largest population for laws restricting smoking and found that some sort of restriction existed in almost all of these cities. In 1990, legislation was proposed in 35 states and the District of Columbia to restrict or increase limits on smoking. Twelve states and the District passed smoking restriction measures.

As the 1986 report of the National Research Council suggests, there are many unresolved questions regarding the issue of ETS and human disease. By contrast, the costs that will result from the enactment of a Clean Indoor Air Act which only address ETS are clear and high. These costs can be broken down into three major categories: the cost to businesses, the cost to the enacting government, and the cost to individuals affected by the law.

The cost to businesses can be usefully broken down further into two major groups: those affecting eating and drinking establishments and those affecting private workplaces, though there are important costs that are common to both. Restaurants can expect to face a significant loss in revenue to fast food and grocery stores, the exact extent and nature of

Table 8.2 State Laws Restricting Smoking

State	Employer's Responsibilities	Enforcement/Penalties	Other Public Smoking Restriction Areas
Connecticut (June 1983)	Establish written rules governing smoking and nonsmoking, post and provide copies to employees. "The rule may include the designation of non-smoking areas."	Not specified for private workplace. Other smoking laws carry $5 fine for violation.	Restaurants (75 + persons), health care facilities, elevators, retail food stores, public meetings, classrooms of public schools or colleges.
Montana (March 1979)	Designate nonsmoking areas, designate smoking areas, or designate entire areas as smoking. Post signs accordingly.	Enforcement by local boards of health. Penalty to employer (added in 1981) maximum $25.	Restaurants, stores, trains, buses, education and health facilities, auditoriums, arenas, public meeting rooms, elevators, museums, libraries, state/local government offices.
Nebraska (May 1980)	"To prohibit smoking in those places of work where the close proximity of workers or the inadequacy of ventilation causes smoke pollution detrimental to the health and comfort of nonsmoking employees" or "to make reasonable efforts to prevent smoking in the workplace" by "arranging seating to provide a smoke-free area," posting signs, asking smokers to refrain upon request of a client or employee suffering discomfort from the smoke.	Department of Health enforces. Fines up to $100 per violation by smoker or employer. Department of Health, local health board or any affected party may ask for injunction.	Restaurants, retail stores, public conveyances, education and health facilities, auditoriums, arenas, meeting rooms.
Utah (August 1976)	Make "reasonable efforts" by posting signs and "arranging seating to provide a smoke-free area." May use existing physical barriers and ventilation.	Enforcement by local boards of health. Fine up to $299 per violation by employer or smoker. Also, up to 90 days in jail for employer violation.	Restaurants, retail stores, public conveyances, health facilities, auditoriums, meeting rooms, buildings supported by tax revenues, any place that proprietor posts as no smoking. Regulations also include hotels, motels, and resorts.
Minnesota (June 1975)	By regulation, "Shall make arrangements for an acceptable smoke-free area: separated by 56" high barrier or by 4' space: or meeting specific ventilation standards; or meeting specific carbon monoxide limits. Must determine preferences of employees and other users, may designate smoking areas proportional in size to preference, using existing physical barriers and ventilation systems.	State and local boards of health enforce. Violation by smoker gets fine up to $100. Injunctive action against employer.	Restaurants, retail stores, public conveyances, education and health facilities, auditoriums, arenas, meeting rooms, state/local government offices. Hotels, motels, and resorts are included by regulation.

Source: The Tobacco Institute

which will depend on the precise nature of the Clean Indoor Air Act in question. Suppose that it is a relatively lax ordinance, and requires merely that a restaurant that permits smoking must provide a separate "smokers only" area. Because the composition of their customers on a given day between smokers and nonsmokers is unknowable in advance, the owner of such a restaurant would be unable to establish a "smoking" section of a size that was always correct. Sometimes he would designate "too much" space for his nonsmoking section, and other times he would designate "too little" (and the same with his smoking section). Consequently, he will frequently face the need of having to turn away otherwise willing customers due to the artificial scarcity of table space the law imposes. In the case of more stringent ordinances like the San Francisco statute, which grant nonsmokers essentially the power to veto *all* smoking on the premises if they so desire, this individual revenue loss is likely to be more straightforward and probably larger: some smokers will simply choose to stay home, or take out food. Other smokers will "vote with their feet" in cases where the restriction only applies to a limited area, and drive into another jurisdiction to buy their meal. Either way, restaurants can be expected to lose significant amounts of revenue, and this revenue loss will in turn represent the imposition of a loss on consumers, who have to spend time finding an alternative restaurant or who choose to eat out less frequently because eating out has become more costly.[5]

Another cost restaurant owners may have to bear is the cost of physically altering their establishments to make them comply with the Clean Indoor Air Act in cases where that Act requires that nonsmoking areas be set aside of a certain size in relation to the building capacity. For example, a study of the Clean Indoor Air Act in Montgomery County, Maryland, reported that about three-quarters of restaurant-owning respondents judged that the law would require them to make physical alterations of their property, and 16 percent estimated costs to amount to over $1,000. Also, the signs some laws require add another small, although in some cases significant, cost to complying with the law.

The costs likely to result from a Clean Indoor Air Act in the private workplace most importantly involve productivity losses resulting from compliance. Again, the actual loss will tend to vary with the actual law, and can be quite substantial. Consider the San Francisco ordinance, which requires employers to provide segregated facilities where smokers can smoke, and effectively requires that businesses also provide "smoking breaks" to smoking employees, instead of simply allowing them to continue to work while smoking. The cost of the physical arrangements together with the time lost to production due to smoking breaks which in turn would be necessary for maintaining the morale of smoking employees, may in some cases prove significant in themselves.

But there is another cost to the firm which is likely to be more difficult to measure, but which could have more important and detrimental consequences. This is the resentment and hostility between smokers and nonsmokers which may result from the imposition of a kind of "tobacco apartheid" in the workplace. If nonsmokers have the legal right to restrict the smoking of their tobacco-smoking fellow workers, resentment between the two groups will necessarily represent a potential problem and could adversely affect morale within the company. This lower morale could in turn be difficult to improve, and could itself result in a decline in productivity. Many firms are engaged in some kind of "team production," and the loss of the team spirit among employees could have serious consequences in terms of firm output.

Finally, Clean Indoor Air Acts will impose significant costs on individuals, though these are likely to be more difficult to quantify than the costs imposed on businesses. Individual smokers who find that the costs of eating out have risen for them, or who find themselves treated like second-class citizens in the workplace, are harmed in a simple and clear cut manner. The existence of a Clean Indoor Air Act brands smokers as social reprobates in the eyes of many who, not having the time or inclination to themselves peruse the technical literature and master its complexities, may trust the assessment of smoking rendered by the elected officials. This will not merely cause smokers undeserved discomfort but will generally tend to reduce the level of civility in society. Such acts add an artificial, additional source of conflict between groups of people who would otherwise have no grounds for dispute with each other. Clean Indoor Air Acts that focus solely on banning smoking serve to create conflicts between smokers and non-smokers where otherwise none would exist. A needless conflict is created which serves no economic purpose, and therefore represents pure waste from the standpoint of society as a whole.[6]

Indeed, the mere wording of Clean Indoor Air legislation sets the stage for such conflict. Consider a bill introduced in Hawaii's House of Representatives: "If a reasonable accommodation which is satisfactory to affected nonsmoking employees cannot be reached in any given office workplace, the preferences of nonsmoking employees shall prevail, and the employer shall prohibit smoking in that office workplace." Such language means that in some cases a single nonsmoking employee can determine the smoking policy of an entire company. The potential for conflict and lower productivity among a workforce is apparent in such a case.

Perhaps even more amazingly, the issue of ETS has been extended to encompass hiring practices. To date, only two state discriminatory hiring policies have been adopted. In 1986, an executive order was issued by the Governor of North Dakota approving the Department of Health's hiring policy, giving preference to nonsmokers for departmental jobs. The second was adopted by the Massachusetts State Legislature requiring all public safety personnel hired after January 1, 1988, to be nonsmokers. In five other states, anti-smoker proposals are still pending (California, Connecticut, Florida, Kansas, and Minnesota). Sixty-nine discriminatory hiring proposals have been introduced in localities around the country. Fifty-two policies have been adopted while seventeen were defeated. In 1977, Alexandria, Virginia, became the first locality to implement a policy requiring newly hired police officers to be nonsmokers. The policies either require future employees to be nonsmokers on and off the job or promote preferential hiring of nonsmokers. Of late, there has been a slight trend in some areas of the country toward prohibiting employment discrimination based on smoking status. Such legislation was introduced in 20 states and the District of Columbia, and was passed in Colorado, Kentucky, Rhode Island, South Carolina, and Tennessee.

What is obviously at stake here is not what a person does on the job, but what he or she does *off* the job. Such blatantly discriminatory hiring practices intrude into the private lives of employees, and, again, set the stage for costly litigation and arbitration, as well as for social conflict on a larger scale. Perhaps, however, we are putting the cart before the horse to some extent. As with all legislation, two issues need to be addressed. First, is there an economic rationale, such as market failure, for such laws? Or, can the market resolve the conflict between smokers and nonsmokers efficiently? Second, if there is no rationale in principle for such laws, why are they passed and who wins and who loses from their enactment? These are the issues to which we now turn.

The Coase Theorem, Ownership Rights, and Markets

The key idea behind Clean Indoor Air Acts is that it makes sense to claim that legally mandated restrictions on the peaceful behavior of individuals acting in markets will increase their welfare. But basic economic theory explains why this common claim is of dubious validity. Where a regime of private property rights prevails, the social costs of ETS are *zero*. Therefore, individuals are *already* maximizing their own welfare (subject to the constraints they face resulting from the existence of scarcity) without state restrictions on indoor smoking, and the enactment of new restrictions can only make people generally worse off.

Consider ETS in the context of privately owned public places.[7] The bar, the restaurant, the airline, and other firms are privately-owned entities with a residual claimant(s). In each case, the owner has an economic interest to provide the kind of environment that workers and customers want. For example, firms hiring employees in a competitive labor market will provide certain workplace environments as part of the optimizing compensation package. This may involve smoker-nonsmoker segregation on the job, investment in smoke-removal devices, paying smokers or nonsmokers a wage premium to work in a given environment, and so on. The point is that the owner will internalize such costs.

Suppose that all workers prefer to smoke on the job, but that the owner of a firm objects strongly to tobacco smoke in the workplace. Clearly, the owner must bear the costs of indulging his preferences. If he requires that his employees not smoke on the job and only offers the going market wage, no one will be willing to work for him. To induce his employees not to smoke, the owner must pay, over and above the competitive wage, a premium that is sufficient to make employment in his firm as attractive as alternative jobs where there are no restrictions on smoking. On the other hand, the owner can offer the market wage, allow smoking on the job, and invest in smoke-removal devices that bring the air quality to his liking. In either case, the costs of imposing a given smoking policy are internal to the owner of the firm.

Now, suppose that the owner is indifferent between smoke and smoke-free environments, but that some of the workers wish to smoke on the job and others prefer no tobacco smoke in the workplace. How does the owner reconcile these conflicting preferences? As one possible option, the owner can ban smoking and pay a wage premium to smokers. Alternatively, he can allow smoking on the job and compensate non-smokers. Yet other options are to segregate smoking and nonsmoking employees or to install smoke-removal equipment. Which of these is chosen will depend on such factors as the mix of smokers and non-smokers in the firm's work force, the cost and effectiveness of air cleaners, and the nature of the firm's production process, with this last consideration dealing with the extent to which co-workers can be separated without having adverse effects on overall productivity. Market forces will lead the owner to select the smoking policy that achieves the desired result at minimum cost. In a competitive market, we would therefore expect to observe a variety of smoking policies adopted across firms, each of which is optimal for the given circumstances.

Exactly the same argument applies to the owner of a restaurant, bar, or any other private firm that serves a public composed of smokers and nonsmokers. The market for dining out, for example, will discipline firms in the restaurant industry to provide preferred eating and drinking environments. This involves the mechanisms mentioned previously: smoker-nonsmoker segregation, smoke removal devices, price-environmental trade-offs, and so on. If the owner bans smoking, smokers will only patronize the establishment if the price-quality combination offered is as attractive as that in alternative eating places where smoking *is* allowed.[8] The opposite applies for nonsmokers if smoking is permitted. The owner can indulge his own preferences at a cost. Thus, a variety of smoking policies will arise in the marketplace, and in the process issues related to smoking in restaurants and bars are minimized.

The Coase Theorem also has implications for the regulation of smoking on airplanes, which is a particular type of indoor environment. For some time smokers and nonsmokers were segregated on airplanes. This system seemed to be working well with proportionately few complaints from passengers. Indeed, this system is still intact in other parts of the world, such as some countries in Western Europe, again with very few complaints, and the system still prevails for flights of over six hours that originate in the U.S. In other words, the market for passengers had worked out a resolution of the problem of public smoking, and individual firms were relatively free to experiment with alternative policies. Indeed, Northwest Airlines introduced a ban on smoking on all of its flights in 1988. All of this is perfectly consistent with the Coase Theorem. Northwest's policy had to meet a market test, and it would have either been good for Northwest's business or not. Other firms were free to experiment as well. What would have evolved would have been a variety of choices with respect to smoking policies and flying. Unfortunately the federal government intervened into this market process by passing legislation which took effect in 1989 which banned smoking on most domestic flights. Such legislation, in the economic sense of the Coase Theorem, can only make matters worse, on average.

In other words, with private property and residual claimants in place, the social costs of public smoking are approximately zero. The situation in the case of publicly owned facilities, managed not by residual claimants but by government bureaucrats with little motive to provide workers or consumers a smoking-nonsmoking environment consistent with their preferences, is admittedly not subject to the same salutary incentive effects. But even in publicly owned buildings, market forces can be expected to operate in a manner that minimizes any possible social costs of ETS. Government agencies must compete for workers with private firms, which as we have seen have strong incentives to provide employees with a work environment consistent with their smoking preferences. Therefore, those agencies must either provide similar accommodations to *their* employees, compensate them with a wage premium identical to what they could receive in the private sector, or they will be unable to attract suitable workers.[9]

So, even if we assume that ETS exposure can affect the health of nonsmokers adversely, rational adults operating in competitive markets will prevent uncompensated harm from occurring to anyone. Of course, some nonsmokers may be less risk averse (and hence more tolerant of those around them who smoke cigarettes) than some opponents of tobacco may consider wise. But one important feature of free society is the protection it affords individuals from busybodies who feel themselves qualified to enforce their own personal preferences on others.[10]

An Alternative Explanation

The need for an alternative interpretation of the origin of laws against public smoking is apparent. Private entrepreneurs have strong incentives to adopt smoking policies that minimize their costs, yet we observe various antismoking activists using the machinery of government to impose additional restrictions on smoking behavior in the workplace and other private establishments. It is plausible in this case, as in the case of many other laws, that the avowed "public-interest" motivation of the nonsmokers may be based on a more ordinary form of self interest. By way of illustration, consider a ban on smoking in the workplace. As a result, nonsmoking employees impose costs on actual and potential smoking employees. To the extent that such bans make the smoking workers less satisfied with their job situation, less likely to be hired, and so on, the wages of nonsmokers will rise relative to smokers. There is thus a simple redistributive basis for laws prohibiting smoking in the workplace -- they transfer wealth from smokers to nonsmokers.

We can see how this effect operates in a few of the possible settings. Take the case where a firm has an established policy of allowing smoking on the job, and is paying nonsmokers a wage premium that is just enough to induce them to work in the firm. Current employees who do not smoke clearly gain from a law which bans smoking in the workplace: the legislation allows them to get both the higher compensation and the working environment they prefer. The wage premium is transformed into a rent; nonsmokers are now being paid more than the amount necessary for them to have been willing to accept employment in a firm where no smoking is permitted. Moreover, potential employees who do not smoke also benefit. It will now be cheaper at the margin for the owner to hire nonsmokers than to pay a wage premium to induce smokers to work in the mandated workplace environment. In short, nonsmokers have made it more difficult for smokers to compete for their jobs.

These gains are of course only transitory. In the long run, competition among nonsmokers for jobs will drive wages down to the amount just necessary for them to accept employment in their preferred workplace environment. In the interim, however, nonsmokers earn rents, and these short-run returns provide a sufficient incentive for them to support no-smoking legislation. And do not think that the transitory, short-run nature of such gains provides only a weak incentive to seek after those gains. For at a 10 percent rate of discount, a gain that lasts seven years is half as valuable as one that would last forever!

Alternatively, suppose the firm has banned smoking and is currently offering a wage premium to smokers. We have argued that this additional compensation was necessary to attract smokers away from their next best alternative, namely, employment in firms that permit smoking on the job. Legislation which mandates the prohibition of smoking across the board reduces the need to compensate smokers. If no employer is able to offer jobs where smoking is permitted, smokers have fewer employment alternatives, and they therefore command smaller wage premiums. Accordingly, smokers suffer a real reduction in their economic welfare.

What about bars and restaurants? Here the argument is only a bit more complicated. In the absence of government intervention, some establishments will offer smoke-free environments while others will allow smoking under various conditions. An across-the-board ban on smoking forces restaurants and bars in the latter category to convert to no-smoking operations. The supply curve of smoke-free eating and drinking environments accordingly shifts to the right and, other things equal, this tends to lower the money price of dining out in a no-smoking atmosphere. Nonsmokers who eat out clearly gain from such an outcome: they obtain their preferred environment at a lower price. On the other hand, smokers and restaurant owners lose. As the price of meals eaten out declines, some restaurant owners will not be able to cover their opportunity costs; they will be forced to exit from the industry. (Exiting firms will most likely be those establishments where the cost of converting to no-smoking operations is high.) Smokers who buy meals out lose to the extent that the market price does not fall by enough to compensate them for having to dine in the mandated restaurant environment. This is just an extension of our earlier argument. A portion of the wealth transferred to nonsmoking employees by general prohibitions on smoking in the workplace comes at the expense of firm owners.

The interest-group explanation thus suggests that firms and smokers will generally oppose laws restricting smoking behavior, while non-smokers advocate them. In particular instances one group wins over the other, depending on such factors as the costs of organizing the respective coalitions and of influencing the political process. In any event, it would appear to be interest groups and wealth transfers and not concern over an externality that drives public policy in this area.

Our basic point is that considerations of redistribution, not economic efficiency, guide legislation about public smoking behavior. The Coase Theorem implies that in most private contexts, the relevant costs of smoking are zero. Bans on smoking behavior appear to emanate from nonsmokers who seek wealth transfers from smokers and from the owners of firms in the economy. In this respect, public policy toward smoking operates like many other regulatory programs, with wealth transfers as its central focus. Any positive explanation of policy in this area must confront this fact.

Tobacco and "Public Health"

In the public debate about environmental tobacco smoke, advocates of legal barriers to smoking continually imply that exposure to smoke is something smokers "do to" nonsmokers. This implication is revealed in language that speaks of nonsmokers "being exposed to" ETS, in contrast to language that speaks of nonsmokers as "exposing themselves to" ETS. This difference in language is important. The former use implies the absence of choice, with exposure to ETS being involuntary. The latter use implies the presence of choice, with exposure to ETS being a consequence of choice. In the days of the military draft it might have been accurate to speak of nonsmoking draftees "being exposed to" ETS. But as a general rule in a free society people "expose themselves to" ETS. To the extent nonsmokers associate with smokers (and encounter tobacco smoke as a result), this reflects their judgment that the benefits of that association at least equal to any claimed costs. In a market economy, individuals will frequently find it to their advantage to have dealings with those whose personal characteristics--whether involving table manners, personal appearance, how often they bathe, or whether or not they choose to smoke--are not entirely pleasing to them. If individuals continue to interact with others with disagreeable personal characteristics, it must be true that they perceive themselves better off by doing so.

This leads us to the basic problem with "public health" arguments as applied to questions involving smoking in public places. The standard public health paradigm is an external disease everyone would like to avoid, but which is transmitted by invisible organisms and which might be spread to innocent victims by means of only a brief exposure to carriers who may be almost impossible to identify as such (and who may not even know *themselves* that they are infected). In economic terms, the information and the transactions costs associated with identifying and avoiding the disease carriers is sufficiently high to prevent the emergence of efficient market mechanisms which allow the non-infected to protect themselves. For this reason, in some cases it is reasonable to require by law that certain measures be taken (e.g., a mandatory quarantine) to prevent the spread of the disease. But it makes no sense to apply the public health paradigm to the case of ETS. Even if we assume that ETS exposure has been shown to lead unambiguously to disease in non-smokers, ETS is clearly visible and gives off a noticeable odor, and lit cigarettes themselves are obvious. People may become exposed to smallpox or polio involuntarily and without their knowledge, but prolonged exposure to ETS cannot be anything but the result of *voluntary choice*.

It is an abuse of language to describe ETS exposure--or the consumption of tobacco more generally--as a "disease." The application of grossly inappropriate public health models to questions of regulation of smoking represents a substitution of ideology for science. The increasing tendency for disputes between those with different tastes to become transformed into "public health" issues of dubious empirical merit, of which the controversy over ETS and the enactment of Clean Indoor Air Acts constitutes an excellent example, should be of great concern to those who support institutions consistent with human liberty. The description of activities or behavior by others that some dislike as "disease" or "a public health menace," on the basis of the limited and contradictory evidence, is an expression of the increasing politicalization of society in which private disputes (which could be settled spontaneously and amicably by the relevant parties) become objects of unrestrained political conflict. Disputes formerly resolved efficiently through the efforts of profit-seeking entrepreneurs in private markets have increasingly become battlefields across which rent-seeking interest groups struggle for political favoritism. The appeal to the "public's health" is essentially just political rhetoric designed to camouflage the coercion. That appeal is not based on science, but rather represents *scientism* -- the articulation of scientific sounding rationalizations to support the use of coercion.[11]   The transition of the ETS question from a minor dispute settled peacefully and civilly by market forces to a violent conflict (which is both unnecessary and wasteful) oriented towards using the mechanism of political force is a sorry example of the politicalization of modern society at its most grotesque.

NOTES

1. For instance, Oster, Colditz, and Kelly (1984) is an attempt to develop individual level calculations of the various costs smokers supposedly impose upon themselves, in an effort to portray to smokers the benefits they could derive from quitting.

2. We are not medical scientists, but it should be stressed that the literature on the potential health effects of ETS is far from a consensus. See National Research Council (1986).

3. One technical point is especially important to keep in mind--namely, ETS is not the only possible factor in indoor air quality. There is a relatively young and new industry called building diagnostics, which conducts audits of the quality of indoor air in major buildings. These indoor air scientists have identified what is known as the "Sick Building Syndrome." The latter are buildings which are poorly ventilated and which have highly polluted indoor air. The key point, though, arising from building audits is that ETS is typically associated with a small number of complaints (2 to 4 percent) in sick buildings and that there are many dangerous substances in indoor air, including ozone, asbestos, fiberglass, bacteria, and fungus. In this context, banning smoking obviously does nothing about these other influences on indoor air quality, and, in fact, people are deluded if they think that banning smoking will improve indoor air quality. The problem is generally not ETS; it is to construct and maintain properly ventilated buildings.

4. Proposition P in San Francisco was the first Clean Indoor Air Act which was neither limited in the range of places covered nor simply required the separation (as opposed to prohibition) of smokers from nonsmokers.

5. There are other potential costs which arise from the same causes mentioned here. Obviously, as restaurants lose business, they will be forced to lay off workers, and unemployment will increase. Also, tax revenue will be reduced as a function of the reduction in restaurant revenues.

6. For a more detailed discussion of the waste resulting from such artificially created conflict, see Den Uyl (1986).

7. Much of the following argument is drawn from Shughart and Tollison (1986). Describing a privately owned business as a "public place" is very apt despite the fact that it is in a sense misleading. Obviously, it is really the *owner's* place. Customers and/or

employees only enter the premises at their own request and of their own free will. This would be true even if the private business in question had significant monopoly power, e.g., the only restaurant in town. But the overwhelming majority of industries that serve the public--and in particular the restaurant industry--is actually *intensely* competitive; owners have no hope of extracting monopoly rents from their customers by either charging excessive prices or not providing smoking/nonsmoking accommodations which are in accord with the preferences of the public. Not only is there likely to be another restaurant across the street eager to take the customer away by charging a lower price and/or offering better service, but there will in many cases be *dozens* of equally eager restaurants within a few blocks. In a competitive market, a privately owned business is literally a "public place" in the sense that the owner has no discretion in his decision making; if he fails to provide the quality of service consumers demand at a competitive price, he faces bankruptcy. For exactly this reason, the vision of (say) restaurant owners intentionally snubbing customers by refusing to provide optimal smoking/nonsmoking arrangements is ludicrous.

8. In other words, smokers will consider the marginal benefits and costs of different restaurants in making their choice of which establishment to visit, and will take all factors relevant to them--the decor, the cuisine, the prices of meals, and provisions for smoking, as well as many others--into account.

9. Admittedly, government managers are not residual claimants in the same sense as are private entrepreneurs, and therefore will have less incentive to search for and retain competent workers than private firms. However, while this will tend to reduce the efficiency of public as compared to private enterprises in the delivery of similar services, it remains the case that even public bureaucratic managers will lose their jobs if they fail to maintain a workforce of adequate size and minimum skills required to perform their assigned tasks. Therefore, even government enterprises are forced to provide working conditions and salaries that are competitive with those offered by private firms.

10. Buchanan (1986) has observed that busybodies may in the end be their own worst enemies by promoting institutional arrangements which may come back to haunt them: "Let those who would use the political process to impose their preferences on the behavior of others be wary of the threat to their own liberties, as described in the possible components of their own behavior that may also be subjected to control and regulation. The apparent costlessness of restricting the liberties of others through politics is deceptive. The liberties of some cannot readily be restricted without limiting the liberties of all" (p. 340).

11. See Buchanan (1986, pp. 340-341).

CHAPTER 9

Advertising, "Addiction," And The Denial Of True Choice

Many scholars question the constitutional validity of an advertising ban on tobacco products. There is also no question that some people seem to think that such a ban would constitute desirable public policy. However, there are several serious questions concerning both the costs and the benefits to be expected from any such restriction. This chapter attempts to compare the claims made for cigarette advertising bans by anti-smoking enthusiasts with the available economic evidence. A close look at the problem reveals several clear conclusions. First, the impact of advertising on consumers has been shown to be marginal and minor; cigarette advertising seems to have little, if any, effect on cigarette consumption. Second, cigarette advertising has not been shown to have a significant influence on smoking by young people. Third, cigarette advertising is a firm-specific phenomenon, which companies invest in for the purposes of competition, particularly in attempting to draw away existing market share from other companies and for promoting loyalty to their own brands. Fourth, the international evidence on smoking ad bans indicates that they have little, if any, effect on levels of cigarette consumption. Fifth, the U.S. Supreme Court has extended the protection of the First Amendment to "commercial speech" in a series of decisions, and any reversal of this trend would lead to a grave Constitutional crisis; and sixth, there is no meaningful link between advertising and cigarette "addiction."

Separating Advertising Myth from Advertising Reality

There is a remarkably durable popular myth about advertising that is repeated endlessly by critics of free enterprise. Ads allegedly brainwash consumers into buying goods they do not truly want; shoddy products are rescued from the incompetency of their manufacturers by clever commercials; and so on. To people who stand opposed to business as a mortal sin, advertising is the Bogeyman. There seems to be no limit to the absurd claims that are voiced about advertising, often by people who should know better.

Contrary to sometimes popular misconceptions, there is overwhelming economic evidence of the relatively negligible power of advertising to influence consumer demand. This extremely limited influence is often very obvious. Major and minor brands fall into obscurity; entire product lines pass into history; and even whole categories of products drop out of the market. The ability of advertising to affect consumer choice among available products is solely at the margin; an effective advertising campaign serves merely to increase slightly the probability that consumers will pay attention to the existence of the advertised product. Ads seek to make a particular brand stand out among a galaxy of other available brands, each competing for the attention--and the dollars--of the intelligent consumer. Further, thousands upon thousands of different products, all competing for consumer dollars, advertise at the same time. In such an intensely competitive environment, only the most modest effect of advertising on the sales of a specific brand of a particular product can possibly be expected.

This competitive environment is one fundamental reason why economists ascribe only a minor role to advertising in determining overall buyer expenditures. Another is that the formation of consumer demand and the structure of preferences among the millions of potentially available goods in the market is a highly complex phenomenon. In modern economies, the range of choice available to consumers is almost infinite. Many factors completely unrelated to advertising make a major impact on how consumers choose to spend their limited budgets, including age, income level, religious affiliation, geographic location, family history, and education, to name only a few. Advertising only stimulates primary demand for a product in very rare and unusual cases, and even this happens only in rapidly growing markets where demand expands for other reasons (e.g., as was the case with videocassette recorders). Obviously, cigarettes are not a "new" product subject to fast-growing demand.

A number of econometric studies have explored the relationship between cigarette advertising and sales, and these generally conclude that total advertising expenditures in a mature, competitive market--such as that in the United Kingdom or the United States--do not expand the total market for cigarettes. In other words, advertising does not increase the total number of cigarette smokers. For example, Sinnott (1979), in a study covering a 25-year period, concluded that no convincing evidence had been reported of a significant association between the total level of media advertising and total cigarette sales in the United Kingdom. Similarly, Chiplin, Sturgess, and Dunning (1981) concluded that the evidence for a causal connection between advertising and cigarette demand is "rather weak (p. 97)."

Data from other developed countries tells the same story. Johnson (1988) estimated the effect of advertising on aggregate cigarette demand in Australia, using a logarithmic demand specification that included a large set of variables designed to distinguish between a large number of possibly relevant factors. He reported that there is no statistically significant evidence linking advertising to cigarette demand in Australia. Advertising may well be important in inducing smokers to switch from one brand of cigarette to another, or to forestall such a switch, but it does not seem to be a means for increasing the share of smokers in the population.

Impact of Cigarette Advertising on Smoking by Youth

Since the evidence indicates that advertising has no impact on the demand for cigarette smoking by adults, and is intended only to influence which brand consumers choose to smoke, advocates of cigarette advertising bans have fallen back on a different claim--that ads lead young people to take up smoking. But recent research shows that this is simply not the case. Advertising has not been shown to be a significant influence on cigarette smoking by young people. For example, Flay *et al.* (1989) reported that peer influence and various social risk factors for smoking were strong predictors of smoking behavior among high school students, advertising was not. Another recent study by Moschis (1989) concluded that there is no clear evidence that advertising creates a desire to smoke on the part of young people, but that smoking tends to be part of a larger pattern of risk-taking behavior and is more prevalent among children of certain cultural and subcultural backrounds.

Two factors seem to be major influences over whether young people will take up smoking: parental smoking habits and peer pressure. In fact, the single best predictor of whether a young person will smoke appears to be whether that boy or girl has a best friend who smokes![1] A recent comprehensive survey of research on adolescent smoking reported that current research shows parental smoking habits also play a key role in whether or not a young person will take up smoking (Cleary *et al.* 1988). Advertising by tobacco companies has not been demonstrated to play a significant role in the decision of young people to smoke. However, the choices made by parents, siblings, friends, and acquaintances--sometimes called "word-of-mouth" advertising--are certainly one form of informal "advertising." The only way to ban "word-of- mouth" advertising would be to institute a totalitarian society.

For its part, the tobacco industry has opposed smoking by young people, and has sought to eliminate all advertising directed at young people. The industry code requires that all models in cigarette ads be and appear to be at least 25 years old. Sports figures and celebrities have been prohibited from ads by the industry's own code since 1964. The industry has even fielded an extensive advertising campaign designed to emphasize that smoking is a choice for *adults only*. More recently, the industry has mounted a 1990 Youth Initiative, which will support a variety of measures designed to limit the access of under-age individuals to cigarettes (both at retail and through vending) and to cigarette advertising. This Initiative also supports state laws restricting the sale of cigarettes to anyone under the age of 18.

Yet anti-smoking zealots are eager to exploit children in seeking their real goal of banning smoking for adults. This aim is particularly obvious in the recent agitation to ban or regulate more closely the sales of cigarettes from vending machines. The supposed reason for such a ban is that children, who cannot legally buy cigarettes in many areas of the country, might possibly buy cigarettes illegally from vending machines.

No convincing evidence is offered that any significant illegal purchases are made by children from vending machines. Why existing laws against selling cigarettes to children should not be enforced is not explained. What children are supposedly doing in bars, night-clubs, and gambling establishments, where most cigarette vending machines are located, in the first place is also left unexplained. The real aim of the anti-cigarette lobby seems clear: to prevent the purchase by adults of cigarettes from vending machines and to make smoking less convenient and more expensive to the grown-ups who prefer to buy cigarettes from vending machines. Proposed advertising bans, just like proposed vending machine bans, are political "Trojan Horses," designed to allow the anti-smoking movement to achieve by deception what it has failed to achieve in an open forum.[2]

Cigarette Advertising is a Firm-Specific Investment

So why do cigarette companies advertise so much if advertising does not increase the total demand for cigarettes? The answer is simple: the cigarette industry does not advertise; rather individual cigarette companies advertise their own, competing brands of cigarettes. Advertising in this industry represents a *firm-specific investment*; it is of no value to other businesses except the advertising firm itself. Companies advertise in an attempt to increase their own share of an existing market for cigarettes. Advertising is aimed at persuading existing smokers to purchase different brands of cigarettes than the brand they currently smoke or to stay with their current brand. Cigarette advertising is aimed at convincing smokers to switch or not to switch brands; it is not a vehicle for converting nonsmokers into smokers.

This situation is not peculiar to cigarettes, but is similar to the problem confronting the manufacturers of many other kinds of goods. For example, the automobile industry does not invest in advertising designed to get car owners to drive more or to buy more generic automobiles. General Motors, Ford, Chrysler, Toyota, Isuzu, and the multitude of other competing car companies all advertise to convince existing car owners that they should exchange their present automobile for a model manufactured by the advertising producer. Ford advertising is intended to sell *Fords*; and so on. The same is true with videorecorders, diapers, soft drinks, and most other goods we could name. The explanation for this pattern involves what economists term the *free-rider problem*: if Ford invested in advertising to convince car owners to buy more cars (of any make), or drive more (again, regardless of the make of their cars), a good part of the benefit from Ford's advertising would be received by other, competing car manufacturers. Advertising which increases the sales of your *competitor's* products is the short road to bankruptcy. Cigarette advertising behaves in exactly the same way. Competing cigarette companies advertise to pry consumers away from other cigarette companies, and to keep their own consumers.

Moreover, this competitive brand advertising improves the welfare of consumers. In a competitive market, advertising provides accurate, reliable information about the characteristics of the advertised product, and allows consumers to make better-informed decisions in the marketplace. For example, brand advertising makes consumers aware of the existence of new products and new product features (e.g., filters, lower tar and nicotine yields, and lighter and novel flavors). The very process of competition itself ensures that consumers will be provided with high-quality goods which improve over time, at the minimum possible cost. Poor quality goods will not survive in a competitive market. Overpriced commodities will quickly lose customers.

"Good quality" in this context is judged from the only standpoint relevant to economic science: that of the consumers themselves. As Ekelund and Saurman (1988, p. 77) explain, advertising is itself a good, and it provides valuable services to consumers:

> The demand for information and for noninformational messages through advertising originates in a market economy in which knowledge and information are not perfect. Information is both costly and beneficial. Advertising is exactly like any other scarce economic resource. In fact, in a world of imperfect knowledge and incomplete information on the part of consumers, *it is impossible to conclude that consumers would be better off with severe restrictions on advertising. While there are gaps in our economic understanding of advertising, it appears that any general notion of the consumer as being manipulated by advertisers will not bear careful scrutiny* (emphasis added).

International Evidence: Cigarette Advertising Bans Do Not Work

Advocates of a cigarette advertising ban in the U.S. are fond of pointing to the numerous foreign countries that have instituted similar bans. The implication is that the U.S. is somehow lagging behind more "progressive" countries, and that freedom of advertising speech is a dinosaur (at least where tobacco is concerned). They fail to point out, however, that international data suggests that cigarette advertising bans do not work.

A study by the International Advertising Association (Boddewyn, 1986) examined and compared the experiences of fifteen countries which have banned cigarette advertising (and includes one country, Sweden, that has no advertising ban, for purposes of comparison). In the seven non-communist countries studied, there was no evidence of any significant change in cigarette consumption resulting from the bans. Trends apparent before cigarette advertising was banned have continued in the period following the ban. In Thailand and Iceland, cigarette consumption has increased steadily *since the ban was imposed,* both overall and on a per capita basis (1.4 percent and 0.7 percent increases respectively). In Singapore, where the ban was less than total, cigarette consumption has similarly continued to grow steadily (a 1.4 percent per capita increase in Singapore since the 1970 ban). In Norway, there was a steady growth in consumption from 1975 (when the ban was imposed) to 1980; after 1980, cigarette consumption fell slightly leading to a slight net per capita drop since the 1975 ban of 0.6 percent. However, other factors greatly distorted the situation, such as a huge 59 percent cigarette price increase between 1980 and 1982 (compared to a general inflation rate of only 29 percent). But even so, the total incidence of adult smoking remained the same.

The IAA study also examined the record in eight communist countries. Cigarette advertising has been banned for more than thirty years in each of these countries, and therefore, communist countries provide a test case for the long-term effects of such bans. The evidence suggests that in the long run, cigarette bans may have the *opposite* effect than that claimed by their proponents. In all eight centrally planned economies, per capita cigarette consumption grew from 1970 to 1981 by an average of 14 percent, and aggregate cigarette consumption increased by 25 percent. At the same time, the nature of the cigarettes sold in those countries remained unchanged. Very little progress has been made in the development and sale of more modern cigarette products, like those with filters and lower tar, while in free market economies where advertising has been permitted such advances have led many product changes and innovations.

Finally, the study considered Sweden, where tobacco advertising is permitted (albeit with some restrictions). The IAA reported that per capita cigarette consumption had fallen slightly between 1976 (a date chosen as a mid-point between the bans in Norway and Finland), and 1982--about 0.6 percent. But the low-tar segment of the cigarette market--i.e., the percent share of cigarettes sold which had from 0 to 15 mg "tar" content--grew much more rapidly in Sweden than in Norway and Finland. By 1982, in the Swedish environment of free commercial speech, 48 percent of the cigarette market was for low "tar" types, compared with only 22 percent for Norway and 32 percent for Finland, where in each case cigarette advertising had been illegal for many years. This situation does not prove that advertising resulted in these changes, but it at least supports the position that advertising bans impede the development of new products.

Short of an outright ban, government can regulate advertising extensively, and has done so aggressively. The results of this regulatory effort have been meager. A recent study of the regulation of cigarette advertising by the Federal Trade Commission over the last 30 years reports that the actual effects have generally been the opposite of those intended. The 1955 advertising guidelines and the "informal agreement" in 1960 (later recinded in 1966) together banned advertisements by cigarette companies of lower tar and lower nicotine, even though cigarettes with such characteristics were widely thought at the time to be of increasing interest to consumers (hence, the interest on the part of the industry in advertising such characteristics). Similarly, the 1971 broadcast advertising ban promulgated by the FTC and imposed on the cigarette industry did not lead to any significant effect on U.S. cigarette consumption. In short, FTC regulation of cigarette advertising has been a history of duds and misses.

The Constitution and the Protection of Commercial Speech

On February 3, 1987, Senator Bill Bradley (D-N.J.) introduced a bill (S. 446) that, if enacted, would have disallowed tax deductions "for any amount paid or incurred to advertise any tobacco products."[3]   The sponsors explained that their goal was to penalize and thereby eliminate tobacco advertising; hence, the bills were effectively cigarette advertising bans under a different name. On June 14, 1990, Representative Henry A. Waxman (D-CA.) introduced an even more sweeping bill in the House that would essentially ban all tobacco product advertising. Many politicians seem to think that a cigarette advertising ban would be an attractive piece of legislation. Hence, we should consider the legal environment such a legislative ban would encounter.

The power of the U.S. Congress to regulate advertising springs exclusively from the Interstate Commerce Clause of the U.S. Constitution, which gives it power to regulate commerce among the states. This congressional power, however, is restricted by protection granted under the Constitution's First Amendment.

Two main bodies of law are particularly relevant here: *sales law* (contract law, including the *caveat emptor* principle) and *communications law* (based on the First Amendment). At first, advertising regulation was related only to the attachment of liability to the use of language in connection with a sales transaction and contract. The prohibition of false, misleading, and deceptive advertising through a variety of statutes (including the 1914 Federal Trade Commission Act and its subsequent amendments) rests on this notion that business must deliver what it promised. In this context, any tobacco advertising that is false, misleading, or makes or implies certain claims which cannot be substantiated might elicit regulatory attention. Since the 1930's, a number of FTC proceedings, proposals, and guides about cigarette advertising have involved these issues.

The term "commercial speech" is a legal term that refers to advertising communication by business. The initial definition of commercial speech began in the 1942 case, *Valentine vs. Chreatensen.* The Court ruled that commercial speech falls outside the ambit of First Amendment protection. The 1975 case of *Bigelow vs. Virginia* (*Virginia State Board of Pharmacy v. Virginia Citizens Council, Inc.*, 425 U.S. 748) established protection for commercial messages and justified that protection on the basis of the public's need for information. In the 1980 case of *Central Hudson Gas & Electric Corp. vs. Public Service Commission* (447 U.S. 557), the Court ruled that any restriction by government on commercial speech must serve its intended purpose and not be any more extensive than necessary.

Most recently, in the case of *Posadas de Puerto Rico Associates vs. Tourism Company of Puerto Rico* (106 S.Ct. 2968, 1986), the Court added another dimension to the test of restrictions on commercial speech: whether or not the underlying conduct that was the subject of the advertising restrictions was constitutionally prohibited and could not have been prohibited by the state. According to the Supreme Court, if an activity is not constitutionally protected, such as gambling, advertising for that activity can be banned--providing that such a ban is in accordance with the criteria outlined in *Central Hudson vs. Public Utilities Commission* (1980), mentioned above (Trauth and Huffman 1988).

Given the standard of protection afforded commercial speech by the Court in that (1980) case, the constitutionality of a total ban on cigarette advertising is questionable. In *Central Hudson*, the Court decision explained:

> At the outset, we must determine whether the expression is protected by the First Amendment. For commercial speech to come within this provision, it at least must concern lawful activity and not be misleading. Next, we ask whether the asserted government interest is substantial. We must determine whether the regulation directly advances the governmental interest asserted, and whether it is not more extensive than necessary to service that interest (447 U.S. at 566).

The first test set out by the court was that commercial speech refer to lawful activities and products and that it not be misleading. This test presents no problem for tobacco advertising since such a requirement is desirable to protect the quality of commercial information and to maintain general respect for the law. Thus, cigarette advertising passes the first two elements of the *Central Hudson* test. We saw above that the third test would also disqualify a cigarette advertising ban: Banning cigarette advertising has not been shown to lead to a reduction in cigarette consumption. A limited reading of *Posadas* leads to the conclusion that the ban would be unconstitutional due to the feasibility of less restrictive alternatives, such as health education programs.

Posadas is a peculiar case for a number of reasons. In the July 1, 1986 case, the Court upheld a ban on advertising of gambling casinos to residents of Posadas in Puerto Rico and ruled that even truthful advertisements for lawful goods and services may be restricted by the state to protect the "health, safety, and welfare" of its citizens. But the actual law in question was itself a dubious proposition. The 1940 Puerto Rican law permitted casino advertising to non-residents, but proscribed ads addressed to residents. Since the average resident of Puerto Rico (in 1940, and even today) was too poor to be of much interest to gambling casinos, which depended on the business of wealthier tourists, this particular law would superficially seem to have been a pointless restriction.

However, the real story behind the law suggests itself when its enforcement is examined. The law was so strictly enforced that the use of the word "casino" was prohibited on matchbooks, napkins, and in telephone books. In other words, casinos were prevented from advertising on the island of Puerto Rico, regardless of whether the intended audience for the ads were residents or tourists. The most likely explanation for this odd law involved the desire by larger, established casinos to restrict entry into the lucrative Puerto Rico gambling market by limiting the ability of newer and smaller casinos to advertise to visiting tourists. Only the larger casinos could afford to invest in advertising directed at the U.S. market, and desired to restrict the ability of smaller, newer casinos from competing away tourist dollars once those tourists were actually in Puerto Rico. The case that reached the Supreme Court stemmed from an action against the Condado Holiday Inn--a hotel with an attached casino--brought by another competing casino. In other words, the law had nothing to do with either the health, safety, or welfare of Puerto Rico citizens, but functioned as an anti-competitive entry barrier benefitting the larger casinos (Mayerowitz 1986).

Meanwhile, it is clear that some members of the present Supreme Court are not neutral parties. The present Chief Justice of the U.S. Supreme Court, William Rehnquist, is on record as being hostile to advertising in general. He has been an opponent of efforts to extend First Amendment protections to commercial speech. He wrote in one case that the First Amendment "demeaned itself" by protecting advertisements! He dissented in *John R. Oates and Van O'Steen vs. State Bar of Arizona* (1977), which struck down a state law against lawyers advertising their services. And he dissented from *Central Hudson*, again claiming that the First Amendment was "demeaned" by being used to protect commercial speech (Colford 1986, p. 12). Thus, it comes as no surprise that the Chief Justice suggested that the logic employed in *Posados* could be used to justify governmental restrictions on products or activities, such as cigarettes, alcoholic beverages, and prostitution.[4]

On the other hand, *Posadas* was carried with a knife-edge 5-4 majority, and is therefore unlikely to provide a basis for sustaining any cigarette advertising ban, or even a quasi-ban. Professor Philip B. Kurland (1987, p. 9), of the University of Chicago Law School has cautioned that *Posadas* should not be relied upon because its reasoning, if taken at face value, "is so inconsistent with everything that has gone before." If one interprets the narrow majority decision as meaning that there are no limits on government's power to suppress truthful speech about lawful products, then almost all of the Supreme Court's commercial speech decisions since 1976 would have to be scrapped.

The values illustrated by the First Amendment are central to the efficient functioning of the economic and political systems of all democratic countries. A ban on the truthful advertising of cigarettes could lead to a general unraveling of the First Amendment protection for speech more generally. The threat to the First Amendment posed by banning cigarette advertising has been succinctly stated by Arthur Spitzer (1989, p. 161):

> A ban on cigarette advertising would be censorship, pure and simple, and it would inevitably lead to the censorship of a variety of other speech...[following such a ban] Some states will ban advertising for handguns. Other states will ban advertising for abortion clinics and condoms. Many may ban advertising for alcoholic beverages. Perhaps Michigan will ban advertising for foreign cars, and maybe Wisconsin ("the dairy state") will ban advertising for margarine and non-dairy creamers. Why shouldn't Florida agree to ban advertising for Idaho potatoes if Maine will agree to ban advertising for California orange juice? Why not ban advertising for eggs, palm oil and other high-cholesterol foods? Why not ban advertising for X-rated movies? Why not for R-rated movies, too?

Spitzer is the Legal Director of the American Civil Liberties Union of the National Capitol Area.

More recent Supreme Court decisions have underscored the serious

First Amendment obstacles to banning or severely restricting tobacco product advertising. One decision, *Peel* vs. *Attorney Registration and Disciplinary Commission of Illinois*, 58 U.S.L.W. 4684 (U.S. June 4, 1990), effectively settles any question raised by *Posadas* or *Fox* concerning the degree of protection afforded to commercial speech under the First Amendment. In *Peel*, the Supreme Court held that, under the First Amendment standards applicable to restrictions on commercial speech, a state may not prohibit a lawyer from advertising his or her certification as a trial specialist by the National Board of Trial Advocacy. Three aspects of the Court's decision in *Peel* are pertinent here.

First, *Peel* signifies that the Court continues to demand rigorous justification of restrictions on commercial speech and painstakingly examines the asserted link between means and ends. Second, *Peel* reaffirms the Court's particular distaste for commercial speech restrictions that smack of paternalism. Third, *Peel* suggests a basic shift on the Court in favor of greater First Amendment protection for commercial speech. In any event, *Peel* suggests a current majority of the Court that would subject to stringent First Amendment scrutiny under *Central Hudson* any attempt to ban or severely restrict tobacco product advertising.

But merely predicting which direction the Supreme Court will jump is really beside the point. There are more fundamental issues here than "handicapping" potential Court decisions as so many legal horse races. Freedom of speech is either an absolute principle, or exists at the whim of politicians and politically-appointed judges. There is no middle ground. When we begin to admit "exceptions" to the Constitutional freedom of speech, the First Amendment will begin to unravel. If "commercial speech" is excluded from the umbrella of First Amendment protection, the freedom of speech of all kinds is jeopardized. Some would also favor redefining the First Amendment to exclude political speech they do not like; others would attempt to exclude speech concerning unpopular religions; and still others would move to ban the expression of unfashionable views about art. We can either have freedom of speech, or give it up. Government cannot just pick and choose, rejecting freedom for speech about things temporarily out of political favor, meanwhile guaranteeing freedom for speech politicians happen to like to hear (today!). Such a political travesty of free speech would be equivalent to replacing the First Amendment with the "rule" that whomever happens to be in power at the moment can decide what speech is permissible. Eastern Europe just underwent a revolution to achieve the kind of freedom some American politicians seem willing to repudiate for momentary electoral advantage.

Advertising and Addiction

Advertising is a commercial endeavor designed to communicate relevant information to rational consumers about the availability, price, and quality of commercial goods. Therefore, if cigarettes are conceded to be an ordinary good, truthful cigarette advertising can only benefit consumers-- and efficient markets will ensure that advertising is truthful. The anti-smoking lobby responds by asserting that cigarettes are not an ordinary good. Instead, they insist that cigarettes are an addictive substance, and therefore advertising of cigarettes leads consumers to adopt a habit which they cannot break. Proponents of the "addiction model" of smoking insist that a ban on cigarette advertising is necessary to break this cycle of addiction.

But this "addiction model" is a house of cards built on quicksand. Rational individuals who are observed to make particular choices are necessarily maximizing their own individual welfare, as they see it. Someone else might not care for the choice a particular individual actually makes, but that someone else has no basis for claiming that a rational person will intentionally choose in such a way as to reduce his or her own welfare. Given the information at their disposal, and the other resources (e.g., money) available, rational actors will always choose what is best for them. The modern teetotalers and Temperance Leaguers have evaded this problem by simply declaring that people who make "wrong" consumption choices are *not* rational. Instead, they are addicts. This pseudo-clinical term allows moralists and busy-bodies to posture like scientists. *Addiction* is a term of opprobrium which sounds like a medical diagnosis. But as we shall see, it is really a vacuous assertion.

If cigarette smoking is called an "addiction," it is a very peculiar one; millions of cigarette smokers have successfully quit smoking altogether, and many millions more have successfully reduced their cigarette consumption. Therefore, cigarette smoking is a form of behavior which is entirely under the control of the smoking individual. The anti-tobacco lobby likes to whistle past this uncomfortable fact, and prefers to complain that the millions of existing smokers would really like to quit but somehow cannot control themselves and smoke anyway. But one could make a similarly specious argument about any activity that some individuals enjoy. Many people enjoy smoking. It is fatuous to deny this obvious fact, and instead to make claims about "addiction." If the term addiction is simply a reference to an activity that one person enjoys although someone else disapproves, then the "problem" of addiction is cured when busybodies learn to mind their own business.

All choosing individuals have at least one thing in common: they make the choices they do in order to maximize their own personal utility. The political junkie judges the advantages of remaining in the U.S. to outweigh the costs, and passes up the opportunity to leave for a different country with an ongoing political campaign. The gardener feels that the costs of moving from Wisconsin are greater than the advantages (including year-round gardening) of living in Florida. The smoker may decide that the advantages of quitting are greater than the disadvantages, including the loss of smoking enjoyment.

Thus, it is sheer nonsense to claim that cigarette advertising leads rational adults to become addicts who are compelled to smoke against their wishes. Adult consumers are intelligent, rational utility maximizers who pattern their choices in a manner which they judge to be optimal given their own preferences and inclinations. Calling the consumer of a good or service you disapprove of an "addict" represents an arbitrary value judgement thinly disguised as a scientific statement. It is language pollution of the worst sort.

The New Economics of Addiction

Recently, economists have begun to argue that there is no good reason for assuming that "addiction" is necessarily "irrational." These writers argue that "addiction" is a useful term for describing the phenomenon of past consumption affecting future consumption, and that this phenomenon can be shown to be quite consistent with rational behavior on the part of the consumer. One of the positive features of this "model of rational addiction" is that it eliminates the moralistic references to "dysfunction" and the like, and focuses solely on the relationship between past and future consumption. Thus, alcohol, cigarettes, and caffeine can be accommodated within this model, as well as other "addictive" activities such as work, eating, music, television, and even a standard of living, to other people, religion, and many other activities. The model has the virtue of explaining a wide variety of "habit-forming" behaviors without imposing external value judgments on the consumers involved. The most important article in this literature is Becker and Murphy (1988).

Addictive goods, in the Becker and Murphy sense, are ones in relation to which consumers tend to be relatively unresponsive to temporary changes in price. But those same consumers tend to be much more responsive to permanent changes in price. The term "addiction" is often taken to imply that the addict is completely unresponsive to changes in price, i.e., the consumer's demand curve is vertical. The price of the addictive good is purportedly irrelevant to the addict. However, Becker and Murphy point out that this stereotype rarely fits with the facts, and is obviously inapplicable to cigarette consumers. Numerous studies have shown quite the opposite in the case of cigarette smoking; the demand for cigarettes is not completely inelastic, that is, unresponsive to price. Estimates of the elasticity of demand for cigarettes range from around .4 to around .6 (see Becker and Murphy 1988, p. 686). An elasticity coefficient of .6 means that for every 10 percent increase in the price of cigarettes, the quantity of cigarettes purchased will drop by 6 percent. For purposes of comparison, the elasticity of demand for cigarettes is only slightly lower than the elasticity of demand for automobiles (.8), somewhat higher than some estimates for the residential demand for electricity (.2), and about the same as the elasticities of demand for such ordinary goods as milk, eggs, and gasoline (Glahe and Lee 1989, p. 81). Cigarette smokers respond to price changes in the same way that rational consumers normally respond to price changes.

Becker and Murphy argue that rational consumers will recognize the money value of expected changes in future utility and earnings induced by current consumption choices, and add these expected costs to the market price of the goods they consume. For example, rational consumers will understand that hang-gliding is associated with certain risks to life and limb, and take these expected costs into account when allocating their resources between hang-gliding and other things. The theory of hedonic markets implies that the market price of the goods will themselves be affected by the perceived costs associated with consumption. This has important implications for the economics of quitting smoking.

Property situated next to a garbage dump will sell at a lower price than similar land located elsewhere, the lower value reflecting the less desirable location. Similarly, a brand of automobile with a better-than-average service record will tend to sell at a higher price than an otherwise similar make and model with a worse service record. In both cases, the market price will tend to reflect the net value of all quality dimensions of the good which are relevant to the consumer. Some consumers will prefer to pay extra for the car with the better-than-average expected maintainance requirements; others may prefer to live on the lower priced, but less pleasingly located, tract. Rational consumers will allocate their scarce resources so as to achieve the best price-quality mix from their own personal perspective. Consumers maximize their utility derived from goods, not necessarily the *quality* of those goods. Sometimes, the utility-maximizing choice will be the one that combines somewhat lower quality with a somewhat lower price.

This is relevant to the question of "addictive" goods. Assume that a person expects to gain enjoyment from consuming some good, but recognizes that this particular good has "addictive" properties--that is, after some period of time, ceasing to consume the good will entail some costs to the consumer. If the consumer expects such a phenomenon to occur, the cost of quitting (i.e., the expected costs associated with ceasing consumption, times the risk that the consumer will actually want to cease consumption at some later date) will normally be fully reflected in the price of the given good.

Some people reportedly experience degrees of difficulty in quitting smoking, although these difficulties vary from person to person. Former smokers often report some temporary weight gain, sometimes become irritable, and generally miss the smoking habit for a period after they quit. These potential difficulties are well understood by normal adults. They also have not prevented millions of smokers from becoming *former* smokers when they decided that non-smoking was the best choice for them. There is even an industry which has grown up to provide quitting-assistance services to smokers who want to stop smoking. The standard contract for this service costs about $400, and "money-back quarantees" are common.

These expected costs must necessarily be reflected in the price of the cigarette product. Simply stated, if the risk of temporary discomfort associated with quitting smoking was zero (and hence, the expected cost of quitting was also zero), the price of cigarettes would be significantly higher than it is. This means that in an efficient market for cigarettes, the expected costs of quitting will have been fully *internalized* into the price. If we choose to describe cigarettes as an "addictive" good (which term has recently come to refer to a vast array of commodities), then the same economic argument applies. To the extent that quitting smoking entails expected difficulties, these expected difficulties are reflected in the lower price smokers will be willing to pay for cigarettes.

The only important exception might occur in a case where the habit-forming substance was marketed by a pure monopoly, in which case the monopolist might engage in "price discrimination," charging a very low price to new smokers (who have not yet acquired a habit), and significantly increasing the price charged for the same kind of cigarettes to long time smokers. Even in this extreme case, however, the scheme would probably be unworkable, because it would be practically impossible to prevent new smokers from buying up cigarettes at the cheaper price, and reselling them to the more habituated smokers at a higher price, thus robbing the monopoly of its profit. But in the real world, the cigarette industry is highly competitive, with numerous different manufacturers marketing dozens of competing brands. Price discrimination cannot work in a competitive, open market.

Consumer Sovereignty or Health Fascism?

The free market economy is founded on the rule of consumer sovereignty: products succeed or fail and businesses profit or go bankrupt on the basis of how well they provide to consumers what those consumers most urgently desire. The freely expressed preferences of consumers guide the allocation of resources among competing possible goals. Businesses compete to satisfy those expressed preferences. An efficient market is a democracy in the best sense; not just the votes of the majority but the "votes" (choices) of literally all consumers carry weight in the allocation of resources.

Free markets have one unavoidable drawback, however. When

consumers are left free to make whatever choices they as individuals perceive to be the best, some consumers will choose patterns of consumption that some other people will not like. There is inevitably some person or group who feels aggrieved at the choices made by others in the marketplace, even in cases where those choices can be shown to have absolutely no measurable impact on the well-being of the objectors. As efficient as free markets are as resource allocators, as long as some people are unwilling to mind their own business, not even the most efficient market possible will ever make everyone happy.

In recent years, smoking has become an activity which some people object to in principle. Many in the anti-smoking lobby would probably oppose tobacco use even if it could be absolutely proven that smoking has no adverse health effects on anyone. Advocates of cigarette advertising bans essentially wish to prohibit choices of which they do not personally approve. Proponents of cigarette advertising bans aim at restricting smoking regardless of the fact that advertising has not been shown to ever have forced any adult to take up smoking involuntarily. To anti-smokers, cigarettes are just *immoral*. It is unfashionable simply to admit that one's opposition to an activity is based on moral grounds. The modern habit is to disguise moral judgements behind the decision to mind other people's business for them by advocating an intrusive public policy as necessary to promote health.

How else are we to explain the behavior of anti-smoking zealots? One of the clearest indications of the religious-like nature of much of the opposition to cigarette advertising are the recent episodes involving the vandalism of cigarette billboards in urban areas. These "protests" are usually claimed to represent the hostility of members of the black community to tobacco products. Ironically, prominent members of the black community are strong defenders of tobacco advertising.[5] The real cause of such violent episodes appears to be the bigotry of anti-smokers, who are willing to sacrifice free speech and the expressed preferences of cigarette smokers at the altar of their anti-smoking religion.

If professional opponents of tobacco simply admitted that they opposed cigarette advertising because they believe smoking is immoral, people would start to ask embarrassing questions, like: says who? Americans are naturally skeptical about any supposed "morality" which presumes that peaceful behavior must be coercively regulated. But this natural skepticism can be cleverly outflanked by packaging the same coercive goal as a "health" measure. This little bit of legerdemain works because references to "health" sound medical, clinical, and scientific. But underneath the rhetoric is the same odious moral presumptuousness: my personal health choices are somehow not my own business.

The anti-smoking movement, and in particular its hue and cry for a cigarette advertising ban at any cost, has at its base an odious philosophical premise: people can and should be coerced to make "healthy" choices. There is no demonstrated evidence that a cigarette advertising ban would have lead to a drop in consumption, and, therefore, presumably a positive effect on the health of smokers or non-smokers. But assume, just for the sake of argument, that some new study comes along and finds that a cigarette advertising ban will reduce the demand for cigarettes and, consequently would supposedly lead to improvement in the health of smokers. Restricting free commercial speech would amount to replacing consumer sovereignty in the free market with government compulsion to make the "right" choices. This violation of human rights is not magically justified by invoking "health." An individual's choices which may affect his or her health represent that person's best efforts to maximize his or her well-being. Forcing individuals to make different choices, whether for reasons of "health," religion, or ideology, necessarily make those same people *worse off*.

Fascism technically refers to a form of state socialism where the government "manages" the economy by making most or all important decisions for individuals (usually for some supposedly "higher purpose") without actually nationalizing all property. The anti-smoking lobby advocates a form of "health fascism," in which Health--irrespective of the desires, goals, and plans of individuals--is touted as the only true aim of government policy. We need to recall the Founding Fathers' dedication to the separation of Church and State, and understand that Public Health has become a secular church, whose followers think individual liberty to be an annoying impediment to their Holy Quest.

NOTES

1. See Glazer (1989, p. 152).

2. It should also be noted that health education programs cannot be shown to reduce smoking in any significant way. See the comprehensive survey of anti-smoking education program results in Cleary *et al.* (1988, pp. 142-149). The authors describe the results of 17 different studies of smoking prevention programs as only showing "modest" effects. and point to numerous methodological shortcomings in the research.

3. On March 11, 1987, Representative Stark introduced a similar bill (H.R. 1563) that would have gone even further, and prohibited deductions for *any* communications about tobacco products.

4. The intensity of the Chief Justice's animosity towards tobacco is evident in his lumping cigarettes and alcoholic beverages with a blatantly illegal activity, prostitution. See Waterson (1986) for further discussion of Rehnquist's views on advertising.

5. See Glazer (1989, pp. 156-157) for a discussion of the widespread opposition in the black community to restrictions on cigarette advertising.

CHAPTER 10

Self Interest,
Public Interest,
And Legislation

W e have suggested in several places that political processes follow an economic logic, and that in so doing the outcomes of political processes often conform quite poorly to the values and norms that are commonly presumed to inform public policy discourse. In this and in the next chapter, we explore more fully this cleavage that often separates normative or value statements about public policy from the empirical consequences of the policy measures that are actually enacted.

Corrective Cigarette Taxation: An Analytical Unicorn

The use of taxation as a tool for social control leads us back to the problem of social cost. Virtually all rationalizations for the taxation of specific goods and services are based on a presumption that voluntary exchange can impose damages on third parties. In light of this presumption, the proper role of government is to force private decision makers, through "corrective" taxation and regulation, to bear the full cost of their activities. As we saw in Chapter 3, however, the language of social cost often serves more as an instrument of political advocacy than as a meaningful category of economic analysis. Such costs do not have prices associated with them and hence are not measurable. Because they are not measurable, social costs can easily become analytical unicorns -- interesting hypothetical situations of little relevance to the real world. Furthermore, even if it were somehow established that an activity generates a cost of $X to some third party, this does not imply that eliminating that cost would be economically efficient, because the effort to do so might cost more than it gains. To the extent that alleged external costs continue to exist over time, it becomes increasingly likely that it would cost the parties involved more to alter the situation than they would gain by doing so. In short, people who support the increased taxation of tobacco products should look elsewhere to rationalize their policy preferences, because claims of social cost are too deeply steeped in mythology to withstand critical scrutiny.

Even if the weaknesses of arguments grounded on the concept of social cost are set aside, the case for the discriminatory taxation of tobacco products is weak. The costs of smoking are private costs borne by smokers. As we have discussed in earlier chapters, the alleged social costs generated by a smoker evaporate upon careful scrutiny. This is so even if it is assumed that there are adverse disease consequences for nonsmokers due to working or otherwise associating with smokers. In a free society people choose those with whom they associate. The persons with whom an individual spends time are those with whom such association is regarded as beneficial on balance. A person may choose to associate with someone who has bad body odor, tells stupid jokes, has poor taste in clothes, or who possesses other personal characteristics found distasteful, because there are gains from that association that outweigh those costs. An additional factor which will be relevant to some people is whether a potential associate is a smoker. If someone continues to associate voluntarily with a smoker, either in the workplace or elsewhere, the benefits that person derives from that association must be assumed to exceed the costs. Smoking is no different than a number of other forms of personal behavior in this sense. The same calculus applies--is this association worth the costs to me?--in cases involving the dressing, drinking, driving, and cursing behavior of others, as well as all other facets of personal behavior which some may find objectionable.

The usual rationalizations for selective taxation as a tool for increasing economic efficiency (by forcing individuals to bear the social costs of their activities) and as a means for paternalistic protection of the unwashed from their vices are not only weak in and of themselves but are also inconsistent with the liberal values on which a free society is based. Americans in particular have traditionally been extremely skeptical of government as a Big Nanny, and in this context the usual arguments justifying selective taxes on goods like cigarettes represent a weak basis for such taxes. This leads to the inevitable conclusion that the rationalizing rhetoric of selective taxation covers up more plausible motivations for such taxes.

What, then, can we infer about the use of such taxes? Are selective excises, which are rationalized by fallacious arguments about correcting for social costs, simply the result of mistaken reasoning? To some extent simple intellectual confusion may contribute to the support for such discriminatory levies, but unless we are willing to abandon the assumption that individuals are rational maximizers--i.e., that people in general are not systematically stupid--confusion alone is not a plausible candidate for a complete explanation. As economists we need to ask, who gains from discriminatory excise taxes, and who loses?

The answer is fairly clear and can be summarized by paraphrasing the Golden Rule: he who has the gold makes the rules. Smoking is more customary among the working class and poor; lawyers, college professors, and legislators are not usually smokers. Smoking is like bowling -- it tends to be a working-class, leisure time activity. But unlike bowling, which non-bowlers largely ignore (perhaps because it is only practiced in bowling alleys), smoking is often conducted in public places and hence offends the sensibilities of many upper-income people. It is irrelevant *why* their sensibilities are offended. They may believe that their own health is harmed by the smoking of others, or that smokers need to be protected from themselves, or simply that smoking is gauche, aesthetically unappealing, and unfashionable. Rules prohibiting smoking in public places are an effective means of discrimination without violating anti-discrimination laws; discriminatory excise taxes on cigarettes help to ensure that "those" people behave "properly." A specific excise tax on polyester clothing would serve the same function, protecting the fashionable from the "bad taste" of the poor.

Unfortunately for them, smokers are a relatively easy target for excise taxation. They face high organization costs with relatively meager resources as a group to fight taxation. Perhaps more importantly, they have been so thoroughly educated about the supposed social irresponsibility of smoking that guilt prevents them from mounting a determined resistance to tax discrimination. This politically immobilizing guilt, carefully cultivated by the opponents of smoking may help to explain why poll data indicate that at any given time large numbers of current smokers claim to be trying to quit. It is only natural to prefer to be viewed as a victim of a "bad habit" than as an intentional social reprobate.

This relative vulnerability is exploited by politicians whose aim is always to increase tax revenues because revenue is the primary raw material for the wealth transfers that have become government's principal activity. In contrast to smokers, other potentially taxable groups of citizens who have higher incomes and are better organized politically can impose higher costs on politicians who seek to tax them. Truck drivers, waitresses, carpenters, and welfare recipients who smoke have little clout. The exploitation of relatively vulnerable groups like smokers with discriminatory taxation increases political revenue at the margin over what it would be in the absence of such discriminatory exploitation.

So discriminatory excise taxes on tobacco products accomplish two distinct but consistent ends. One is that such duties help to keep people with offensive tastes in line, reducing their tendency to engage in distasteful and unfashionable activities which offend the same people who regard bowling alleys as museums of primitive culture. The other is that the revenue from such taxes can be extracted at relatively low political cost by legislators who have demands to fund transfers to special-interest groups. The fashion-mongering snobs and the rent-seeking politicos form an unholy alliance, the outcome of which is the imposition of a highly regressive tax on those with lower incomes, for the different but compatible purposes of social control and revenue maximization.

An Economic Approach to Legislation and Regulation

Legislation as an Economic Process: An Overview.   For almost two hundred years it was common for most economists to assume that the realm of economics was the wide world outside the hall of the legislature and the other offices of government. Private interest ruled the economic world, but the decision making of government was guided by the public interest calculated by selfless public servants who constantly strove to improve the welfare of society. The revolution in economics known as Public Choice changed all this. The decision making of government was now admitted to be part of the economic universe. Government officials were recognized as being neither better nor worse than ordinary private citizens, as being motivated by neither more nor less noble goals.

One of the most important developments to arise from the public choice revolution has been the extension of economic analysis to the process by which legislation is actually produced in legislatures. A growing literature has shown that the process of legislating by a legislature can be effectively modeled as the output of a kind of market, with unusual characteristics to be sure, but nevertheless conforming to the same economic principles as production in more ordinary kinds of markets.[1]

A basic principle as well as a basic problem informs the demand for legislation. The principle is that groups who can organize for less than a dollar in order to obtain a dollar of benefits from legislation will be the effective demanders of laws. The problem is that economists have little idea of how successful, cost-effective interest groups are formed. That is, how do groups overcome free rider problems and organize for collective action so as to be able to seek a dollar for less than a dollar?[2]

One theory that attempts to answer this issue is the by-product theory of group collective action.[3] According to this theory, an association provides a private service to its members that cannot be purchased competitively elsewhere. By pricing the service in a monopolistic fashion, the association raises money for lobbying.[4] Alternatively, George Stigler suggests that an asymmetry of firm sizes, products, and interests in an "industry" tends to promote more effective collective action by the industry (e.g., a larger association budget).[5] He argues that participation is mandated by the desire to protect specialized industry interests. These are interesting and useful arguments, but they only begin to solve the difficult analytical problem of group formation and the demand for legislation. At best, one can take the existing array of interest groups and associations in the economy as an expression of such a demand function. Somehow, these groups have become organized as demanders of legislation and other types of government action.

Indeed, for whatever reason organization is undertaken, lobbying for special legislation becomes a relatively low-cost by-product of being organized. For example, a firm is an example of an organization that can be used for lobbying purposes. Laborers may organize to bargain collectively and then find it relatively easy to set up a Washington office to advocate favored union policies. Lawyers may agree collectively to a code of ethics to address such matters as attorney-client privilege and then proceed to adopt provisions in their code that restrict competition among lawyers.

In the interest-group theory, those who "supply" wealth transfers are individuals who do not find it cost effective to resist having their wealth taken away. In other words, it costs them more than a dollar to resist having a dollar taken away. This concept of a supply curve of legislation or regulation suggests that the costs of political activity to some individuals exceed the potential gains (or avoided losses). The supply of legislation is, therefore, grounded in the unorganized or relatively less-organized members of society.

The individuals who operate the market for legislation are politicians, bureaucrats, and other political actors. These individuals may be conceived of as brokers of legislation, and they essentially act like brokers in a private context--they bring together those who have a demand for legislation with those who are able to supply it. In the usual logic of the interest-group theory, brokers will concentrate on legal arrangements that benefit well-organized and concentrated groups for whom the pro rata benefits are high at the expense of diffuse interests, each of which is taxed a little bit to fund the transfer or legislation. By efficiently pairing demanders and suppliers of legislation, the political brokers establish an equilibrium in the market for legislation. Obviously, mistakes can be made in this process. If "too much" legislation is passed, some parties will find it cost effective to organize and to remove inefficient and overreaching brokers in the next election.

For better or worse, then, legislatures are a kind of marketplace. Legislators supply output in the form of legislation to demanders who bid against one another for bills in a kind of auction. These demanders are various interest groups who may represent huge industries, or major labor unions, or individual companies, or even individuals seeking a tax break. Legislation supplied--that is, bills actually passed--are thus not the result of some Olympian deliberation by white-robed, selfless legislators, but the result of vigorous competitive bargaining and haggling in which interest groups bid against one another for legislative favors.

Most would agree that many laws passed as the result of this competitive bidding process among interest groups are effective and serve important purposes which enhance the welfare of society. However, there are other bills that pass the legislature as well, which simply transfer wealth from taxpayers to favored interest groups in one way or another, and in the process reduce economic efficiency and therefore harm social welfare. These are the bills which undertake to do things like establish mandatory licensing for barbers which serves not to protect the public but only to protect present barber shop owners from future competition. Real world legislatures pass numerous laws which erect entry barriers, establish legal monopolies, subsidize certain activities at taxpayer expense, and in other ways generate financial gain for favored interest groups while harming the interests of society at large. By enacting measures of this kind, legislatures produce wealth transfers at the expense of wealth creation and lower the efficiency of the overall economy.

Wealth Transfers Versus Wealth Creation. There are two major categories of economic activity. The one which has traditionally interested economists involves the creation of wealth through the pursuit of gains from trade. This form of economic activity represents a gain in welfare for all participants. In a free market context, all economic activity increases the perceived wealth of the voluntary participants; otherwise, they would not engage in the activity. Some wealth will take a physical and tangible form (e.g., iron ore mined from the ground) while other kinds will take forms which are less tangible and much harder to measure, such as increases in the satisfaction of consumers (e.g., the increased well-being supplied to parents as the result of baby-sitting services) or improvements in organization and management which permit the more efficient use of scarce resources. Legislative activity which improves the security of contracts, makes the enforcement and adjudication of the law more efficient, or otherwise helps to make market exchange less costly also represents wealth creation.

The other form of economic activity, wealth transfer, does not represent mutual gain, but rather represents one person gaining at someone else's expense. Rather than becoming wealthier through providing a service of value to someone else, wealth is acquired by taking *someone else's* wealth. The paradigm of wealth transfer activity is pickpocketry. Anyone who has read Dickens is aware of the investment in specialized training, the rational weighing of risks versus benefits, and the general businesslike attitude of the successful pick-pocket. Picking pockets for profit is just as much a rational, deliberate economic activity as running a steel mill or selling greeting cards. But unlike these other activities, the pick-pocket does not increase the net wealth of society, but just transfers the wealth created by someone else to himself. Also, to make matters worse the picking of pockets causes the net wealth of society to *decrease* by the amount of the investment of time and resources by the pick-pocket in his profession as well as the investment by potential victims to protect their wallets, both of which are a waste from the standpoint of society.

We do not deny that morality may play an important role in curbing outright thievery, for those who refrain from theft do so as the result of their moral training and belief that stealing is wrong. Nonetheless, the decision to engage in wealth transfer instead of wealth creation (or vice-versa) by a particular individual is economically understandable without making moral assumptions. People specialize in different activities because they have different talents, interests, and abilities, and those things which allow the individual to earn the highest return will be different for different individuals. Economists refer to this phenomenon as the law of comparative advantage. Some people will earn the highest return they can as plumbers, others as architects. Some will earn the most as doctors, others as pick-pockets. And of direct relevance to our concerns here, some will have a comparative advantage in actively competing for profit in the marketplace, and others will have a comparative advantage in lobbying for transfers in the legislature.

Democratic Politics and Tax Policy

The economic theory of legislation provides a basis for understanding both the process by which tax policy is enacted in a democracy and the outcomes of that process. As stressed above, the legislature is viewed not as a selfless and dedicated servant of something called "public interest," but rather is a set of ordinary people pursuing activities that offer the highest rewards. The realities of tax policy formation as one subset of legislative outcomes contrast sharply with the various normative theories of taxation which are often touted by those who feel that taxes should be employed by government as tools for social engineering. Progressive tax rate structures have often been defended on the basis that the capitalist free market system will, when left alone, generate an inequitable distribution of income; for the sake of equity, government should tax the rich at higher rates and redistribute the revenue to the poor, thereby making the income distribution more equal.[6] Another, related view holds that government should tax the rich at higher rates because the marginal utility of money diminishes as wealth increases; one more dollar may be of inconsequential importance to a millionaire but may make the difference between making the rent or getting tossed out on the street to a poor person (an intuitively plausible view that most economists reject as being based on invalid intuition).[7]

When these claims concerning the nature of a just tax system are compared with reality, an obvious chasm appears. Virtually all loopholes in the form of exemptions and deductions benefit middle- and upper-income individuals. At the same time current tax law places substantial impediments on the efforts of the poor to become self-supporting and self-sufficient. But, of course, it is meaningless to look only at the net tax burden without taking into account the *consumption* of tax revenues. If a particular group pays $X in annual taxes but the government spends $X+N on that group subsequently, the group is net tax *consumer* in the amount $N.

In this latter sense, the current tax system not only directly increases the poverty problem but increases the difficulty the poor face in attempting to pull themselves out of poverty. Clark and Brownstein (1985) report that according to Census calculations in 1982, the combined effects of federal, state, and local taxes pushed the incomes of 3.2 million taxpayers below the federal poverty threshold. According to Pechman (1985), the average rate of tax by states and localities on families in the lowest 10% of the income distribution actually rose from 1966 to 1985 (due mostly to increases in the level of excise taxes). Danzinger and Gottschalk (1985) found that the effective federal tax rate facing the poor (defined as total federal tax as a percentage of family income) has increased from only 1.3% in 1975 to 10.1% in 1984. The combined effects of federal, state, and local taxation reduce the effective earnings of the working poor and reduce their incentives to leave welfare programs by moving up the economic ladder.

Rent Seeking, Tax Resistance, and Social Waste

Review of the Excess Burden Literature. When the government collects a dollar in revenue from a tax on tobacco products, the disposable income of consumers is reduced by one dollar. However, the burden the tax imposes on the economy will exceed the amount of tax revenue collected by the government. The additional burden represents a social waste in the sense that it represents value foregone--i.e., it does not go to anyone. This waste is usually termed the excess burden, or deadweight cost, due to the tax.

As outlined in Chapter 2, this deadweight cost results from the differential between the price per pack of cigarettes after the tax and the value to consumers of alternative forms of output relative to an additional pack of cigarettes. If the price of an additional pack of cigarettes with the tax is $1.50 and the cost in terms of alternative output foregone to produce that pack is $1.10 (which in a free market will tend to be equal to the pretax price), consumers are made worse off *beyond* the 40 cent tax ($1.50 - $1.10 = $.40) by the extent to which the value they place on additional cigarettes exceeds the cost of producing those additional cigarettes. This is the excess burden; it is the lost utility consumers *would* have received if they had been permitted to purchase a quantity of cigarettes up to the point where the value of the last cigarette to them equaled its cost of production.

There is an important corollary to the theory of excess burden which is commonly cited in the case of tobacco taxation: the magnitude of the excess burden associated with a tax on a specific commodity will tend to be inversely related to the elasticity of demand for that commodity. Hence, the excess burden resulting from a tax on a commodity subject to a very elastic demand (e.g., newspapers) will tend to be relatively high while the excess burden resulting from a tax on a relatively inelastically demanded commodity (e.g., cigarettes) will be relatively low. This is because the more inelastic the demand for the good, the less likely it is that the tax will have any effect on consumer behavior. A tax on newspapers will cause many consumers to shift to substitutes (they will listen to the radio, watch TV, or buy weekly news magazines). The shift to these available substitutes which provide the consumer with lower satisfaction than newspapers did at the pretax price will create a significant deadweight cost. In contrast, because few close substitutes are available to cigarette smokers, the tax will have relatively little impact on their consumption choices, and consequently the aggregated deadweight cost of this tax will be relatively low.

This is the conventional account of the social waste resulting from excise taxation. However, in recent years economists have begun to recognize that the conventional account ignores an important source of additional tax-related social loss, and therefore seriously underestimates the true magnitude of the total social waste resulting from excise taxation. This additional source of inefficiency is the rent-seeking loss to which we now turn.

Rent Seeking in General. One of the propositions of economics best understood by the general public is that profits associated with a given business activity will inspire competition by other suppliers eager to earn profits for themselves. If ACME Pest Control invests and markets a better mouse-trap and thereby receives large profits, other pest control firms will strive to market similar (or even superior) products to consumers in order to compete away some of ACME's profits for themselves. As a result of this competition, motivated by simple self-interest on the part of competing firms, consumers benefit from better and cheaper mouse-traps, to say nothing of the similar benefits from millions of other goods and services. The market economy, with its enormous productivity and inventiveness, is rooted in the profit-seeking endeavors of individuals and firms.

One of the important developments which has arisen out of the public choice revolution during the last twenty-five years has been the extension of the same basic paradigm of economic analysis to the political realm. The political process is not somehow magically insulated from the economic world, but rather operates according to the same basic principles. The reason for this is that politics is populated by the same self-interested, rational maximizing individuals who populate the ordinary marketplace. The theory of public choice represents the extension of the profit-seeking paradigm to the political realm, and the theory of rent seeking is an important subset of the theory of public choice, for it is concerned with explaining the wealth transferring activities of government.

The key proposition relevant here is that all governmental decisions and policies tend to transfer wealth within society. Simply stated, any government action creates winners and losers. This will be true even of policies not explicitly designed to redistribute wealth. Rent-seeking analysis emphasizes that economic actors will invest resources in competition for these wealth transfers (or rents) in much the same way that business enterprises compete for consumer dollars.

A little background will help to clarify terminology. In economic analysis the definition of economic rent is a payment to a resource owner above the amount his resources could command in their next best alternative use. An economic rent is a receipt in excess of the opportunity cost of a resource. Over time, the presence of economic rents provides the incentive for resource owners to seek out more profitable allocations of their resources. When competition is viewed as a dynamic, value-creating, evolutionary process, the role of economic rents in stimulating entrepreneurial decisions and in prompting an efficient allocation of resources is crucial. "Rent-seeking" or profit seeking" in a competitive market order is a normal feature of economic life. The returns of resource owners will be driven to normal levels (on both the intensive and extensive margins) by competitive profit seeking as some resource owners earn positive rents which promote entry and others earn negative rents which cause exit. Profit seeking and economic rents are inherently related to the efficiency of the competitive market process.

The task at hand is to distinguish rent seeking from profit seeking. Suppose a king wishes to grant a monopoly right in the production of playing cards. In this case artificial scarcity is created by the state, and as a consequence, monopoly rents are present to be captured by monopolists who seek the king's favor. Normally, these rents are thought of as transfers from playing card consumers to the card monopolist. Yet in the example, this can only be the case if the aspiring monopolists employ no real resources to compete for the monopoly rents. To the extent that real resources are spent to capture monopoly rents in such ways as lobbying, these expenditures create no value from a social point of view. It is this activity of wasting resources in competing for artificially contrived transfers that is called rent seeking. If an incipient monopolist hires a lawyer to lobby the king for the monopoly right, the opportunity cost of this lawyer (for example, the contracts that he does not write while engaged in lobbying) is a social cost of the monopolization process.

Such rent-seeking costs must be added to the standard welfare-triangle loss associated with monopoly to obtain an estimate of the total social costs of monopoly and regulation. Rent seeking is thus the expenditure of scarce resources to capture an artificially created transfer. "Real" rents are different from "government" or "fake" rents because rent seeking has productive implications in the first case but not in the second.

Alternatively, consider the development of that proverbial better mouse trap by ACME Pest Control. As a result of ACME's efforts, its customers are better served and its owners get wealthier. Rather than seeking for that better mouse trap, however, ACME could have directed its efforts into such activities as lobbying the International Trade Commission to place restrictions on the importation of mousetraps from Taiwan. Or it could have lobbied the Consumer Product Safety Commission to set minimum standards for mousetrap safety; by eliminating cheaper mousetraps from the market, these standards would generate increased business for ACME. Yet again, ACME could lobby the Food and Drug Administration to refuse to approve use of some new rodent poison that, if approved, would reduce the market for conventional mousetraps. In these kinds of ways, ACME would also increase the net worth of its owners, only it would do so at the expense of its customers, who would be unable to choose from potentially cheaper and better options.

Rent-seeking activity will have an important consequence in terms of the excess burden associated with a particular tax or regulation. As we noted in Chapter 2, according to the conventional analysis, excess burden would be approximately equal to one-half the product of the increase in price and decrease in output brought about by the tax. But this understates the amount of wasted resources associated with the tax or regulation. All resources invested, by both those in favor and those opposed, in lobbying about the measure in question are also a pure waste from the standpoint of society as a whole. These resources have been devoted not to efforts to increase the stock of wealth but only to efforts to affect the process by which a portion of the existing stock of wealth is reallocated. These resources have been lost to the productive economy. As we argued above, in the limit this rent-seeking investment will be equal to the expected value of the wealth transfer resulting from the tax or regulation.[8] Hence, the potential excess burden from a tax is much higher than conventionally measured, for tax revenues raised by the tax can also be a gauge of the extent of social costs.

Rent Seeking Applied to Tax Resistance. As the preceding discussion suggests, the existence of a transfer rent implies not only that potential recipients will make some level of investment in competing for that rent, but also that the potential victims will make some investment to prevent or at least reduce that transfer. Both the offensive pursuit of rents through legislation and the defensive effort to avoid losing rents through the rent-seeking efforts of others are rational economic activities that stem from the ability of the legislature to transfer wealth through taxation and regulation. It must be recognized that the ability of those adversely affected by governmentally imposed restrictions to engage in defensive rent-seeking activity is vital to the protection of their rights and liberties in a free society. Nevertheless, from a strict economic perspective, such investment is analytically equivalent to rent seeking.

But when anti-rent seeking, tax resistance activity--like rent seeking a net waste from the standpoint of society--is taken into account, the conventional claim that a tax on the most inelastically demanded goods or services is the least wasteful tax becomes dubious. Consumers will be most likely to organize to fight a tax imposed on the most inelastically demanded goods. A commodity for which the demand is highly elastic is one for which good substitutes are readily available. The imposition of a tax on such a commodity will lead consumers readily to shift to the nontaxed alternative product that is nearly as satisfactory as the taxed product. The availability of such alternative products reduces the potential gain from tax resistance. By contrast a commodity for which demand is inelastic is one that has no close substitutes. In this case consumers will have more to gain from resisting the tax through political activity.

At the same time, suppliers of commodities for which demand is highly elastic are unlikely to be earning supranormal profits. Because of the availability of close substitutes for the output they produce, they will be unable to set price above the marginal cost of production. Since they are not earning supranormal profits (rents), they have minimal incentive and resources to organize themselves to oppose the tax. But the suppliers of inelastically demanded goods will probably be able to set price *above* marginal cost because close substitutes are *not* available. Because they will therefore be earning supranormal profits (rents), they will have an incentive to invest resources to defeat (or reduce) the tax which would otherwise reduce the magnitude of this rent flow. When the demand for a commodity is relatively elastic, neither consumers nor producers are likely to have an incentive to invest significant resources in efforts either to prevent the imposition of a proposed excise tax or to eliminate an existing tax. But when the demand is relatively inelastic, both consumers and producers will have a stronger incentive to invest in opposing the tax or increases in it. When this is taken into account, it becomes problematical in general whether excise taxes on elastically demanded goods (with low anti-rent seeking investment but large excess burden) or inelastically demanded goods (with high anti-rent seeking investment but low excess burden) will generate greater social waste. In some cases taxing relatively inelastically demanded commodities (e.g., tobacco products) will tend to generate the maximum social loss.[9]

The Social Cost of Tobacco Taxation: A Recalculation

The foregoing argumentation suggests that the conventional analysis of the excess burden which results from taxes--in particular cigarette taxes--grossly understates the true economic cost of the tax. As noted in Chapter 2, what is often claimed as the excess burden resulting from the taxation of cigarettes is about 7 percent of the revenue raised by the tax. But the full potential extent of the excess burden also includes the revenue raised by the tax. This is because the entire amount of the transfer of wealth associated with the tax will be "up for grabs," and rent-seeking interest groups will invest up to their expected value of this amount in competition for it. Consequently, the total amount of excess burden when rent-seeking costs are included could exceed *the amount of revenue the government generates from the tax*. In terms of the numerical illustration used in Chapter 2, the government's revenue will be limited to $11.2 billion ($.40 x 28 billion packs sold), but the total excess burden plus rent-seeking loss could be as high as $12 billion ($11.2 billion + $800 million excess burden).

In practice, it is unlikely that the total waste resulting from a tax will reach this magnitude. Efforts to influence legislative outcomes are subject to significant transaction costs as compared with ordinary markets, and the greater uncertainty that thus results will tend to lower the level of rent-seeking investment somewhat. But even if these costs are likely to be somewhat smaller than our simplified example implies, they nevertheless could be quite large.

Economic Principles and the Anti-Cancer Bureaucracy

Economic Principles of Bureaucratic Conduct. A government bureau may seem superficially to be the opposite of a business firm in a market economy, and hence necessarily to be impervious to economic analysis. On the surface a bureaucracy is a hierarchy ruled from top to bottom, with all decisions being made centrally, and with members acting on orders from their superiors and not through voluntary exchange. Even some economists have used bureaucracy as an example of the antithesis of the marketplace.

However, in recent years a number of economists have succeeded in extending economic analysis to the decision-making process within bureaucracies. Although such organizations are not markets in the ordinary sense, meaning that they are not characterized by competition within the context of explicit prices for goods and services, they do function nonetheless according to ordinary economic principles.

A bureau differs from a private firm in one important respect. A bureau, unlike a firm, does not have profits that can be directly appropriated by owners. This is a major difference to be sure, but there are nevertheless major similarities between the two types of organization. There are powerful incentives in each for managers to act in ways that increase the relative power of the organization at large. Managers in firms are rewarded with promotions and increased salaries when they increase the firm's profits by expanding sales. Bureaucratic managers are similarly rewarded with promotions and increased salaries when they succeed in expanding the "sales" of their bureau in terms of its political influence and public support. Larger bureaucratic organizations tend to provide higher rates of pay and perquisites to management. Also, the political influence of a bureau, as well as its ability to serve interest groups who can reward management with promises of lucrative future contracts or employment, if not actual bribes, will tend to be a function of its size. For these reasons government bureaus will tend to be dominated by the economic interests of their management, and behave in economically predictable--although often inefficient--ways.[10]

The Anti-Cancer Bureaucracy in Public Choice Perspective. The debate about the regulation and taxation of smoking is intimately related to various claims concerning the alleged adverse health consequences associated with smoking. Essentially all of the opposition to smoking is ultimately based on various claims regarding these alleged consequences. The most important of these claims involve the alleged relationship between cigarettes and cancer.

Generally, studies concerning the alleged links between smoking and cancer are produced by the cancer research community, which includes both private and public establishments and which is heavily subsidized by the federal government. Because of the enormous level of federal government involvement in this research, it is useful to describe this research establishment as a single bureaucracy, even though a number of distinct private and public organizations are involved.

While it may seem obvious that these principles of bureaucratic behavior should apply to units like the Registry of Motor Vehicles or the Department of Defense, some might balk at the logical extension of them to such other units as the cancer research bureaucracy, by which we refer to government bureaucracies like the National Institutes of Health as well as private-sector organizations like the American Cancer Society, the American Lung Association, and various other foundations and research institutes. But the economic principles of bureaucracy are as applicable to these agencies as they are to other agencies more commonly considered "bureaucratic."

As they apply to the anti-cancer bureaucracy, the economic principles of bureaucracy suggest that, as compared with organization through market competition, the anti-cancer bureaucracy will face weaker incentives to find and develop effective treatments of and cures for cancer, as well as facing incentives to magnify the risks of cancer. The first point is more subtle than merely noting that a cure for cancer would put many cancer bureaucrats out of work, even though a consideration of such perverse incentives has led at least one critic of the medical establishment to suggest that the cancer bureaucracy is the last place to look for a cancer cure.[11] There are, of course, several occupations that are dependent upon a continuation of a state of affairs that its practitioners seek to eliminate, but for which universal success would end the occupation.

Divorce lawyers and family counselors would go out of business if people were to learn how to get along together. Physicians may advise people how to stay healthy, but healthy people would have little demand for physicians. In these and related cases, what provides the incentive for individual practitioners to promote the interests of their clients, an incentive that clashes somewhat with the interests of the entire group of practitioners, is the competitive organization of service delivery. (We pursue this theme in greater detail in the next chapter.)

There is clearly competition among cancer researchers, but those researchers are in a somewhat different position than ordinary market competitors. Competitors must always seek to please their customers. In ordinary market arrangements these customers are numerous and decentralized. It would be the same with cancer research if the sponsors of that research were numerous and decentralized, but such sponsorship is centralized and largely monopolized. While individual researchers have incentives to find cures for cancer, they also have incentives to please their sponsor--and the dominant sponsor is a government bureaucracy and not the numerous and variegated buyers who constitute a competitive market.

The second point is a mere recognition of the application of individual profit incentives in a nonprofit setting. In bureaus larger budgets are generally preferred to smaller budgets. One means of gaining larger budgets is to "advertise," as it were. With respect to the cancer bureaucracy, one form such "advertisement" can take is to magnify the likely risk of cancer. The more successful the bureaucracy is in portraying an image of the ubiquitousness of cancer, the larger will be governmental appropriations and charitable donations.

The apparently spurious nature of many recent claims about the risks of cancer which has been made by even prominent researchers have been the subject of a recent book by Edith Efron (1984). She reported that even the most absurd claims with the weakest empirical support tended to be seized by the public and the media as fact, and that standards of scientific rigor were habitually relaxed virtually to the point of abandonment by cancer researchers. Virtually every imaginable substance and practice, both man-made and natural, has been claimed by some representative of one of the major cancer research institutes (either the National Cancer Institute, a federal government agency, or some other institution) to be carcinogenic. This list includes virtually all the chemicals known to exist,[12] all forms of energy generation (including solar cells and solar heating and cooling systems),[13] most major components of foods (including salt and sugar),[14] and even numerous naturally occurring substances in the air we breathe (including oxygen itself).[15] Efron contends that the overwhelming majority of these claims are based on flimsy evidence or no reliable evidence at all. Scientists (sometimes even those associated with major cancer research foundations) who held reservations about the validity of some of the more extreme claims made by their colleagues concerning cancer risks expressed reluctance about mentioning those reservations in public for fear of being ostracized or branded as tools of industry.

Again, it is not strictly relevant whether the conscious motives of cancer researchers are pristine and sincere or cynically self-interested. The point is that any increased level of perceived cancer risk among the general public is likely eventually to increase their pecuniary incomes. Efron (1984, p. 232) concludes that "basic" or "pure" science has been partially supplanted by something she terms "regulatory science":

> In principle, basic science is concerned to explain the biological mechanisms of cancer; its goal is understanding. But "regulatory" science is concerned with the legal elimination of carcinogenic substances in the environment whether biological understanding exists or not...The basic scientist, whether he works for the government or at a university, is an intellectual explorer in search of truth, and coercion is no part of his repertoire. The "regulatory" scientist, whether he works for the government or at a university, is an intellectual policeman whose judgements, if accepted by regulators, are backed up by the guns of the state.

If the "regulatory scientist" is actually an intellectual policeman, there is a simple economic explanation for his unscientific behavior. He is protecting his existing rents in the form of his salary and status, which have been artificially increased by his encouragement of cancer fears that have dubious validity, not to mention the protection of possible increases in future rents resulting from the expected expansion of the cancer bureaucracy. When viewed from the perspective of a competitive marketplace or from that of some notion of public interest, this is a questionable way to run a scientific research establishment, and is clearly inconsistent with the basic integrity of science as a whole. But when viewed from the perspective of the economic theory of bureaucracy, it nonetheless represents perfectly rational behavior.

What Does the Surgeon General Optimize?. We ask this question seriously, though in doing so we look upon the Surgeon General as an example of a wider phenomenon. Although not the actual administrator of the National Institutes of Health or any of the other major components of the federal research bureaucracy, he is the chief public representative of a bureaucratic empire which will tend to expand in size and scope as its budget increases. It is obvious that the budget will be functionally related to the perceived risk of cancer and other diseases within the Congress and the general public. It takes neither a Machiavellian imagination nor a Ph.D. in economics to conclude that the Surgeon General has a built-in incentive to magnify the risk of cancer.

If the research community were largely independent of government funding, notably including funding from the National Institutes of Health, any statements by the Surgeon General, which should have a strong basis in research findings, would be vulnerable to attack by alert and technically competent critics. But, of course, this competitive organization of funding is not even remotely the case. For 1991, the federal government projects spending $8.7 billion on health research; $6.7 billion of this through the National Institutes of Health.[16] The Surgeon General is not the actual administrator of this vast research bureaucracy, but he is the chief public spokeman for this bureaucracy's interests. We do not expect employees of General Dynamics to be totally disinterested witnesses to the probity and honesty of General Dynamics' management. Why should we apply different standards to the medical research community?

The Surgeon General could be described as the nation's chief doctor. He is basically a representative of the interests of the medical profession at large. The medical profession, like all professions, may at times face perverse incentives with regard to the services it provides. Auto mechanics may be expected to exaggerate the mechanical defects present in a car they have been assigned to repair. However, they face the constraint of competition. Auto mechanics compete vigorously, have no national organization designed to limit competition, and are not heavily subsidized by the government in such a manner that they are rewarded for finding more "broken" cars, so that the perverse incentives which they face are kept under tight control. These controls would seem to be much slacker in the case of medical research, because of the dominant position of the government as the purchaser of medical research.

Tobacco Taxation and Regulation: A Realistic Approach

The anti-smoking lobby portrays itself as engaging in a crusade to save smokers from themselves and at the same time seeking to rescue non-smokers from the "social costs" imposed on them by smokers. We have attempted to argue that the "social cost" justifications for the anti-smoking crusade are pseudo-science masquerading as economic analysis. It seems unlikely that such specious arguments actually inspire the intellectual commitment of large numbers of rational and articulate people such as many of those who promote restrictions on smoking.

This leaves us with paternalism as a major motivational factor. But this too seems unconvincing. Many of the same people in the forefront of the anti-smoking movement are known for their long-time commitments to civil libertarian positions like freedom of speech, civil rights, and skepticism of governmental intrusion into the personal lives of individuals in general. Rank paternalism has rarely appealed to Americans, and it seems particularly inconsistent in the case of many of those prominently identified with the anti-smoking movement. The rhetoric used by the anti-smoking movement would seem to have little to do with what the movement is actually about.

As we saw in Chapter 8, with private property and residual claimants in place, the "social costs" of smoking in public are approximately zero. Owners of private establishments have an incentive to provide the kind of environment most satisfactory to their customers. Therefore, in the absence of government smoking regulations, private rules concerning smoking, segregation of smokers from nonsmokers, and investment in smoke removal devices will tend to be economically efficient. Some restaurants will cater to smokers, some to nonsmokers; some businesses will establish a smoke-free workplace, some will not; and private property owners in general will provide the degree of smoke-free environment that their customers and employees most prefer because only by doing so will they maximize their own profits.

But even if the profit-seeking decisions of private entrepreneurs will tend to provide for an efficient mix of rules regarding smoking and no-smoking, nonsmokers may still stand to gain from making no-smoking rules universal and compulsory. We must face the fact that some people simply do not like the fact that other people smoke, for whatever the reason. In the absence of wage effects, which we will consider below, nonsmoking workers may prefer that smoking be banned outright if the price to themselves is low enough. If a nonsmoking worker were to bear the full cost of achieving a smoke-free workplace, he might decide that although he would *ideally* prefer that *no* one smoke, he would actually *choose* a situation where the cost to him of reducing smoking equaled the benefits to him of that reduction--which point, if we make the usual assumptions about rising marginal cost curves, will probably be one where some smoking is still permitted. In practice it may well be much more expensive for a business to prohibit smoking altogether than to segregate smokers from nonsmokers or to allow smoking only in designated areas. Non-smokers may not be willing to bear the cost of such measures (i.e., they may be unwilling to accept lower wages in return for company enforcement of nonsmoking rules), but they might still favor legislative action to ban smoking if they perceived that it cost themselves little or nothing.

Anti-smoking rules may find support among nonsmoking workers for another reason. There is data suggesting that smokers are relatively efficient workers. In some cases they have lower rates of absenteeism than nonsmokers (Solmon 1983).[17]   A recent study indicates that smokers tend to be relatively more productive workers (Dahl, Gunderson, and Kuehnast 1984).[18]   Other research reports that smoking may enhance the ability to concentrate on assigned tasks (Spielberger 1986).[19] The movement to exclude smokers from the workplace may be motivated in part by the fact that nonsmokers can expect to gain in wages by excluding higher productivity smokers from competing with them in the workplace.

To the extent that no-smoking rules make smokers less productive on the job, as well as less likely to be hired in the first place, the wages of nonsmokers will tend to rise relative to that of smokers. Hence, laws restricting or prohibiting smoking have a simple redistributive basis--they transfer wealth from smokers to nonsmokers. Of course, these gains will only be transitory. In the long-run, competition among nonsmokers for jobs will drive wages down to the amount just sufficient for them to accept employment in their preferred workplace environment. In the interim, however, nonsmokers earn rents, and these short-run returns may provide a sufficient incentive for them to support no-smoking legislation.

So nonsmokers gain in two ways from no-smoking rules. They obtain a working environment they most prefer at a zero (or very low) price, and receive restriction rents (at least in the short run) which increase their wages. Non-smoking consumers tend to benefit in similar ways from smoking bans. Legal restrictions on smoking in bars and restaurants tend to shift the supply curve to the right which, other things equal, tends to lower the money price of dining out in a no-smoking atmosphere. Under such conditions, nonsmokers who eat out not only obtain a more preferred environment but enjoy a lower price as well. On the other hand, smokers and restaurant owners lose (Shughart and Tollison 1986).

While there are data suggesting that high-skilled male workers (including white collar and professional workers) who smoke are relatively more productive than their nonsmoking colleagues, smokers are disproportionately found among the ranks of the lower-skilled, the poor, and the young. The incidence of tobacco taxation tends to fall heavily on lower-income groups, and this burden decreases the disposable income available to poor individuals to allocate to human capital development through education and training for themselves and their children. In consequence, the probability is lessened that such individuals and/or their children will acquire the skills necessary to allow them to enter and compete in the skilled labor force where they face the best chance for improving their long-run income status. Existing skilled laborers--particularly the members of labor unions--stand to receive reduced wages in the long run from competition with new entrants into the skilled labor force from the ranks of the previously poor and unskilled. Discriminatory taxation imposed on the poor, like tobacco taxation, tends to function as a form of entry barrier which generates monopoly rents for relatively wealthy skilled workers.

Anti-smoking measures also tend to function as a form of racial discrimination. A disproportionate share of smokers are black and

Hispanic. Measures which discriminate against smokers effectively act to discriminate against members of these minority groups. In modern America overt racial discrimination is prevented by law; Jim Crow was killed by the civil rights movement of the 1960's. But anti-smoking rules allow a form of discrimination against members of minority groups which evades federal and state laws designed to eliminate discrimination along racial lines. A business may not be able to refuse to hire blacks because of their race, but it may be able, legally, to refuse to hire a smoker who refuses to quit if the firm has a "no smoking" policy, or if the local law requires a "smoke free" workplace even though the worker is black.

NOTES

1. See McCormick and Tollison (1981) and Peltzman (1984) for reviews of the literature.

2. The free rider problem refers to the issue of why an individual should join the group seeking government benefits if he cannot be excluded from the benefits once the law is passed. If all group members reason this way, no group action would be forthcoming; therefore, one object of the group is to spend resources to deter such behavior.

3. See Olson (1965).

4. This analysis, however, ignores a potentially troubling question: What about rival associations with lower prices?

5. See Stigler (1974).

6. See Boadway (1979, Chapter 12) for a technical summary of these arguments.

7. Although the law of diminishing marginal utility applies to specific goods--a given unit purchased provides less utility to the consumer than the unit purchased before it--it does not apply to goods in general. Money represents command over goods in general. While in some individual cases, each additional dollar may generate less utility than the one before it (e.g., in the case of a monk), it is possible that in other cases the utility associated with each additional dollar actually *increases*. Therefore, even if we could measure and compare utility across persons--which is impossible--it is possible that we would find that the additional dollar generated more utility for the millionaire than it did for the chimney sweep. The point is simply that one cannot generalize across people about the value of additional income or command over goods and services

8. The case where rents are exactly dissipated represents an example of competitive rent-seeking. This does not mean, however, that all rent-seeking contests are perfectly competitive in nature. There are models where rent-seeking is imperfectly competitive in the sense that the competitive process for rents leads to over- or under dissipation of the available rents. These cases are interesting, and they are obviously generated by assumptions about limitations on the number of bidders, imperfect information, and so on.

9. For a more detailed argument, see Lee and Tollison (1985).

10. See Tullock (1968), and Niskanen (1971) for a more detailed analysis.

11. Szasz (1978) has made this observation on numerous occasions.

12. Joseph Califano, then HEW Secretary, put the number at seven million in 1978. See Efron (1984, p. 97).

13. *Ibid.*, p. 102.

14. *Ibid.*, p. 160.

15. *Ibid.*, p. 166.

16. See OMB (1990, p. 5-116).

17. Solmon reported that the 1976 National Health Survey showed that smokers of less than 15 cigarettes per day had an absenteeism rate of 2.6 days, compared with 4.3 days for nonsmokers, and notes that the 1979 Surgeon General's Report indicated that male smokers of less than 11 cigarettes per day were absent less than nonsmokers, and women aged 17 and older who were presently smokers had less bed disability than nonsmokers. See Solmon (1983, pp. 1-2).

18. Dahl, Gunderson, and Kuehnast (1984) studied a group of 55 financial managers at Minnesota's Farm Credit Services, and reported that smokers were significantly more productive than nonsmokers; smokers were reported to be 2.5 percent more efficient in allocating their time to assigned tasks.

19. Spielberger (1986, pp. 106-107) reports the results of a survey given to 424 college students who were current smokers. They indicated that reasons they continued to smoke included perceived relaxation, stimulation, and the facilitation of thinking aided by smoking.

Interest Groups
And The
Public's Health

W hile there is now an extensive body of scholarship on the interest-group approach to political processes, public health is one significant area of governmental activity that, to our knowledge, has not been brought under such analytical scrutiny.[1] Partly this is what we sought to do in Chapter 10, especially when we discussed issues involving bureaucratic behavior. We seek to close the circle in this chapter by exploring the extent to which collective choices concerning public-health budgetary and regulatory processes can be brought within the rubric of the interest-group theory of government. To advance a private-interest explanation of public-health processes is not to deny that those processes may serve some notion of public interest. Rather, the point is simply that any public-interest outcome can be reconciled with, and derived from, the pursuit of self interest by participants in public-health processes.

Overview

There are some obvious respects, at least based on casual observation, in which the provision of public health might appear to be concerned more with the supply of public goods than with the self-interested pursuit of wealth transfers. For instance, the control and prevention of contagious diseases has long been the paradigmatic example of public health, and this can readily be brought within the framework of the theories of externalities and public goods. However, the battle against contagious

193

diseases has largely been won, at least in the West. Nonetheless, the budgets of public-health agencies continue to increase, and regulatory processes operate to convey a portrait of a world increasingly imperiled by risks to health and life. Perhaps this public-health hype can be understood as a public-interest representation of the need to maintain the hard-earned gains of the past. But, alternatively, it might be better understood as a component of rent seeking, or of rent protection, by factor suppliers.

In this chapter we examine three main elements of public-health processes from the perspective of the self interest of those engaged in the supply of public health services. First, we consider the possibility of market failure, either in the market for wellness or in the market for public-health research, as explanations for public-health expenditure and regulation. In the process of doing so, we explore the probable impact of self interest on the operation of such processes. Second, we consider investment in such non-profit health organizations as the American Heart Association and the American Lung Association. It is certainly possible to conceptualize such investment as being one illustration of the market provision of public goods. But such investment might alternatively operate as a means of increasing the earnings of the input suppliers who provide the services financed by those organizations. Third, we examine the possibility that public-health processes which seek to extend life beyond what would result through ordinary market processes might also be a means of increasing the real incomes of input suppliers. After all, raising the age at which people die does not change the fact of death, but it may lead to a more medically intensive method of dying, one that at prevailing rates of interest may be a worthwhile investment by medical input suppliers, particularly if those investments are financed through taxation rather than by the input suppliers themselves.

There are at least three hypotheses that can be advanced about the operation of public-health processes. One is that those processes are concerned with the provision of public goods and the correction of market failures, and so are to be understood in terms of a logic of welfare economics or public interest. A second is that these processes are concerned with promoting the self-interests of input suppliers, and so would largely reflect the interests of certain physicians, pharmaceutical companies, and the like. In this case, public-health processes would be understood in terms of a logic of self interest. Moreover, paternalism is sometimes advanced as a third type of explanation for the supply of public health. In this case suppliers seek to do good for recipients, even though the recipients may not seek to have the service supplied to them. The reduction or elimination of smoking might be an illustration. Paternalism is a forced transfer, so we should expect input suppliers to be less wealthy to the extent that paternalism pervades public-health processes.

Market Processes and Personal Health

Wellness in a Market Economy. In a market economy in which public-health programs were absent, one subset of that economy could be conceptualized as a market for health or wellness. Just as one speaks about the properties of the market for housing or shoes, so is it reasonable to speak about the properties of the market for wellness or health. Some aspects of this market would be directly observable, as illustrated by visits to physicians, the sponsorship of pharmaceutical research, and the purchase of exercise bikes. Other aspects would be reflected in such things as the foods people eat, the beverages they ingest, and the proportion of bicycle riders in the population.

In any case, given the preferences of the population and the state of knowledge about the production function for wellness, there will exist a particular pattern of wellness within the population. These features of the market process could in turn be described by such outcomes as life expectancies, days of sickness, hospital beds occupied, enrollments in medical schools, subscriptions to health magazines, and purchases of exercise equipment. Medical knowledge and technology would exert important impacts on the outcomes of this market, as would the preferences of the population. Changes in information about the health consequences of foods would be reflected in the structure of market activity. If red meat comes to be viewed as exerting a negative impact on health, the population of steers will decline, as will the employment of butchers. If eating oat bran comes to be viewed as a means of securing better health, the amount of land planted in oats will increase.

Personal preferences regarding health would likewise be reflected through the market process. Health is doubtlessly valued, but so are other things; it is quite reasonable in an economic sense for people to exchange health for other things. The terms on which people are willing to make this exchange would be reflected through market processes. Walking to work is safer than driving, as well as healthier, but people typically drive, and in so doing are trading off life and health for comfort and convenience.

Within this framework people can choose to live in relatively more or less healthy manners. It is reasonable that people could have chosen to live longer and in a healthier manner, but preferred other things instead. They could have drunk only distilled water and eaten tofu patties for dinner, but drank whiskey and ate marbled beef instead. They could have chosen relatively stress-free lives as telephone installers, but chose the stressful life of an investment banker. Zemper (1989) reports that 32 percent of college football players in 1986 and 1987 were injured at least once, with the median number of days lost being 4 in 1986 and 3 in 1987. The players could have chosen to avoid football, but chose to sacrifice health for the fun -- and possibly glory and profit -- of doing so. Similarly, injury rates are 50 percent greater on artificial turf; the choice to play on artificial over natural turf likewise represents a conscious sacrifice of health for such other things as lower maintenance costs.

It is possible to have too much of a good thing. In strictly economic terms, added life and better health can be worth less than what they would cost. In any event, extra years of life are a private good, as the benefit accrues to the longer-living individual. This proposition is unaffected by a recognition that others may benefit, or perhaps bear costs, of that longer life, as illustrated by friends and relatives. Familial and friendship relationships fall into an almost completely Coasian part of the economy, where the relevant external effects are worked out by private bargaining. If a wife demands that her husband exercise, he can either buy more life insurance or start jogging. In either case, property rights are clearly defined, and economically efficient outcomes will result. Hence, longevity is a private good and is not a candidate for public provision. And what holds for longevity would seem to hold *ipso facto* for health or wellness.

Among other things, the public-health concept of "premature death" would be meaningless, for all deaths would be efficient from an *ex ante* perspective. There is no loss or waste to death, in contrast to what a concept of *premature* death would seem to require or imply. People make choices concerning diet, exercise, and occupation in light of their preferences and knowledge, and the resulting pattern of death is but one element of the overall pattern of market outcomes. If it is "known" that eating red meat or smoking cigarettes may shorten life expectancies, people can choose how much meat to eat or whether to smoke in light of their preferences for such activities relative to their preferences for longer life. Should some people die before some such arbitrary age as 65, there is nothing wasteful or premature about those deaths, at least in an economic sense. Rather those deaths are simply one aspect of rational personal conduct within market processes.

"Failure" in the Market for Wellness?. Contagious diseases provide the exception to the argument about the private goods nature of health and longevity for two distinct reasons. One person's choice in matters relating to personal health may affect the likelihood that that person will become a carrier of a contagious disease. If so, personal choices in the direction of reducing health relative to other things will impose costs on others. For instance, suppose a failure to get enough sleep and exercise increases the probability that that person will contact a contagious disease. In consequence, the probability that people who are careful to get enough sleep and exercise will catch the disease is also increased. To the extent that diseases can be transmitted in this manner, the market for wellness may be subject to a source of market failure.

Communicable diseases can also be sources of market failure for reasons relating to the theory of public goods. This case perhaps conforms a little more closely to the standard paradigm of public health. In this case it is not so much a matter that individual choices regarding personal health characteristics influence their susceptibility to communicable diseases, as it is a matter that such diseases simply arise exogenously. While the onset of the disease may be independent of personal choices, these are diseases that everyone would like to avoid, but which are transmitted by invisible organisms and spread to innocent victims by means of only a brief exposure to carriers, who may be almost impossible to identify as such (and who may not even know themselves that they are infected). In this case the control of the disease may present a public goods problem, in that individuals cannot purchase immunity through their market choices but rather must act in concert. Spraying to control mosquitos and the encephalitis they may carry might serve as an illustration.

Self Interest and Public Health. The standard public-health paradigm, particularly as it regards communicable diseases, would seem to have relatively limited applicability these days, especially in the West. And neither would there appear to be any market failure in the provision of information about personal health. Indeed, the standard proscriptions for health and longevity have been around for a long time, and largely have the status of conventional wisdom: lose weight, eat a balanced diet, stop smoking, drink less alcohol, avoid stress, and so forth. Physicians can freely give this type of advice, and individuals can read and research such matters for themselves.[2] Out of this decentralized process, individuals will collect data and organize their lives accordingly, expecting to live for some preferred period of time. Individuals, as it were, "choose" their expected lifetimes.[3] As constraints and preferences shift, individual behavior will change. For example, alcohol consumption may rise in wartime.

If there is no market failure in the provision of health and longevity, the addition of public-health spending to the market provision of those services may lead to excessive expenditures to promote health and longevity. If public and private provision are perfect substitutes, public-health activities will simply substitute for private activities. There will be no net effect on health and longevity. In this case self interest can manifest itself through transfers of income. Suppose the population can be divided between health nuts and gluttons. Average incomes are the same for both groups, though the gluttons have lower life expectancies. The health nuts spend a larger share of their income on health-promoting goods than do the gluttons. To the extent they can secure public provision of health-promoting goods, they will be able to secure a wealth transfer from the gluttons, in that those who consume relatively large amounts of health-promoting goods will gain at the expense of those who do not. If such goods are supplied at constant cost, the operation of self interest is limited to the uses of income.

In contrast, if health-promoting goods are produced under conditions of rising supply prices, self interest can also operate on the sources of income. In this case the expansion in the production of health-promoting goods that results from collective provision increases the price of those goods, thereby creating rents for infra-marginal suppliers of those services. Indeed, there are generally strong grounds for thinking that these supply-side sources of self interest will be stronger than the demand-side sources. Input suppliers are more concentrated and face lower organization costs than consumer groups. Being more concentrated, the per capita value of any given value of rent will be higher for input suppliers than for consumers. This is certainly not to deny that public provision can take place even though supply curves are horizontal because of the redistribution that can result on the demand side of the transaction. Rather it is simply to assert that the pressures for collective provision will be stronger if supply prices are rising because specialized input suppliers can then acquire concentrated gains.

Is Health Research a Public Good?

Public Goods Justifications for Health Research. Suppose it were accepted, at least for purposes of argument, that wellness is a private good that is supplied efficiently through market processes. In other words, assume there are no problems of externality and public goods with regard to the control of diseases. It is still possible to argue that there is an important place for government in public-health processes because the research that generates new knowledge about health might be a public good.

The investment in the acquisition of knowledge will conform to the same economic principles as all other activities. Someone investing in dietary research will do so to the extent that such research is anticipated to be profitable. Yet that anticipated profitability depends on the extent to which the benefits from that research can be captured by the developer of that knowledge. For instance, someone exploring the dietary properties of different strains of tomatoes will pursue such research to the point where the anticipated marginal return equals the marginal cost. Suppose this research culminates in the form of recipes for the use of tomatoes in casseroles and other dishes, which if consumed twice weekly, will lower cholesterol by 20 points.

Once this knowledge is made available to one person, it can be readily passed on to other people. The extreme form of this case is that once it is communicated to one person, it can be costlessly communicated to everyone else. In this setting, the incentives to acquire such knowledge would be weak, and would essentially be limited to the pursuit of hobbies. Once it is recognized that communication is costly, it is possible for the inventor to capture some of the gains, which in turn will give stronger incentive to invest in developing such knowledge. For instance, the knowledge may be transmitted through magazines and books, for which the inventor can receive a royalty payment. But absent copyright laws, good ideas can be copied by others without payment to the inventor.

Much of the economic literature on research, copyrights, and patents has focused on the ways in which market processes can operate to overcome what would otherwise be the public goods nature of research. Copyrights can serve to give the inventor a property right, thereby strengthening the incentive to undertake research into such things as the health properties of foods. Likewise, patents can do the same for such things as research into the health properties of different forms of exercise equipment. To be sure, there is a significant governmental presence in the enforcement of copyright and patent laws, though in principle the cost of administering these laws could be charged to the holders of the patents and copyrights. And scholars seem to hold different opinions about the extent to which market processes might be able to operate to convert research into an appropriable activity. But no one seems to think such appropriability can be complete, which means that there will be some public goods element to such research, even though there may be considerable room for questioning the extent of such publicness. But whether the public goods component of health research might be relatively large or relatively small, there will surely be a public goods component to such research.

But to accept this argument about public goods is not necessarily to affirm that the actual provision of such research operates to provide those public goods or that such provision is free of interest-group influences. The actual conduct of the bureaus that administer research programs, as well as the legislative committees that sponsor those bureaus, may conflict with the public-goods justifications advanced in their support. Those justifications envision government acting as a substitute for the competitive organization of inquiry, in a setting where market competition is subject to failure. But actual governments may act quite differently than idealized governments. A world in which government is a monopsonistic supporter of research may differ significantly from a world in which research is supported by a large number of independently acting and financed donors (Tullock, 1968).

Monopoly, Competition, and the Organization of Inquiry. For instance, consider research into the relationship between smoking and health under two alternative organizational settings: (1) research is sponsored by a large number of independently financed organizations, and (2) research is sponsored by a single government bureau that is financed by a single legislative committee. To be sure, reality lies somewhere between these polar types. But a focus on the polar types serves to clarify our point about the distinction between justificatory argument in support of government sponsorship of research and explanatory argument about the actual consequences of such sponsorship.

Knowledge about the alleged health consequences of smoking is obviously of great interest to people, and this interest extends to non-smokers because of claims that they can be harmed by environmental tobacco smoke. There are many hypotheses that might be advanced about these alleged health consequences of smoking, as well as about the properties of alternative ways for mitigating or avoiding those consequences. One possible line of inquiry could be based on a premise that smoking causes lung cancer. Such a line of inquiry is clearly the predominant one in the cancer research community. The observation that the preponderance of diagnosed lung cancer cases are smokers makes this line of research appear to be fertile ground. But it is also the case that the predominant number of "heavy" smokers do not contract lung cancer, which in turn might suggest the value of a research program into why most smokers do not get lung cancer. Such a program might look to differences between smokers and nonsmokers. Or it might look to psychological or personality differences, much as one research program concerning heart disease distinguishes between type A and type B personalities.[4]

The number of research possibilities could be multiplied greatly. For instance, within the context of a program that operates on the assumption that smoking causes lung cancer, some could explore different ways of quitting smoking, others could investigate the possibilities that different forms of diet or exercise might diminish or even eliminate the allegedly toxic effect of smoking, and yet others might examine the prospects for reversal of that allegedly toxic effect through genetic engineering. All of these lines of research, and many others, might find support within a truly competitive organization of inquiry. What would result would be unknowable independent of actually allowing such a process to operate. What would seem likely to emerge would be a wide variety of findings and suggestions. There would be claims made for smoke-free environments. Treatments to help people stop smoking would be developed. Others would sell books and appear on talk shows telling how the diet they developed apparently greatly reduces the likelihood that smokers will get lung cancer.

The conduct of research would proceed much differently if it were sponsored by a monopsonist. As we noted above, cancer research, or research into health generally, is not a monopsonistic endeavor. But it is also far from a competitive endeavor, for the federal government is clearly the dominant sponsor; the federal government is perhaps more dominant in the sponsorship of health research than AT&T once was in the provision of communication services. The data concerning the alleged relationship between smoking and lung cancer, for instance, is generated by the cancer research community, which includes both private and public establishments and which is heavily subsidized by the federal government. Because of the enormous level of federal government involvement in this research, it seems a useful and essentially non-distorting simplification to describe this research establishment as a single bureau, even though a number of distinct public (e.g., National Institutes of Health) and private (e.g., American Cancer Society) organizations are involved.

Legislative Sponsorship of Health Research. In seeking to understand how the direction of public health research might differ as between organization through competitive market processes and organization through a monopsonistic government process, it is important to distinguish between the legislative sponsors of research and the bureau to which responsibility for the conduct of that research is given. The incentives of each are important to any effort to gauge the course of governmentally-dominated research and to compare it with what would emerge from a competitive market process.

Within the context of the interest-group theory of government, the legislative committees that appropriate funds for health research are responding principally to the interests of input suppliers. This is not to deny that consumers can receive some benefit from such sponsorship, but is only to note that it is the interests of suppliers that drive the process. Granted, there can be many input suppliers who vie for legislative sponsorship. Some competitors in the case of cancer research might be those who emphasize medical programs, others who emphasize dietary programs, and yet others who emphasize psychological programs.

Scholarship in the interest-group theory of government would say that the winning suppliers will generally be those to whom government sponsorship is the most valuable net of the cost of lobbying. Suppose this turns out to be those who stress medical programs--physicians. This means that the legislative committees that oversee health research and rule on appropriations will be doing so in a way that advances the general interest of physicians. In turn, the bureau that administers health research will serve largely as an agent of its legislative sponsor, although such relationships may not be controlled fully by the sponsors.

Bureaucratic Direction of Health Research. Within an interest-group model of government, it seems possible to characterize the monopsonistic sponsorship of health research by government as a program run by physicians predominately for the benefit of physicians. Again, this is not to deny that customers or patients may derive some benefit through the products of such research, but is only to assert that it is physicians and not customers whose interests motivate and drive the process of research sponsorship.

Once this step is taken, it is easy to see that the economic principles of bureaucracy suggest that, in comparison with an industry of profit-seeking firms, the anti-cancer bureaucracy will face weaker incentives to find and develop effective treatments of and cures for cancer and will face incentives to exaggerate the risks of cancer. To some degree, this point involves a subtle variation on the theme that finding a cure for cancer would put many cancer bureaucrats out of work. There are, of course, several occupations that depend on a continuation of a state of affairs that its practitioners seek to eliminate but for which universal success would end the occupation. Divorce lawyers and family counselors would go out of business if people were to learn how to get along together. Physicians might advise people how to stay healthy, but healthy people would have little demand for physicians.

In these and related cases, what provides the incentive for individual practitioners to promote the interests of their clients--an incentive that clashes somewhat with the interests of the entire group of practitioners-- is the competitive organization of service delivery. Auto mechanics, for instance, may be tempted to exaggerate the mechanical defects present in a car they have been asked to repair. However, they face the constraint of competition. Auto mechanics compete vigorously, have no national organization designed to limit competition, and are not heavily subsidized by the government in such a manner that they are rewarded for finding more "broken" cars. As a result, the perverse incentives they might face as a group are kept under control.[5]

The medical profession, taken as a collective group, may similarly face perverse incentives with regard to the services it provides. There is clearly competition among cancer researchers, but those researchers are in a somewhat different position from ordinary market competitors. Competitors must always seek to please their customers. In ordinary market arrangements these customers are numerous and decentralized. It would be the same with cancer research if the sponsors of that research were numerous and decentralized. But such sponsorship is centralized and largely monopolized. Although individual researchers have incentives to find cures for cancer (the Nobel Prize), they also have incentives to please their sponsors--and the dominant sponsor is a government bureaucracy, not the numerous and variegated buyers that constitute a competitive market.

Moreover, the sponsor may well have an incentive to act as an agent for the collective interest of physicians. In the case of medical research, this interest is surely advanced more fully by exaggerating the risks of cancer than by rhapsodizing over how the world is becoming ever safer. In bureaus, larger budgets are generally preferred to smaller budgets. One means of gaining larger budgets is to "advertise," as it were. With respect to the anti-cancer bureaucracy, one form such "advertisement" can take is to exaggerate the risk of cancer. The more successful the bureaucracy is in portraying an image of the ubiquitousness of cancer, the larger its governmental appropriations and charitable donations will be. It is obvious that the budget will be functionally related to the perceived risk of cancer and other diseases within the Congress and the general public. It takes neither a Machiavellian imagination nor a Ph.D. in economics to conclude that if the Surgeon General is acting as an agent of the medical community, he has a strong incentive to stress the risk of cancer, as we argued in Chapter 10.[6]

Public Health and the Collective Interests of Physicians

The individual physician has a competitive incentive to cure his patients and otherwise to give them reliable health care. This incentive derives from the competitive pressure provided by competing physicians in the market for health care.[7] Nonetheless, the medical profession has historically gone beyond services of individual physicians to patients and has organized as a group for collective action. The American Medical Association (AMA) is the lobbying arm of the medical profession. In this aspect of their behavior, physicians as an organized interest group may have quite different incentives than the individual physician has with respect to his patients.[8]

In fact, the AMA has historically behaved like a physicians' interest group seeking to control the supply of new physicians, the price of medical services (through, for example, seeking an exemption from the antitrust laws), the price of complements and substitutes for physicians' services, and a variety of other competition-suppressing schemes. All of these activities are consistent with increasing the wealth of doctors.[9]

The medical profession is a strong driving force behind the modern expansion of the public health bureaucracy, that is, of government programs ranging from basic research in health sciences to the dissemination of information about the reported health consequences of activities such as diet, smoking, drinking, and so on. While public-interest rationales for public health cannot be dismissed totally, as we noted earlier, it is surely also reasonable that a more complete understanding of public-health processes requires a consideration of how those processes affect the wealth of physicians.

The effort to place public health within an interest-group model of government suggests that a great deal of what constitutes public health can be understood more sensibly as a method of transferring wealth from taxpayers and consumers in general to physicians and other specialized inputs involved in the supply of medical services, than as a means of providing public goods and internalizing externalities. One point in this respect is that congressional sponsors of public health have particularly strong demands for public health because their constituencies have relatively high concentrations of physicians. Physicians are not distributed geographically in proportion to the general population. There are some places where physicians are concentrated relatively heavily. For example, a cursory inspection of the data shows that physicians are disproportionately concentrated in those states where a senator sits on the Senate's Labor and Human Resources Committee, which oversees a variety of public-health programs (approximately 196 non-federal physicians per 100,000 of population as compared to 180 in all other states). Those very same states also have a significantly greater concentration of nursing homes (approximately 327 to 285) and beds (59 per 1,000 of population over age 65 to 56). The distribution of public health spending is thus concentrated in those states that have representation on the Labor and Human Resources Committee. The members of that committee can be thought of as having a relatively high demand for public health spending, in reflection of particularly strong interests of their constituency in such spending.[10]

A more subtle self interest of physicians in public health programs concerns the impact of such spending on aggregate spending for physicians and their services. Suppose that public-health spending achieves its purported effect of increasing the longevity of the population. The population may be healthier in some overall sense, but spending on medical services can increase nonetheless. This could happen if medical-care expenditures rise with the age of the population. If this follows, then it can be said that it is in the direct self-interest of the medical profession to support public health programs designed to increase the longevity of the population. In this respect, the medical profession's support of public health programs is analogous to its support of Medicare and Medicaid. There may be a public interest rationale in both cases, but one's intuition is to look at the impact of such programs on physicians' wealth.

A great deal of public-health activity designed to increase longevity involves the advocacy and dissemination of information about "healthier lifestyles." Thus, individuals are advised not to smoke, to avoid fatty foods and obesity, to exercise, to limit alcohol consumption, and so on. The primary purpose of such advice is to increase the lifetimes of those who follow the advice, or at least so it is claimed. Under one alternative, an individual can live it up and be merry and then die at a younger age with consequent medical expenses. Under the other, he can follow the proscribed advice of the medical sages and die at an advanced age with consequent medical expenses. It is possible to test whether the present value of medical expenses in the latter case exceeds those in the former. Should this turn out to be so, the hypothesis about physician support for public-health spending would not be refuted. Indeed, such an argument has a degree of plausibility. Instant death from a heart attack at age 55 will not compare in medical expenses to death from a lingering illness at age 80.[11]

Public health programs cannot, of course, abolish the fact of death. All they can do is perhaps alter the timing and the cause of death. That people will die is invariant; when they will die and from what may be variable within limits. It is the possibility of this variation that creates an important relationship between public health and the general or class interest of physicians. For public health programs may operate to transform deaths from medically-unintensive to medically-intensive categories. One way this might work is simply a product of age: if the demand for medical services increases with age, an increase in longevity will translate into an increased demand for medical services, which in turn will generate rents for suppliers of specialized inputs. A second way is through a shift in what might be called the disease structure of a society. Even if longevity is unaffected by public health, programs that shift deaths from low-cost to high-cost (in terms of medical resources) forms will also generate rents for specialized medical inputs. To be sure, both types of changes are likely to be present; there is likely to be covariance between the age of death and the form of death. Nonetheless, it seems useful to keep the conceptual distinction between the two types of transformation in mind.

Consider first the effect of increasing age on the demand for medical services. Suppose that the aggregate demand for medical services is disaggregated into age categories. For any given price of medical care, there will be an amount demanded by people at each age category in the population. Further suppose that the amount demanded rises monotonically with age. A public health program that postpones death will increase the aggregate demand for medical services. So long as medical services are produced under conditions of rising supply price, that increased demand will generate rents for medical input suppliers that face inelastic supply conditions.

The basic facts do not refute this line of reasoning. In 1984, health care expenditures for urban consumers rose consistently with age, ranging from $305 per year for ages 24 and under to $1,487 per year for ages 75 and over (Bureau of Labor Statistics 1984). While such a result may hardly seem surprising, it does put the effort to extend life expectancies beyond what would result through market processes into a somewhat different perspective.[12]

An obvious question arises with respect to whether such a rent-seeking investment by physicians is economically sensible. In other words, at prevailing interest rates, does an investment in an increase in medical spending by promoting a longer-lived population make sense for physicians as an interest group? The answer, in general, is that it is rational for physicians to lobby for older populations and hence increased medical expenditures so long as the rate of increase in spending exceeds the real interest rate. The data mentioned above from the Bureau of Labor Statistics (1984) suggest that this can be the case. For example, suppose an alcohol abuse program resulted in an increase in life expectancy of four years, from 58 to 62. The BLS data suggest that annual per capita spending on medical services would increase by some 15 percent. Given historical levels of real interest rates, this hypothetical investment in an alcohol abuse program could represent a wise investment for doctors. Also, it must be borne in mind that longevity promotion is mostly a free lunch for doctors; physicians themselves bear only a miniscule portion of the tax-financed costs of public health. Therefore, longevity promotion (over some relevant range) in the absence of any market failure in the wellness market will almost always pay for physicians as a whole. [13]

Consider the possible impact of public health upon the disease structure within a society, independently of any effect on the average age of the population. This would describe a world in which a reduction in the incidence of one disease would be exactly offset by an increase in the incidence of other diseases. There would be no effect upon morbidity or mortality rates. If, for instance, the incidence of lung cancer is reduced, the incidence of kidney disease will be increased offsettingly. In point of fact, a shift in the structure of disease will also produce a shift in life expectancy. The removal of a disease that would have killed people at age 60 will lead to its replacement by some other disease that will kill them nonetheless, but it is likely that death would occur at some later age. Within the context of a public-interest model of public health, the allocation of treatment and prevention resources between the two diseases will be governed by relative consumer valuations. But within a physician-interest model, the allocation of public health resources will be biased toward the less medically-intensive disease. If this is lung cancer, public health will be more fully aimed at lung cancer than consumers would direct, because the resulting lowered incidence of lung cancer would transform those patients into demanders of the more expensive treatment for kidney disease. The basic idea is to change the disease structure of society in a way that increases the demand for medical services and to do so through public health programs.[14]

Self Interest in Public Interest Organizations

To this point we have treated input suppliers as homogeneous. In particular, we have referred to the general or class interests of physicians as something that can be advanced through public-health processes. But physicians themselves have various interests, and those interests can surely conflict in many ways and along many margins. Public-health processes may operate to generate rents for physicians, but those rents need not be distributed proportionately throughout the population of physicians. Some physicians may gain more than others. In particular, physicians who are particularly well organized politically and for whom factor supplies are relatively inelastic will gain relative to other physicians. All physicians may gain through public health, but some may gain more than others.

One of the notable things about public-health processes is the participation of non-profit, public-interest organizations. Examples are the Cancer, Lung, and Heart associations. What is the place of such organizations in the provision of public health? Can such organizations be located within the context of the interest-group theory of government? Are such organizations as the American Lung Association and the American Cancer Society illustrations of the interest-group theory of government? Or are they empirical illustrations of the limits of that theory?

To start, the designation of some organization as being "non-profit" is a legal, tax-related designation and not a designation with economic content. There may be many particular reasons why people invest in non-profit and in profit-seeking enterprises, but the same economic principles would apply in both cases: people will choose a portfolio that equates the anticipated risk-adjusted returns at the margin. The same principles that govern investment in companies that manufacture medical equipment govern investment in lung associations and the like--to say nothing of governing investment in politicians through campaign contributions, donations of time, and the like.

For instance, most hospitals are organized with a non-profit legal status. But this does not mean that the transactions in which those hospitals participate stand outside ordinary economic incentives and motivation. For there are several ways in which non-profit hospitals can serve as vehicles for advancing the interests of physicians who staff the hospitals. This was demonstrated by Mark Pauly and Michael Redish (1973), who explained how the non-profit hospital can be used as a vehicle for profit maximization by the physicians who effectively owned the hospitals. The hospital would have no net income to show. But this does not indicate non-profit status, but only shows that what could alternatively have been shown as income and then distributed to shareholders was captured directly by the physicians in the first place. Pauly and Redish showed that it would be misleading to treat non-profit hospitals as independent, charitable agencies. While they may be organized on a non-profit basis, they are also essentially owned by the physicians who staff them. Pauly and Redish explained how physicians could use the hospital as an input in their own profit-maximizing activities.

Something similar might be said about the public-health bureaucracy, including such private components of that bureaucracy as the Cancer, Lung, and Heart Associations. For instance, the American Lung Association might be seen as an agency that increases the aggregate demand for pulmonary services, just as the American Cancer Society operates to increase the demand for oncological services. There are a number of ways in which such a process might operate, all of which can be seen in one way or another as increasing the demand for the services of the medical specialities they represent. For instance, what constitutes proper diagnostic and testing procedures is influenced by patient perceptions of risk and value, by malpractice awards, by insurance company policies, and by governmental requirements, among other things.

A paternalistic view of such non-profit organizations would suggest that the net worths of the physicians they are related to have been reduced through an essentially charitable transfer program. A self-interest view would expect to find that those incomes have increased. Those physicians who deal with heart disease should find their incomes increasing by virtue of the activities of the American Heart Association. This could be because the efforts of the association increase the amount of heart-related tests in standard diagnostic procedures, which in turn induces an increased demand for medical inputs.[15]

Although the activities of physicians, as represented by the AMA, have long been viewed from a self-interest perspective by economists, public health processes have not been subjected to such an examination. But just as the conduct of ostensibly charitable hospitals cannot be examined independently of the interests of the physicians who staff them, so too, we think, the conduct of public health bureaus should not be examined in isolation from the interests of the medical community that they represent. An interest-group interpretation of public health would look to the ways in which public health processes increase the aggregate demand for medical services, thereby generating quasi-rents for specialized input suppliers.

NOTES

1. One effort to explore some of the relevant conceptual issues is Tollison and Wagner (1991), from which the arguments in this chapter are drawn. For complementary descriptive material based principally upon examinations of the American Heart Association, the American Lung Association, and the American Cancer Society, see James Bennett (1990).

2. It is worth noting that much of the recent dietary revolution emphasizing the reduction of saturated fat and the increased consumption of complex carbohydrates in the diet was pioneered by such non-physicians as Nathan Pritikin.

3. "Choice," of course, is not so simple as described. But while certainly more complex than described, the general idea is that individuals pursue their objectives, whether longer life or more fun, with purpose and efficiency.

4. For a wide ranging description and discussion of a variety of hypotheses, see Eysenck (1986).

5. See the development of this theme in Darby and Karni (1973).

6. This process of exaggerating risk in order to secure larger appropriations is inherent in all the risky and uncertain activities of government. Thus, the Department of Defense will stress the risk of losing or falling behind in the arms race, the Justice Department will exaggerate problems of crime, and so on.

7. We abstract here from issues concerning barriers to entry in the medical profession and whether there is a competitive supply of physicians.

8. As discussed in Chapter 10, groups like physicians may organize initially for quite productive reasons, such as the promulgation of professional standards. Yet once organized, the marginal costs of collective action to cartelize and to raise prices are low. Such a pattern of historical evolution is apparent in the history of many interest groups.

9. Of course, the issue of motivation can be debated. Why do physicians support government health-care programs such as Medicare and Medicaid? Is it because they support health-care programs for the poor for altruistic reasons or because such programs increase the aggregate demand for medical services? And could the latter effect be an unintended consequence of public-spirited behavior by physicians? Are doctors doing well by doing good? Reasonable people could disagree about the answers to these questions, but the historical behavior of the AMA suggests clearly that economic incentives and the impact of its efforts on physicians' wealth have been an important factor.

10. This pork-barrel type result is not at all unusual in public choice analyses of congressional behavior. See Plott (1968), Stigler (1976), and Crain and Tollison (1977) for related studies.

11. We have been speaking as if physicians have homogenous interests. This is not the case, as we note more fully in the next section. Physicians will have various interests depending upon their specialities, and so a more elegant version of an interest-group theory would account for struggles among physicians within the physicians' interest groups. Some physicians, for example, will specialize in treating heart attack victims, others in treating lung cancer victims, and so on. In this context our hypothesis is that the replacement of early deaths through heart attack and lung cancer by later deaths in other manners increases the net incomes of physicians. A related point is that age-related illnesses are subsidized by government health-care programs, which implies greater consumption of medical care at later ages.

12. Should there be some failure in the market for wellness, such life extension might be worthwhile. The rents for physicians would in this case be the vehicle for motivating the market correction. But if there is no failure in the market for wellness, as we argued previously, such life extension would not be worth the cost.

13. Obviously, the incentives of physicians to lobby for longevity promotion will be a function of the real interest rate and the rate of increase of medical spending with age, as stressed above (less the present value of their pro rata tax costs). This suggests that physicians will be sensitive to the way medical spending behaves with respect to longevity. They will not rationally invest, for example, in more longevity where that longevity initially results in an extended period of zero medical spending by the older population and is followed years later by an increase in such spending. Rational investments by physicians will generally require smoothly rising medical expenditures with respect to age, and even in this case, the increase must at least offset the interest rate, or physicians will

not rationally support it. Hence, policies might be pursued that would promote increases from age 65 to 75 but not from 75 to 80.

14. Indeed, in a public-interest model relatively greater emphasis would probably be placed on the more costly diseases. At base, public health resources would be allocated such that at the relevant margins, marginal treatment costs would be reduced equally per dollar of expenditure.

15. Non-profit organizations in the health area have also sometime ventured into the business of selling testing devices or programs related to stopping smoking and the like. It is not clear how general profit-seeking by the non-profits is, but this is surely an issue worthy of further empirical research.

CHAPTER 12

Principle And
Expediency In
Public Policy

In the traditional, pre-public choice approach to public policy, the creation of policy was seen as exogenous to the economic process. Within this exogenous perspective, there was no scope for a theory of economic policy or political choice as such. The analytical task was not to explain the central characteristics of the policy choices that emerge from a political process, but rather was to advise the policy maker on the characteristics of desirable policy measures. To this day, the central core of what is called welfare economics has consisted of specifying the characteristics of "good" policy measures. The creator of public policy stands outside the economic process, and the task for the economic analyst is to suggest ways for the policy maker to improve the operation of the economic process. Presumably, the more benevolent or public spirited the policy maker, the more fully the policy measures actually enacted will advance the economic welfare of the nation.

But once the production of public policy is itself treated as an ordinary economic activity, as the public choice approach does, public policy becomes endogenous to the economic process, and the characteristics of public policy measures become objects of explanation. In this case what primarily governs those characteristics are the incentives that politicians face. For a given set of incentives there will tend to be a particular set of policy measures that will represent a political equilibrium. This statement is equivalent to the proposition that for a given set of preferences, resource availabilities, technologies, and property rights, there will exist an economic equilibrium. In the familiar economic case, we say that for changes in the structure of production to take place, there must be preceding changes in such things as preferences, resource availabilities, technologies, and property rights. But in similar fashion, we can say that changes in the characteristic outcomes of the political process require changes in the same things, only in this case "property rights" refer to the whole set of institutional rules constraining the operation of political processes.

A constitution is the set of social institutions or rules within which individuals operate and interact with one another. All societies must have some sort of constitution under which social interaction is regulated and disputes between individuals with competing ends resolved. A society without a constitution is not really a society at all, but a jumble of individuals at best and a mob at worst. The social constitution is analogous to the rules of the game in sports. Brennan and Buchanan develop this analogy:

> A game is described by its rules--its constitution. These rules establish the framework within which the playing of the game proceeds; they set boundaries on what activities are legitimate, as well as describing the objects of the game and how to determine who wins. It is clear intuitively that the choice among alternative strategies that a player might make in the course of a game is categorically quite distinct from his prior choice among alternative sets of rules. A tennis player after hitting a particular shot may reasonably wish that the net was lower, yet prior to the game he may have agreed to a set of rules in which the height of the net was specified (1980, p. 3).

It is important to emphasize that *all* social orders are ultimately based on some sort of constitution. Hence, the social constitution is not necessarily related to the document by that name which often serves as the legal basis for government; the constitution of society in America may be thought to include, but is not the same as, the U.S. Constitution. The social constitution refers to all of the "rules of the game" which affect social interaction and regulate disputes among individuals, not just laws but also all other relevant social conventions which constrain individual behavior.

A constitutional perspective implies that since the production of public policy conforms to an economic logic, "improvement" in the type of policy measures produced is much more a matter of changing the incentives constraining political processes than it is a matter of giving policy makers better advice. For this reason, a constitutional perspective focuses on an analysis of social interaction which explicitly takes into account the constitutional constraints affecting social behavior, and pays particular attention to the effects resulting from changes in these constraints over time. Constitutions are not the result of divine intervention nor are they laid on us by exogenous but benevolent despots. Rather they arise from interactions among utility-maximizing individuals pursuing their self-interest, each of whom must accommodate to the fact of others acting in a similar fashion. Constitutions arise from the purposive action of rational, self-interested individuals and not from selfless law-givers. For this reason, constitutions may change over time in ways which serve the interests of restricted subsets of society at the expense of the common interest, as represented by the substitution of rules and policies that emphasize the transfer of wealth for rules and policies that emphasize the creation of wealth.

Principles of Constitutional Political Economy

Constitutions form the basis for all social activity. Therefore, all economic production is ultimately a function of the constitutional order in place in a given society. Economists have traditionally maintained that production requires some combination of three basic inputs in order to take place: land (i.e., all natural resources), labor, and capital (the result itself of a combination of land and labor over time). But, in fact, the constitution is another basic and vital "factor of production." The extent to which economic activity can be conducted efficiently is limited by the nature of the constitution. Regardless of the stock of labor and natural resources available within a country, the degree of freedom and economic opportunity available to its citizens and the rates of economic growth and development it is capable of achieving depend upon the constitutional constraints in place, for these govern the relative incentives of wealth-creating and wealth-transferring activities. There are many examples of unfree and undeveloped countries with anemic economies, which are nevertheless endowed with abundant labor, land, and natural resources (e.g., the Soviet Union or the People's Republic of China), as well as of free, rapidly developing countries with robust and energetic economies with meager endowments of natural resources and land (e.g., Japan and Hong Kong). The difference in economic performance arises to an important extent because countries like Japan have constitutional and institutional arrangements that encourage and nurture freedom and economic opportunity for individual consumers and producers, while countries like the People's Republic of China have constitutional and institutional arrangements that stifle and repress freedom and economic activity.

But as previously noted, constitutions do not result from divine intervention. The same factor which dominates the determination of outcomes in private markets--the driving force of rational self-interest--is also the primary factor determining outcomes in constitutional "markets." Laws, conventions, and all other forms of social regulation are the outcome of the competition among various individuals, each seeking to maximize his own utility.

However, there is a vital difference between two kinds of constitutional competition. This difference reflects the fact that the social constitution can be separated into two fundamentally different parts. The first part is composed of those rules which are the result of a voluntary agreement between all participants, and are in a sense analogous to rules in sports. Every one who plays baseball, for example, has agreed of his or her own volition to obey a certain set of rules of that game. Otherwise, they would not agree to play in the first place. The "voluntary" rules are the result of spontaneous agreement among all participants, and represent a quite literal "social contract." Like ordinary contracts in private markets, no coercion is involved in securing agreement. Everyone involved agrees to abide by the rules in question because in each individual case they perceive themselves to be better off by so doing. Most customs, social conventions, and informal rules of social interaction--e.g., manners--are examples of the "sports-like" portion of the social constitution.

The other part of the constitution is determined and enforced through political processes. This includes laws, government regulations, and the actual, written constitution of the government in question. Unlike the "sports-like" portion of the constitution, this portion is not formulated as the result of completely voluntary agreement among all participants across free markets. Rather, it is the result of decisions made in the political sector, and imposed on society whether all individuals agree or not. This portion of the constitution is based on coercion.

Despite this major distinction, the two portions of the constitution of a society are not by their nature fundamentally incompatible. The use of some coercion may be necessary in order to provide for the efficient operation--and even the existence--of a free society. For example, in the case of certain public goods, such as national defense, voluntary market exchange may not provide optimal quantities. A modification of the social constitution in such a way as to allow for a government to function to provide such necessary goods may represent an efficient solution. The protection of property rights by means of the formulation and enforcement of criminal law may be another similar example of a necessary governmental function requiring modifications to the social constitution in order to allow a certain and precisely delimited amount of coercion by government. Such forms of "coercive constitutionalism" may actually *increase* the level of individual liberty in society by protecting and extending the functioning of the free marketplace. Such coercive, political portions of the social constitution may form a necessary bulwark for a free market and a free society by serving to protect the rights of individuals from force and fraud.

However, there is another, darker side to the political constitution. What Caesar gives Caesar can also take away. Because modifications to the political portion of the social constitution do not require the consent of all participants in the social order, modifications can occur which do not improve the welfare of all individuals. This is not the case with voluntary, "sports-like" constitutional rules: if changes in the rules did not benefit all participants, they would not voluntarily agree to those changes. But in the case of changes in the political constitution, voluntary agreement on the part of all participants is irrelevant. Even if a large minority vigorously object to a given rule (whether statute, regulation, or other form), their objections are irrelevant as long as the measure in question has sufficient political support--in a democracy, a majority of the voters; in a nondemocracy, like most countries in the world today, perhaps much less--to ensure its passage. Those who object will simply be coerced into acceptance.

Hence, the major difference between the two types of constitutional change is obvious. Changes in the voluntary, spontaneous, "sports-like" constitution must, by definition, benefit all participants; otherwise, they would refuse to agree to the changes. By contrast, changes in the political portion of the constitution *do not* necessarily benefit all participants. They may benefit only the relatively small subset of society that is sufficient to ensure enactment of the changes, because the rest will be forced to accept them. In both constitutional realms, people are assumed to be rational and self-interested, and to be seeking to maximize their own utility within a process where they are competing with other individuals with similar motivations. The same economic principles describe the operation of competition in the market for rules with equal validity. The only important difference is that in the first realm the competition is limited to the pursuit of voluntary agreement by means of persuading others; in the latter competition can extend to the use of force to provide the means to coerce compliance.

The Self-Ownership Foundations of a Democratic Polity

There is a logical dichotomy at the base of all discussions of political obligation which is very simple, but which can be ignored only at our peril. This is that, economically speaking, all resources that have value *are* owned by someone. Extending this simple maxim to individuals provides the basis for this dichotomy: individuals either own themselves, or someone else owns them.

The United States was founded on the premise--clearly expressed in both the Declaration of Independence and the Constitution--that each individual in society owns himself. This implies both that individuals are free to pursue their own unique goals, and at the same time that they are responsible for the consequences of their own actions. One of the most important of these responsibilities is respecting the equal freedom of other individuals to pursue their own ends similarly.

Other nations in the world today (though a dwindling number) are founded on a different premise: that individuals do not own themselves but are, in effect, owned by the state. The state makes all important decisions regarding economic and social affairs, and individuals have no rights at all. Individuals only have whatever privileges those who control the state deign to grant them, for as long as those in control find convenient.

Unfortunately in the real world, the line of demarcation between these two extremes can become blurred. This is particularly the case in free societies with constitutions which have established democratic decision-making structures. There is a necessary tension between individual liberty and democracy which can tend to dilute the power of self-ownership of free individuals if not carefully controlled. A free society does not necessarily require democratic governmental structures, but such structures are probably the best available for ensuring that the power of government is effectively constrained by the preferences of citizens. But democracy is like a fire. Carefully constrained and limited, it can be a valuable tool for accomplishing productive ends, as in clearing farmland of useless brush; when it is not carefully constrained and limited, it can be immensely destructive of life, limb, and property.

Democracy only necessarily protects the freedom and property of the *majority*; without express protection, minority interests will be unprotected from the depredations of the majority. But even worse, the majority which is protected today may be a different group of people than that protected yesterday or than that protected next week. In other words, majorities are not likely to be stable over time. This week, A and B may gang up on C and steal him blind; next week, B and C might do the same to A; and on and on. In the absence of effective constitutional constraints on the actions of government--bounds which clearly establish which uses of political coercion are legitimate and acceptable and which are illegitimate and unacceptable--democracy can be transformed from a useful social decision-making device to a kind of majoritarian tyranny based on the unrestrained hunt for plunder of vulnerable minority interests.

There is sometimes a tendency to use the term democracy as a synonym for free society. This is dangerously misleading. Even though free societies commonly find some variant of democratic decision making the most efficient means for controlling government, democracy in the absence of effective limits is just another form of tyranny. The Founding Fathers worked long and hard on the thorny problem of how to establish a democratic form of government which would be effectively restrained from running roughshod over the rights of minorities (a term, as noted above, that refers to those unfortunate enough to be outside of the majority coalition at the time in question). The American Constitution was designed as a strong leash on a form of government that the Founding Fathers envisaged as a powerful, vicious dog--dangerous if allowed to roam free, but potentially an effective protector of the rights and property of the individuals who constitute the society.

Considerations from the Economic Theory of Legislation

As we saw in Chapter 10, the modern economic theory of legislation has as its basis the fact that competition for legislation and regulation is affected by the same forces that affect competition across ordinary markets for other goods and services, and that the outcomes of political competition are as much the outcomes of market processes as those that flow from the ordinary, private marketplace. The same rational, self-interested, utility-maximizing individuals inhabit both worlds.

One implication of this analysis is that legislative outcomes normally tend to be the result of intense competition among interest groups which expect either to gain or to lose tangible and significant amounts of income from the passage (or nonpassage) of a law or regulation. In the real world, legislatures are unlikely to pass a law for the simple and altruistic reason that they expect that it will somehow make "society" better off. Legislatures typically act as a kind of brokerage firm, supplying wealth transfers to competing interest groups, thereby making some people in society better off at the expense of others.

It should be noted that this process of rent-seeking competition among interest groups is perfectly consistent with democracy. Interest groups must purchase in one way or another the votes of a majority in order to have the measures which benefit themselves passed. Democracy by itself places little constraint on the process of rent-seeking competition in the political sector, for it means only that policy measures must receive majority approval in a legislative assembly. However, it is fully possible for measures to receive majority approval in a legislature that would be rejected overwhelmingly in a referendum or plebiscite.

All political processes will necessarily be vulnerable to increasing control by rent-seeking interest groups unless there are effective constraints on what government coercion can be used to do as well as on what it is prohibited from doing. Otherwise, activity by government which reduces the welfare of society at large and tramples on the rights and liberties of individuals is not only possible but probable, if such activity would tend to benefit some interest group.

The political portion of the social constitution in general, and not just laws passed by legislatures *per se*, will be determined in such an environment. Under ordinary circumstances, we should expect that changes are advocated in the political constitution of society primarily by groups that are seeking rents which they expect to flow to themselves as a result. Constitutions are a battlefield on which rent-seeking interest groups compete for coercive wealth transfers they expect to result from the operation of the political process.

This has two major implications in terms of the constitution of society discussed above. First, any tendency towards shifting matters from the voluntary, "sports-like" constitutional arena to the political and coercive portion of the constitution will necessarily involve subjecting those matters to rent-seeking competition by interest groups that are striving for wealth transfers. Fantasies of disinterested, public-spirited politicians and regulators with a single-minded determination to enhance the welfare of society by enacting enlightened legislation and regulation disintegrate after exposure to the real world. If government's power to intervene in society is kept tightly limited, this rent-seeking competition will be held in tight check as well. But in the absence of such constitutional limits on government, rent-seeking interest groups will almost inevitably come to dominate the process in their pursuit of wealth transfers. Second, while there is a natural tendency for matters left in the former realm to be resolved in a manner which is consistent with the rights and preferences of all, there is no such tendency in the latter. The former is the world of peaceful persuasion and cooperative competition; the latter that of coercion and conflict.

Implications for Public Policy Toward Tobacco

The implications of the constitutional perspective on social decision-making for public policy with respect to tobacco products should also be obvious. As we have seen in the earlier chapters, there is no proven economic basis for claiming that smokers impose costs on nonsmokers. We saw that with respect to environmental tobacco smoke, there is no valid economic basis for asserting that smokers allegedly impose uncompensated costs on nonsmokers. And we saw that if we assume that smokers have themselves by smoking any possible costs are borne economically by those smokers and not by nonsmokers.

Suppose that sometime in the future evidence becomes available which indicates that smoking seriously harms the health of *both* the smoker and those exposed to environmental tobacco smoke. Would this fact make any difference as far as restrictions by government on tobacco consumption by adults is concerned? Unless one is willing to reject the basis of the free society of self-owning and self-responsible individuals, it should not. Adults who smoke do so of their own free will, and bear voluntarily whatever risks are associated with that activity. A case could always be made that smokers who do not understand the risks should be protected by government, because government possesses better information. However, such claims about knowledge seem far-fetched in the case of tobacco products. The federal government has engaged in a widely-publicized, concerted campaign for 25 years to convince the general public that smoking is dangerous. If there is any misinformation on the part of smokers, it may well be a substantially *exaggerated* idea of the riskiness of smoking. The same may be true for nonsmokers, many of whom may be nonsmokers *only* because the same informational bias leads them to hold exaggerated perceptions of the risks associated with smoking.

The fact remains: people who smoke do so because the value they place on the benefits they receive from smoking exceeds the cost of smoking to them, including the perceived risk of health consequences. Similarly, nonsmokers who choose to expose themselves to ETS for extended periods do so because the benefits that they receive from relationships with smokers exceed the costs of so relating. To pretend that either in the case of smokers or nonsmokers it is proper and necessary for government to protect the public from cigarettes is tantamount to assuming that normal adults are incapable of making rational and coherent decisions regarding the conduct of their own lives. Even if smoking could be proven to generate significantly increased health risks for either smokers or for nonsmokers through ETS, mandatory restrictions on the behavior of smokers ostensibly based on grounds of "protecting the public health" would imply that adult individuals in general were somehow unable to assess risks rationally and to make responsible decisions.

Of course, political events do not just fall from the sky. Much anti-smoking rhetoric is likely to be window-dressing designed to help in the pursuit of rents through politics. Nonsmokers can be expected to gain higher wages as the result of "Clean Indoor Air Acts" that focus solely on banning smoking at the expense of smokers, as the mandatory regulations act as a barrier to entry that generates monopoly rents. Politicians who view tax revenue as the raw material for wealth transfers which they can supply to favored interest groups will gain from the proceeds from tobacco taxes ostensibly enacted to improve the public health. Large restaurants may favor mandatory segregation of smokers and nonsmokers in order to impose relatively high costs on small restaurants, and thereby to reduce the competition they face. But whatever the real motivation behind the movement to restrict the consumption of tobacco products, it represents a fundamental rejection of the principles of individual liberty upon which a free society is ultimately founded.

Implications for Public Policy More Broadly Considered

Social Costs: A Slippery Economic Slope. The analysis of social costs -- of smoking, drinking, eating fatty foods, and other consumption activities -- has recently become a growth industry. Many studies have purported to show that various different goods and pastimes generate huge costs to society, over and above the costs individual consumers may face.

We have already reviewed the various studies which attempt to evaluate the so-called social costs of smoking. But there are various other applications of social cost analysis. One study maintains that the social cost due to medical care for victims of motorcycle accidents was over $10 billion in 1985, not counting the social cost resulting from accident deaths. If the full cost of deaths due to motorcycle accidents (including the value of lost wages, the cost of medical intervention, and so on) were added, the estimated cost would probably be approximately doubled (Rivers, *et al* 1988). Alcohol consumption has also attracted a great deal of attention from social cost analysts. It was recently reported that about $1.2 billion per year is spent in the United States on alcoholism treatment programs alone (Gunby 1987). A different study indicates that the annual cost of automobile accidents precipitated by drunk driving exceeds $9.4 billion.[1]

As Americans become increasingly health conscious, a number of studies have considered the "social cost" of excess fat. Obesity is a major contributing factor in death from heart disease, and may increase the obese individual's risk from cancer. Overweight individuals are much more likely to require medical intervention for these, as well as a host of other ailments; furthermore, such persons may generally require a longer period of recovery from illness or accidental injury. One study conservatively estimates that obesity adds approximately $27 billion to annual health care costs in the United States (Edmondson 1987).[2]

The basic point however, is that these analysts of social cost are guilty of a glaring inconsistency. They have failed to recognize that the very same methodology they have applied to activities like smoking and drinking can readily be applied to many other forms of consumption. If this idea of social cost makes any sense, it can be extended to a plethora of activities which have heretofore escaped the attention of analysts. As discussed below, similar cost estimates can be calculated for sports participation. Sporting injuries are a major source of hospitalization costs. Attendance at sporting events and other fan-related activities (e.g., listening to a baseball game on the radio instead of concentrating on the job at hand) decrease worker productivity. There is no valid economic reason to claim that smoking produces social costs, but that sports do not. The fact that many people disapprove of smoking, while sports activity is highly regarded, is not relevant to the economic analysis of costs to society.

The methodology of social cost estimation can be consistently applied to a variety of everyday activities, like sports, computer hobbyism, pleasure driving, and so on. Existing studies of social cost tend to emphasize the various economic losses alleged to be associated with high-profile, emotional issues like smoking and drinking. But the same principles can apply to almost any activity. If the concept of social cost is economically valid, there is no logical reason to restrict it to forms of consumption which happen to attract the analyst's personal disapproval.

If social cost principles are considered a useful economic approach, we must recognize that virtually all activities can be shown to generate large costs to society. Furthermore, if it is claimed that government ought to restrict activities which produce social cost, we must recognize that this principle may imply the restriction by government of a vast range of activities and behaviors, goods, and services. This is the slippery slope of social cost analysis.

Consider the example of sports. Sports is a leisure-time activity which is widely regarded as wholesome. Sports are often claimed to represent a spiritually and morally uplifting endeavor; at worst, sports are sometimes argued by critics to be unpleasantly violent. But unlike activities traditionally regarded by some as "sinful," "unhealthy," or "wasteful," there is essentially no significant opposition to sporting activity (except, perhaps, boxing). However, substantial resources are allocated to sports activity each year. Perhaps the most obvious cost involves attendance at a sports event. In 1986, Americans devoted at least 807,030,000 hours to attending sports events. (This does not include time spent traveling to and from those events.)[3] Paid admission fees totaled $3,100,000,000 for spectator sports in that year (U.S. Bureau of Census 1988).

However, the largest "cost" associated with attending events is the value of potential labor effort which is thereby sacrificed. Regardless of whether a sporting event is held during the afternoon on a weekday or on a weekend, a sports fan gives up some amount of potential wage income by going to the game instead of going to work. Naturally, some attending fans are not participants in the labor force, either because they are too young or too old (i.e., retired). A conservative estimate of the percentage of sports event attendees who are actual or potential members of the labor force is the percentage of attendees between the ages of 17 and 55. In 1986, 58.86 percent of total sports attendees were in this age group.[4] Translating this percentage into hours attended, leads us to conclude that approximately 475,022,050 hours of potential work effort were sacrificed to attend sporting events. The value of this time, assuming 1986 average hourly wages, was $4,161,193,100.[5] This is probably a significant underestimate because it is based on the average hourly wage for both men and women together; the average hourly wage for men was higher, and men constituted the overwhelming majority of attenders at sporting events (although unfortunately data on attendance by gender are unavailable).

Americans not only attend sporting events but also participate in them. Unfortunately, statistics on the total time allocated to sports participation are unavailable. In 1986, 214,818,000 Americans participated in some sporting event more than once; approximately 125,536,000 of these participants were between the ages of 18 and 54 (National Sporting Goods Association 1987). If we assume that each of these persons devoted an average of 20 hours a year (24 minutes a week) to sports participation in 1986, the total wage income lost (and the approximate value of lost economic output) was $21,993,907,000. This does not include possible costs resulting from injuries, travel to and from the events, equipment, and so on. This figure is only an informed speculation, but surely represents a reasonable lower bound estimate of the cost of time devoted to engaging in sports.

In order to participate in sports, American spend money on certain goods and services which they expect will enhance their enjoyment of such activities. In 1986, Americans spent $3,931,000,000 on athletic and sporting clothing, and $3,119,000,000 on athletic and sporting footwear. However, special shoes represented a relatively minor expense compared to athletic and sports equipment (e.g., bowling accessories, camping gear, golf equipment), which totaled $9,477,000,000; and recreational transport (excluding pleasure boats), which totaled $6,635,00,000 (National Sporting Goods Association 1987). Americans especially enjoy sports involving water. The most expensive of these, pleasure boating, had 1986 sales of $14,500,000,000 ($7,372,000,000 of which represented the cost of boats) (U.S. Bureau of the Census 1988). The total cost of these listed sporting goods and supplies was $37,373,000,000.

In addition, there are certain other large expenditures made on sports activities which are separate from sporting goods sales. In 1986, $1,130,000,000 was spent on ski lessons, lift tickets, and rentals of ski equipment and $200,000,000 was spent on baseball and other trading cards (*Sports Inc.: The Sports Business Weekly* 1987). Adding these additional expenditures to the previous total leads to a figure of $38,703,000,000. All of these listed costs are either based on reliable Census survey data, or else are conservatively estimated lower bound estimates of relevant cost dimensions. Other researchers have found larger costs per year associated with sports. An econometric study developed by WEFA

Econometrics in conjunction with the magazine *Sports Inc: The Sports Business Weekly* (1987) found that in 1986 total spending on sports reached *$47,250,000,000*, or more than 1 percent of GNP.

The sports example is, of course, silly. As we have repeatedly emphasized throughout this book, such analyses are misapplications of basic economic principles. Nonetheless, the sports example could obviously be extended to almost any other common everyday activity that individuals find rewarding (worth the alleged costs). The point of this discussion is simple -- the errors in the social cost analysis of smoking are quite dangerous. They portend the use of such faulty analysis to argue for the regulation of common everyday behavior, which most people find innocuous. Smoking may not be very popular, but it is best to put the errors in the economic analysis of smoking to rest now, rather than to confront them again in some future misguided debate about the social costs of everyday life.

Indeed, if adults cannot be expected to make rational and responsible decisions about tobacco products without coercive government supervision, how can they be expected to make rational decisions concerning nutrition, child rearing, job selection, gardening, or house-painting, among the myriad decisions they must make? Indeed, how can democracy be trusted to work well if people are such poor judges of their own self-interest? Should we not qualify universal adult suffrage if people are so incapable of wise choice? Perhaps smokers should be denied the right to vote. If government has the power to protect people from making choices that are perceived to involve relatively high risks, why stop at tobacco consumption? What about skiing, mountain climbing, hang gliding, drinking alcohol, and working long hours? Are risks "too high"? By whose standard? Some people are literally so risk averse that they rarely venture out of their own homes.

Just from the above discussion, one could conjure up a case for, say, placing an excise tax on the production of red meat (cattle and hogs), the consumption of which can contribute to obesity, high blood pressure, elevated levels of cholesterol, and so forth. The idea of social costs, used in this way, would probably not make for happy reading in farm country. Yet we allow such a faulty analysis of smoking to go unchallenged. Or take an issue such as skin cancer. Exposing one's self to sunlight is the alleged culprit in this case, and sunbathing is exactly analogous to smoking. It is a voluntary activity with which certain risks are reportedly associated. Again, we would easily conjure up a case for the regulation of sunbathing based upon a faulty application of the principles of social cost. The danger in such procedures to a free society should be apparent.

Paternalism: A Slippery Political Slope. An old saying goes that sauce for the goose is sauce for the gander.[6] Just as there is a slippery slope of economic analysis associated with the issue of smoking, there is also a slippery political slope. It seems clear that most instances of social interdependence among people in a free society are mediated through voluntary private adjustments by individuals. Matters like dress, personal habits, and so forth come to be regulated by what might be called common courtesy and common sense. If individuals do not like the ties that we wear, then several avenues of adjustment are open to them. They can shun us because our ties are so garish; they can offer to buy us more preferable ties in the form of birthday presents; they can ignore our ties and still be our friends because the benefits of friendship continue to outweigh the cost of looking at our ties; and so on. Obviously, there are innumerable interdependencies of this sort that are solved by voluntary private adjustments in every day life.

We have argued in this book that smoking could be treated in this same way. Indeed, we have argued that this is how the smoking issue *should* be handled. Unfortunately, this is not how the issue of smoking has been addressed. The issue has been intensely and heavily politicized. What this means in practice is that a political mechanism is being used by one group of people (nonsmokers) to impose their preferences on another group (smokers). And with smokers representing a minority proportion of the population, it is easy to see how this could happen under majoritarian politics. There is an inherent danger in applying majoritarian politics to inherently private issues regarding social inter-dependencies. This danger resides in the prospect that all such issues will be politicized, and that as this process runs its course, everyone will end up worse off and less free in their personal behavior. What little comfort the nonsmoker finds in regulating smoking today will be lost tomorrow as rules regulating some aspect of the nonsmoker's behavior are promulgated by future meddlesome majorities. The long-run welfare of everyone is best when all cease and desist from trying to use the state to regulate aspects of the personal behavior of others. If individuals do not heed this lesson, we will end up with a totally regulated society.

Private and voluntary processes to resolve issues of social interdependence confront individuals with the relevant costs and benefits of their preferences about what others do. Politicization of such issues breaks this link between costs and benefits and opens the door to a society totally dominated by the regulation of personal behavior. This is a slippery slope best to be avoided, a slope the nature of which was articulated clearly by Ludwig von Mises:

> Opium and morphine are certainly dangerous, habit-forming drugs. But once the principle is admitted that it is the duty of government to protect the individual against his own foolishness, no serious objections can be advanced against further encroachments. A good case could be made out in favor of the prohibition of alcohol and nicotine. And why limit the government's benevolent providence to the protection of the individual's body only? Is not the harm a man can inflict on his mind and soul even more disastrous than any bodily evils? Why not prevent him from reading bad books and seeing bad plays, from looking at bad paintings and statues and from hearing bad music? The mischief done by bad ideologies, surely, is much more pernicious, both for the individual and for the whole society, than that done by narcotic drugs (von Mises, pp. 733-34).

The Real Issue. As important as are questions involving the liberty of tobacco consumers to act on their free choice and mind their own business, there is another, much more important aspect to the tobacco question which extends far beyond cigarettes. Put simply, if government is going to be allowed to enact coercive measures which arbitrarily restrict the liberties and trample the rights of smokers, where will employment of this restrictive power end?

If government is not expressly prohibited from interfering with the free expression of voluntary choice by peaceful adults in the case of tobacco, what is to restrain the government from similarly imposing restrictions on political expression or religious practice? What is to prevent a conservative government from making liberal speech illegal, or vice-versa? Sadly, the First Amendment to the Constitution may not be a sufficient answer. The First Amendment did not prevent the exclusion of tobacco advertising from television. The point is not that amendments to the written Constitution are necessarily without effect--surely they can be vitally important--but rather that the one-time passage of such an amendment, no matter how stringent it sounds, may not be enough. If the general public is unwilling to oppose the tendency of the political sector, driven by the demands of rent-seeking interest groups, to expand beyond its necessary and proper domain, even a seemingly strong, written, constitutional constraint enacted sometime in the past may prove ineffective.

If a broad social consensus exists which acquiesces to the legitimacy of governmental intrusions into the liberties and rights of individuals, further such intrusions are much more likely. The liberty of all depends on drawing a line over which government may not cross. That line needs to represent the rejection by the general public of the principle of unlimited governmental intervention into the peaceful domain of social life. Tobacco regulation is only one example. Every time governmental power extends beyond the realm of the simple protection of individuals against force and fraud, the very existence of the free and competitive social order is increasingly threatened. Tobacco regulation may not itself constitute Pandora's Box, but to the extent that the liberties of tobacco consumers are increasingly whittled away, the Pandora's Box of statism is cracked open a little bit more.

NOTES

1. This includes about $5.28 billion from accidents resulting in deaths, and another $4.195 billion from accidents resulting in injury but not death.

2. The strong association between obesity and TV watching (Tucker and Friedman, 19889) could well be used to argue for taxes on TVs, a restriction in the number of hours during which signals can be broadcast, and possibly even the abolition of TV and the restoration of a TV-free America.

3. This number includes attendance at major league baseball games, college basketball games (both men's and women's), professional basketball games, college and professional football games (including NFL and USFL), National Hockey League games, horse races, greyhound races, and jai alai. Not included, because of lack of data, were soccer, high school and elementary school sporting events (as well as youth sports activities like Little League), minor league baseball games, and the many other spectator sports which each attract relatively small numbers of the public annually. Therefore, this is a very conservative, lower bound estimate of attendance at sporting events. We assumed that the average

length of attendance at each sporting event listed was three hours. See U.S. Bureau of the Census (1988, p. 218).

   4. Calculated from data presented in National Sporting Goods Association (1987).

   5. Average hourly wages in the United States in 1986 were $8.76. See U.S. Bureau of the Census (1988, p.288).

   6. The discussion in this section draw upon Buchanan (1986).

References

Alchian, Armen A. and Demsetz, Harold. "Production, Information Cost, and Economic Organization." *American Economic Review* 62 (September 1972): 777-95.

Arrow, Kenneth J. and Scitovsky, Tibor. *Readings in Welfare Economics.* Homewood: Richard D. Irwin, 1969.

Atkinson, Anthony B. and Stiglitz, Joseph E. *Lectures on Public Economics.* New York: McGraw-Hill, 1980.

Atkinson, Anthony B. and Townsend, Joy L. "Economic Aspects of Reduced Smoking." *The Lancet* 3 (1977): 492-95.

Ault, Richard W., Ekelund, Robert B., Jackson, John D., Saba, Richard S., and Saurman, David S. "Smoking and Absenteeism: An Empirical Study," *Applied Economics,* forthcoming.

Baumol, William J. *Welfare Economics and the Theory of the State,* 2nd ed. London: G. Bell and Sons, 1965.

Baumol, William J. "On Taxation and the Control of Externalities." *American Economic Review* 62 (June 1972): 307-22.

Becker, Gary. "A Theory of Competition Among Pressure Groups For Influence."*Quarterly Journal of Economics* 98 (August 1983): 373-400.

Becker, Gary S. and Murphy, Kevin M. "A Theory of Rational Addiction." *Journal of Political Economy,* 96 (August 1988), pp. 675-700.

Bennett, James T. *Health Research Charities: Image and Reality.* Washington: Capital Research Center, 1990.

Blair, Gwenda. "Betting Against the Odds: Addiction to Gambling Destroys Lives and Ruins Businesses." *The New York Times Magazine,* 137 (September 25, 1988): S57.

Boadway, Robin W. *Public Sector Economics.* Cambridge, Mass.: Winthrop Publishers, 1979.

Boddewyn, J.J. (ed.). *Tobacco Advertising Bans and Consumption in 16 Countries.* New York: International Advertising Association, 1986.

Brennan, H. Geoffrey and Buchanan, James M. *The Power to Tax.* Cambridge: Cambridge University Press, 1980.

Buchanan, James M. "Public Finance and Public Choice." *National Tax Journal* 28 December 1975: 383-94.

Buchanan, James M. *Public Finance in Democratic Process.* Chapel Hill: University of North Carolina Press, 1967.

Buchanan, James M. "The Economics of Earmarked Taxes." *Journal of Political Economy* 71 (October, 1963): 457-69.

Buchanan, James M. *Cost and Choice.* Chicago: Markham, 1969.

Buchanan, James M. "Politics and Meddlesome Preferences." In Tollison, Robert D. (ed.) *Smoking and Society: Toward a More Balanced Assessment* Lexington, Mass.: Lexington Books, 1986, pp. 335-342.

Buchanan, James M. and Tullock, Gordon. *The Calculus of Consent.* Ann Arbor: University of Michigan Press, 1962.

Chiplin, Brian, Sturgess, Brian, and Dunning, J.H. *Economics of Advertising.* New York: Holt, Rinehart and Winston, 1981.

Cleary, Paul D., Hitchcock, Jan L., Semmer, Norbert, Flinchbaugh, Laura J., and Pinney, John M. "Adolescent Smoking: Research and Health Policy." *Milbank Quarterly,* 66 (1988): 137-171.

Coase, Ronald H. "The Problem of Social Cost." *Journal of Law and Economics* 3 (October 1960): 1-44.

Colford, Steven W. "Rehnquist Slams Ads First Amendment Shield." *Advertising Age* 57 (June 30, 1986): 12.

Committee on Ways and Means. *Hearings on User Fees, Revenue Proposals Contained in President Reagan's 1986 Budget, and Other Revenue Measures.* Washington: U.S. Government Printing Office, 1986.

Cowell, M.J. and Hirst, B.L. "Mortality Differences between Smokers and Nonsmokers." *Transactions of the Society of Actuaries* 32 (1980): 185-261.

Crain, W.M. and Tollison, R.D. "The Influence of Representation on Public Policy." *Journal of Legal Studies* 6 (June 1977): 355-361

Dahl, Tor, Gunderson, Barbara, and Kuehnast, Kathleen. "The Influence of Health Improvement Programs on White Collar Productivity." Working Paper, University of Minnesota, Minneapolis, 1984.

Darby, Michael R. and Karni, Edi. "Free Competition and the Optimal Amount of Fraud." *Journal of Law and Economics* 16 (1973): 67-88.

Den Uyl, Douglas J. "Smoking, Human Rights, and Civil Liberties." In Tollison, Robert D. (ed.) *Smoking and Society: Toward a More Balanced Assessment* (Lexington, MA: Lexington Books), 1986, pp. 189-216.

Doernberg, Richard L. and McChesney, Fred S. "On the Accelerating Rate and Decreasing Durability of Tax Reform." *Minnesota Law Review* 71 (1987): 913-62.

Edmondson, Brad. "Health Care Costs of Obese People." *American Demographics* 9 (October 1987).

Efron, Edith. *The Apocalyptics: Cancer and the Big Lie.* New York: Simon and Schuster, 1984.

Egger, Gary. "Increasing Health Costs from Smoking." Health Commission of New South Wales, Australia, May 1978.

Ekelund, Robert B. and Saurman, David S. *Advertising and the Market Process: A Modern Economic View.* San Francisco: Pacific Research Institute, 1988.

Epstein, Richard A. *Takings: Private Property and the Power of Eminent Domain.* Cambridge: Harvard University Press, 1985.

Eysenck, Hans J. "Smoking and Health." In Tollison, Robert D. (ed.), *Smoking and Society: Toward a More Balanced Assessment* (Lexington, MA: Lexington Books, 1986), pp. 17-88.

Ferrara, Peter J. *Social Security: The Inherent Contradiction.* Washington: Cato Institute, 1980.

Flay, Brian R., Koepke, David, Thomson, Shirley J, Santi, Susanne, Best, J. Allan, and Brown, Stephen. "Six-year Follow-up of the First Waterloo School Smoking Prevention Trial." *American Journal of Public Health* 79 (October 1979): 1371-1376.

Garrison, Michael J. "Should All Cigarette Advertising Be Banned? A First Amendment and Public Policy Issue." *American Business Law Journal* 25 (Summer 1987): 169-205.

Glahe, Fred, R. and Lee, Dwight R. *Microeconomics: Theory and Applications.* New York: Harcourt Brace Jovanovich, 1989.

Glazer, Sarah. "Who Smokes, Who Starts -- And Why." *Editorial Research Reports* (March 24, 1989): 152.

Goodin, Robert E. *No Smoking: The Ethical Issues.* Chicago: University of Chicago Press, 1989.

Gray, Wayne B. "The Cost of Regulation: OSHA, EPA, and the Productivity Slowdown." *American Economic Review* 77 (December 1987): 998-1006.

Gunby, Phil. "Nation's Expenditures for Alcohol, Other Drugs, in Terms of Therapy, Prevention, Now Exceed $1.6 Billion." *Journal of the American Medical Association* 258 (October 1987): 210-22.

Hettich, Walter and Winer, Stanley. "Economic and Political Foundations of Tax Structure." *American Economic Review* 78 (September 1988): 701-12.

Holcomb, Harry S., III and J. Wister Meigs. "Medical Absenteeism among Cigarette, Cigar, and Pipe Smokers." *Archives of Environmental Health* 25 (October 1972): 295-300.

Hutt, W. H. "Unanimity Versus Non-Discrimination (As Criteria for Constitutional Validity)." *South African Journal of Economics* 34 (June 1966): 133-47.

Johnson, Lester W. "Cigarette Advertising and Public Policy." *International Journal of Social Economics* 15 (1988): 20-22.

Keeton, William R. and Kwerel, Evan. "Externalities in Autommobile Insurance and the Underinsured Driver." *Journal of Law and Economics* 27 (April 1984): 149-79.

Koplan, J.P., Powell, K.E., Sikes, R.K., Shirley, R.W., and Campbell, C.C. "An Epidemiologic Study of the Benefits and Risks of Running." *Journal of the American Medical Association* 248 (December 17, 1982): 3118-21.

Kristein, M.M. "How Much Can Business Expect to Profit from Smoking Cessation?" *Preventive Medicine* 12 (1983): 358-81.

Kristein, Marvin M. "Economic Issues in Prevention." *Preventive Medicine* 6 (1977): 252-64.

Kurland, Phillip B. "Interview." *New York Times*, (February 22, 1987): Section E, 9.

Landes, W. and Posner, R.A. "The Independent Judiciary in an Interest-Group Perspective." *Journal of Law and Economics* 18 (December 1975): 875-901.

Lavoie, Don. *Rivalry and Central Planning: The Socialist Calculation Debate Reconsidered.* New York: Cambridge University Press, 1985.

Lee, Dwight R. "Rent Seeking and its Implications for Pollution Taxation." *Southern Economic Journal* 51 (1985): 731-44.

Lee, Dwight R. and Tollison, Robert D. "Towards a True Measure of Excess Burden." Center for Study of Public Choice Working Paper, 1985.

Leibenstein, Harvey. "Allocative Efficiency vs. X-Efficiency." *American Economic Review* 66 (June 1966): 392-415.

Leoni, Bruno. *Freedom and the Law.* Los Angeles: Nash,1960.

Leu, Robert E. and Schaub, Thomas. "Does Smoking Increase Medical Care Expenditure?" *Social Science and Medicine* 17 (1983): 1907-14.

Leu, Robert E.. "Anti-Smoking Publicity, Taxation, and the Demand for Cigarettes." *Journal of Health Economics* 3 (1984): 101-16.

Lewit, E. M. and Coate, D. "The Potential for Using Excise Taxes to Reduce Smoking." *Journal of Health Economics* 1 (1982): 121-45.

Luce, Bryan R. and Schweitzer, Stuart O. "The Economic Costs of Smoking-Induced Illness." National Institute of Drug Abuse Research Monograph Series, No. 7, Department of Health, Education, and Welfare, December 1977.

Luce, Bryan R. and Schweitzer, Stuart O. "Smoking and Alcohol Abuse: A Comparison of Their Economic Consequences." *New England Journal of Medicine* (March 9, 1978): 569-71.

Manning, Willard G., Keeler, Emmett B., Newhouse, Joseph P., Sloss, Elizabeth M., and Wasserman, Jeffrey. "The Taxes of Sin: Do Smokers and Drinkers Pay Their Way?" *Journal of the American Medical Association*, 261 (March 17, 1989): 1604-1609.

Mayerowitz, Steven A. "The New Threat to Advertising Freedom." *Business Marketing*, 71 (October 1986): 20-22.

McAuliffe, Robert. "The FTC and the Effectiveness of Cigarette Advertising Regulations." *Journal of Public Policy and Marketing* 7 (1988): 49-64.

McCormick, Robert E. and Tollison, Robert D. *Politicians, Legislation, and the Economy*. Boston: Martinus Nijhoff, 1981.

McMahon, Walter W. and Sprenkle, Case M. "A Theory of Earmarking." *National Tax Journal* 23 (September, 1970): 255-61.

Minarik, Joseph J. *Making Tax Choices*. Washington, D.C.: The Urban Institute Press, 1985.

Mishan, E. J. *Welfare Economics*. New York: Random House, 1964.

Moschis, George P. "Cigarette Advertising and Young Smokers." *Journal of Advertising Research* (April/May 1989): 51-60.

Musgrave, Richard A. *The Theory of Public Finance*. New York: McGraw-Hill, 1959.

National Research Council, Committee on Passive Smoking, Board on Environmental Studies and Toxicology. *Environmental Tobacco Smoke: Measuring Exposures and Assessing Health Effects*. Washington, D.C.: National Academy Press, 1986.

National Sporting Goods Association. *Sports Participation in 1986: Series I*. Mt. Prospect, Illinois: NSGA, 1987.

Office of Management and Budget. *Budget of the United States Government, Fiscal 1990*. Washington, D.C.: Government Printing Office, 1990.

Olson, Mancur. *The Logic of Collective Action*. Cambridge: Harvard University Press, 1965.

Oster, Gerry, Coliditz, Graham A., and Kelly, Nancy L. *The Economic Costs of Smoking and Benefits of Quitting*. Lexington, MA: D.C. Heath, 1984.

Ostrom, Vincent. *The Political Economy of A Compound Republic*, 2nd ed. Lincoln: University of Nebraska Press, 1987.

Pauly, Mark, and Redish, Michael. "The Not-for-Profit Hospital as a Physicians' Cooperative." *American Economic Review* 63 (March 1973): 87-99.

Peacock, Alan T. and Rowley, Charles K. *Welfare Economics: A Liberal Restatement*. New York: John Wiley, 1975.

Pechman, Joseph A. *Who Pays the Taxes?* Washington, D.C.: The Brookings Institution, 1985.

Peltzman, Sam. "Toward More General Theory of Regulation." *Journal of Law and Economics* 2 (August 1976): 211-240.

Peltzman, Sam. "Constituent Interest and Congressional Voting." *Journal of Law and Economics*, 27 (April 1984), pp. 181-210.

Peston, M.H. "Economics and Cigarette Smoking" *The Second World Conference on Smoking and Health*, 1971.

Plott, Charles R. "Some Organizational Influences on Urban Renewal Decisions." *American Economic Review* 58 (May 1968): 306-321.

Posner, Richard A. "Taxation By Regulation." *Bell Journal of Economics* 2 (Spring 1971): 22-50.

Rivers, P. Rivara, Dicker, Barbara G., Bergman, Abraham B., Dacey, Ralph, and Herman, Clifford. "The Public Cost of Motorcycle Trauma." *Journal of the American Medical Association* 260 (July 8, 1988).

Robertson, A. Haeworth. *The Coming Revolution in Social Security.* Reston, VA: Reston Publishing Co., 1981.

Schelling, Thomas C. "Economics and Cigarettes." *Preventive Medicine* 15 (1986): 549-60.

Seltzer, Carl C. "Smoking and Coronary Heart Disease: What Are We to Believe?" *American Heart Journal* 100 (September 1980): 275-80.

Sen, Amartya K. "The Impossibility of a Paretian Liberal" *Journal of Political Economy* 78 (1970): 152-57.

Shillington, E. Richard. *Selected Economic Consequences of Cigarette Smoking.* Ottawa, Canada: National Ministry of Health and Welfare, 1977.

Shughart, William F., II and Savarese, James M. "The Incidence of Taxes on Tobacco." In Tollison, Robert D. (eds.), *Smoking and Society: Toward a More Balanced Assessment* (Lexington, MA: Lexington Books, 1986), pp. 285-307.

Shughart, William F., II and Tollison, Robert D. "Smokers versus Nonsmokers." In Tollison, Robert D., (ed.) *Smoking and Society: Toward a More Balanced Assessment* (Lexington, MA: Lexington Books, 1986), pp. 217-224.

Shoven, John B., Sundberg, Jeffrey O., and Bunker, John P. "The Social Security Cost of Smoking." National Bureau of Economic Research, Working Paper Series, May 1987.

Sinnott, Patrick. *The Relationship Between Total Cigarette Advertising and Total Cigarette Consumption in the United Kingdom.* London: Metra Consulting Group, 1979.

Solmon, Lewis C. "The Other Side of the Smoking Worker Controversy." *Personnel Administrator* 28 (March 1983): 72-82.

Spielberger, Charles D. "Psychological Determinants of Smoking Behavior." In Tollison, Robert D. ed., *Smoking and Society: Toward a More Balanced Assessment* (Lexington, MA: Lexington Books, 1986), pp. 89-134.

Spitzer, Arthur B. "At Issue: Should All Tobacco Advertising Be Banned?" *Editorial Research Reports* (March 24, 1989): 161.

Sterling, T. and Weinkam, J. "Smoking Characteristics by Type of Employment." *Journal of Occupational Medicine* 18 (1976): 743-54

Stigler, George J. "Free Riders and Collective Action: An Appendix to Theories of Economic Regulation." *Bell Journal of Economics and Management Science* 5 (Autumn 1974): 359-365.

Stigler, George J. "The Theory of Economic Regulation." *Bell Journal of Economics and Management Science* 2 (Spring 1971): 3-21.

Stigler, George J. "The Sizes of Legislatures." *Journal of Legal Studies* 5 (January 1975): 17-34.

Stoddart, Greg L. *et al.* "Tobacco Taxes and Health Care Costs: Do Canadian Smokers Pay Their Way?" *Journal of Health Economics* 5 (1986): 63-80.

Szasz, Thomas. *The Theology of Medicine.* New York: Colophon Books, 1978.

Taylor, Daniel T. "Absent Workers and Lost Work Hours, May 1978." *Monthly Labor Review* 102 (August 1979): 49-53.

"The Cost of Being a Sport." *Sports Inc: The Sports Business Weekly* 1 (December 7, 1987).

Tobacco Institute. *The Tax Burden on Tobacco*, Vol. 24, 1989. Washington: The Tobacco Institute, 1985.

Tollison, Robert D. "Public Choice and Legislation." *Virginia Law Review* 74 (1988): 339-71.

Tollison, Robert D. "Regulation and Interest Groups." Unpublished manuscript, 1989.

Tollison, Robert D. and Wagner, Richard E. "Romance, Realism, and Economic Reform." *Kyklos* 44 (1991) 57-70.

Tollison, Robert D. and Wagner, Richard E. "Self Interest, Public Interest, and Public Health." *Public Choice* 69 (1991): 323-43.

Tollison, Robert D. and Wagner, Richard E. *Smoking and the State.* Lexington, MA: D.C. Heath, 1988.

Trauth, Denise M. and Huffman, John L. "The Commercial Speech Doctrine: Posadas Revisionism." *Communications and the Law* 10 (February 1988): 43-56.

Tucker, L.A. and Friedman, G.M. "Television Viewing and Obesity in Adult Males." *American Journal of Public Health* 79 (No. 4, 1989): 516-18.

Tullock, Gordon. *The Organization of Inquiry.* Durham, NC: Duke University Press, 1968.

Turvey, Ralph. "On Divergencies between Social Cost and Private Cost." *Economica* 30 (1963): 309-13.

U.S. Bureau of the Census. *Statistical Abstract of the United States: 1988.* Washington, D.C.: Government Printing Office, 1988.

U.S. Bureau of the Census. *Survey of Current Business,* July 1988.

U.S. Department of Labor, Bureau of Labor Statistics. *Consumer Expenditure Survey: Diary Survey, 1980-81,* September 1983.

U.S. Department of Health and Human Services. *Smoking and Health: A National Status Report.* Rockville, Maryland: Office on Smoking and Health, 1989.

van den Doel, Hans. *Democracy and Welfare Economics.* Cambridge: Cambridge University Press, 1979.

Vaughn, Karen I. "Economic Calculation under Socialism: The Austrian Contribution." *Economic Inquiry* 18 (October 1980): 535-54.

Vogel, Alfred. "Are Smokers Really Less Productive than Nonsmokers?" *Legislative Policy* (Summer 1985): 6-8.

Wagner, Richard E. "Parchment, Guns, and the Maintenance of Constitutional Contract." In Charles K. Rowley, ed., *Democracy and Public Choice: Essays in Honor of Gordon Tullock* (Oxford: Basil Blackwell, 1988), pp. 105-21.

Wagner, Richard E. "Fiscal Principle, Fiscal Politics, and Consumption Taxation." In Manfred Pose, ed., *Heidelberg Congress on Taxing Consumption* (Berlin: Springer-Verlag, 1990), pp. 247-69.

Wagner, Richard E. (ed.), *Charging for Government: User Charges and Earmarked Taxes in Principle and Practice* (London: Routledge, 1991).

Waterson, M.J. "A New Threat to the Freedom to Advertise: Report on Developments in the United States, July 1986." *International Journal of Advertising* 6 (1987): 67-71.

Weaver, Carolyn L. *The Crisis in Social Security: Economic and Political Origins.* Durham, NC: Duke University Press, 1982.

Weis, W. L. "No Ifs, ands, or Buts: Why Workplace Smoking Should Be Banned." *Management World* (September 1981): 339-44.

Williams, Walter E. *South Africa's War Against Capitalism.* New York: Praeger, 1989.

Wright, Virginia B. "Will Quitting Smoking Help Medicine Solve Its Financial Problems?" *Inquiry* 23 (Spring 1986) 76-82.

Zemper, Eric D. "Injury Rate in a National Sample of College Football Teams." *The Physician and Sports Medicine* 17 (November 1989): 100-13.

Author Index

Legal Cases

Legal Cases Cited

Subject Index